How to get things cheap

by
Wilma Fraser

&

Where to get things fixed

by
Patrick Conlon

Designer: Steve Manley
Design Assistant: Greg Butler
Cover Art: Roger Hill
Illustrations: Stephen Toth,
 Barbara Solowan

Photo Credits:
Lynn Johnston — p 9, 19, 34, 49, 52, 59, 69,
73, 76, 87, 92, 93, 94, 120, 122, 123,
137, 139, 143, 147, 148, 149
Leo Hausman — p 11
David Lawrence — p 29
David Lloyd - p 86
Paul Orenstein — p 43.

© Toronto Life
Greey de Pencier Publications,
59 Front Street East, Toronto
Printed in Canada
ISBN 0-919872-29-8
Printed in Canada 1977

Canadian Cataloguing in Publication Data

Fraser, Wilma 1944 –
 How to get things cheap in Toronto

Includes index.
ISBN 0-919872-29-8 pa.

1. Shopping — Ontario — Toronto — Directories.
2. Consumer education — Ontario — Toronto.
3. Repairing — Directories. I. Conlon, Patrick, 1938 –
Where to get things fixed. II. Title.
III. Title: Where to get things fixed.

HF5429.6.C3F73   381'.025'713541   C77-001226-4

Table of Contents

How to get things cheap in Toronto

Introduction. 6

1. Recycling for Fun and Profit . . . auctions / bazaars & special sales /   **7-17**
flea markets / garage sales / rummage sales / pawnshops / thrift shops.
SIDEBARS: recycling for profit / the Gold Shoppe / the art of haggling

2. Food . . . markets / bakeries / cheese / chocolate / eggs / fruits &   **18-31**
vegetables / meat & poultry / health foods. **SIDEBARS:** eating better for
less / grocery comparison chart / pick your own, fruits & vegetables /
alternatives to supermarket shopping

3. Restaurants . . . Chinese / fish / French / German / Greek /   **32-43**
Hungarian / Indian / Indonesian / Italian / Japanese / Jewish /
vegetarian / special occasions

4. Home . . . furniture & appliances / carpets / china / dry goods / kitchen   **44-67**
things / plants / stereos / wicker / household rentals / for do-it-
yourselfers / handyman rentals. **SIDEBARS:** annual sales / apartment
rental tips / salvage / it's your move / landlord & tenant disputes /
mortgages / saving energy & dollars / in the kitchen / cutting your heating
bill / free firewood

5. Clothing . . . clearance outlets / mostly recycled / children's clothing   **68-80**
new & used / furs / shoes. **SIDEBARS:** free haircuts / bargain haircuts

6. Leisure . . . cheap movies / free movies / "home" movies / recreation,   **81-96**
cheap & free / YMCA, YWCA, YMHA, YWHA: Y's / sporting goods /
books & records / toys / hobby supplies. **SIDEBARS:** if you can stand the
crush Sam's got 'em or the great boxing day sale

7. Of Consuming Interest . . . special information directory / municipal **96-113**
government information / information centres / community information
centre of Metropolitan Toronto / volunteer service centres / multi-service
centres / legal & bankruptcy counselling / legal, consumer & human rights
services / medical & dental / University of Toronto Dental Clinic / pets.
SIDEBARS: when things go wrong / tips for would-be borrowers / the
children's storefront / credit / cheap credit: the subtle art of chargemanship / where the cheapest loans are / make your own toothpaste / cars:
some facts to know

Where to get things fixed

Introduction. **116**

Listings A - Z **117-155**

Advice from some Experts

Lynn Gordon

"As a consumer, there's a different set of questions for every business. Learn what to ask."

"Be as aware of pennies as you are of dollars..."

"I don't believe that consumers get just what they deserve. We were taught to believe in an honest system and not to complain. Until recently complainers were labeled trouble-makers and neurotic. Consumerism's just getting started."

"We were taught never to ask questions of those in authority..."

"Never take a package deal until you itemize everything."

"Ask questions even if it's someone you respect. If you're in the dentist's chair don't be afraid to jump out of the chair and discuss charges face to face. How can you talk with his head in your mouth?"

Rod Goodman, Editor Star Probe

"We get around 50,000 *valid* complaints a year from dissatisfied consumers."

"When it comes to complaints, black and white is best. Write a letter — phone calls are generally forgotten. The higher you go the better."

"Treat your name as the most valuable thing you've got. Don't treat it lightly. If you think this way you won't sign anything you don't read first."

How to get things cheap

by
Wilma Fraser

Introduction

Raising three kids on my own in Toronto taught me three things: you *can* stretch a dollar beyond your wildest expectations; there's always one more way to trim your budget; and yes, you are really able to live as well as you used to on less money.

And that's what *How to Get Things Cheap* is all about. It's a personal compendium that tells you where to find the best, cheapest places in town to shop, eat and play, tells how to beat the high cost-of-living in style and how to squeeze the last ounce from your budget without feeling the pinch. It includes the cheapest entertainment in town, and where to take your problems, get free hairdos and next-to-nothing dental care. It's about things that make Toronto special, like the St. Lawrence Market, L'Élégante (the most elegant used clothing establishment around) and the biggest annual free-for-alls in the world, the Hadassah and the TSO bazaars. Nobody has paid to be included in this book — they're here because they deserve to be and for no other reason.

As you read, I hope you'll find that it's more than a shopping guide. Although I've focused on many cheapies and freebies, I've tried to make it a "dollars and sense" guide to Toronto. There's a quick course on the subtle art of chargemanship consumerism and recycling your old stuff for profit. And much more.

Due to limited space, I've excluded large department stores, chain stores and discount stores, so you won't see familiar names like Eaton's, Simpsons, The Bay, Woolco and Tower's. But that's the point — they *are* familiar to you and to tourists. (You can bet the first stop on a tourist's agenda will be the new Eaton Centre.) Of more interest to readers of this guide will be smaller, less well known outlets. Finally, although some of my "cheap thrills" were revealed in previous *Toronto Life* articles ("Cheap Thrills" and "Where to Get Stuff Cheap") many new ones have been uncovered in my most recent fascinating dollar-stretching searches. And I'd like to share them with you along with the knowledge that you *can* live a pretty good life as a bargain-hunter.

A Word About Prices

The prices throughout this book have been painstakingly checked, and are as accurate as they can be as of June 1977. Inflation will more than than likely make liars of us before this book is even printed. The prices, however, have been included to help you make your own mind up about the best bargain places we've mentioned. And even if they're all 10% low when you read them they're still likely relative to other prices around town.

Acknowledgements

I'd like to thank the people who worked so hard and so long: my co-author Pat Conlon, publisher Annabel Slaight for her guidance, patience and good humor, Maralie Martin, Claire Gerus and Barbara Holmes, my daughter Alison, and Valerie Frith. And a special thanks to Wayne for his advice, encouragement and moral support.

Wilma Fraser

1. Recycling for Fun and Profit

Recycling's much more than stomping on cans, re-using containers and using recycled paper. It's also distributing and buying things like used clothing, lumber salvage, plumbing and building supplies, toys and household goods. In this chapter, we take you on a tour of Toronto's great recycling money-savers: auctions, bazaars, garage sales, rummage sales, flea markets, thrift shops and wreckers like Teperman's and Greenspoon's. Learn how best to sell your old stuff and you'll discover that recycling can be fun — and profitable.

Auctions

Auctions are fun, free and worthwhile, by far the best place to buy used furniture, appliances, antiques, TVs, silverware, china and paintings — even the kitchen sink. They're way ahead of junk shops, antique stores and pawnbrokers for sheer variety and reasonable prices. And even if you don't buy, you learn about the value of furniture, art and collectibles.

Toronto has a large selection of fine regular and special catalogue auctions. (You'll find them advertised in the classified section of the newspaper.) First, attend the preview — it's a *must* because you get a chance to look over the display, choose the items you want and inspect them carefully for flaws. Remember, caveat emptor: There are no guarantees and no refunds. Then list your articles by number and set a price. It's tempting but not wise to bid beyond the price you've set. If in doubt, watch the dealers — they seldom if ever overbid.

After three or four hours in a crowded, smoke-filled room, you sometimes wonder if it's really worth it. But a leisurely stroll along Queen Street's antique row east of Jarvis and west of University will convince you it is. For example, a tiny, oblong mirror with a gilt frame that sold at Waddington's auctioneers for $3 was priced elsewhere at $21.

Yes, although dealers like to deny it, they're regulars at auctions. (Auctioneer Gerald Bone estimates that no less than 40% of his business is with dealers.) You'll see them at almost every auction, an assurance that you're getting your money's worth. After all, they have to make a profit, you don't.

Abbey Auctions Ltd.
About 80% of Abbey Auctions Ltd.'s finer goods arrive via containers from England: English china, silver, carpets, furniture, antiques and collectibles — and they're carefully mixed in with fair-to-middling household goods at each regular auction. Abbey auctions are fun to attend. Auctioneer Gerald Bone is quick and amusing, and his customers are soon "bidding furiously," as he puts it.

If you miss the preview, you can roam around and inspect the merchandise while the auction's in progress — Bone will tolerate almost anything but noisy kids — and you

Auctions

W. Jacques Auction Services

can pay for and remove your bargains while the auction's in progress, if you don't care to stay. Bidding is by number and you register as you enter, and refreshments are available. Here's a sample of Abbey bargains: an oak buffet, $12; two floor polishers, $10; a walnut drop-leaf dining room table, $50; six matching side chairs, $10 each. Catalogue sales are advertised in the papers.

Regular auctions Tuesday at 9:30 a.m. and Thursday at 7 p.m. Previews Tuesday and Thursday from 8:30 a.m. to sale time.
2 Thorncliffe Park Drive, Unit 46 (425-7055)

Irving and Associates
Irving and Associates' regular auctions are a dependable and consistent supply of fine, consigned household goods and furniture. You can count on a large selection of antiques, near-antiques and collectibles plus some not-so-near but serviceable antique china, paintings, furniture and oriental rugs. Ray Irving gleans his goods from trust companies, lawyers and the like and dispenses them with considerable charm, poise and alacrity — he's probably the fastest auctioneer around town. Be sure to check the papers for lists of sale items.

There are several outstanding catalogue sales each year, an annual silver sale and other specials, such as a vintage car sale where a Model T Ford sold for $3,000. Irving's specializes in Canadiana and Victoriana. Register as you enter. Opening bids start as low as $2. Some samples: oak washstand, $40; an old Victrola (in working condition), $18; a large oak refectory table, $70 with four matching chairs at $20 each; and a piano for just $60.

Regular auctions Tuesday and Thursday at 8 p.m. Previews at 7 p.m.
1599 Bayview Avenue (481-0878)

W. Jacques Auction Services
Don't be surprised to see a one-armed bandit at one of their many fine sales — that's just the first of many surprises. To start, auctions are held downtown on Sunday when there's lots of parking and little else to do. And there's always lots of Canadiana, collectibles and household furniture and refreshments. Auctioneer Wayne Jacques, a very practical and

Auctions

innovative young man, holds regular specials like Canadiana sales, featuring pine furniture, primitives, old glass and copper, and nostalgia sales with gum machines, old posters and advertising trays (and the one-armed bandit). Recent prices: a pine washstand, $30; a large, earthy mug, just 25¢; a drop-leaf table, under $50; and a pine washstand, $30. Watch the papers for catalogue sales and specials. You won't be sorry.

Sunday noon. Previews: Saturday noon to 5 p.m. and Sunday 10 a.m. to noon.
40-42 Lombard St. (469-2688)

Waddington's
Waddington's regular auctions are an artful blend of objets d'art, household goods, and just plain junk. There's always a fine selection of rugs and carpets on the walls, paintings and prints of better and lesser quality, furniture for every room of the house (with the possible exception of the bathroom), china, silverware, appliances and TVs. And there are usually things you don't expect to find: artists' portfolios, tripods, film editors — even a completely equipped canoe.

Owner-auctioneer Ronald McLean is smooth, witty and keeps things moving. Bids are a simple nod or wave of the hand, so be careful! If your bid wins, your name and a cash deposit are required to hold your purchase for you. You can pick up your treasures after the auction. (Incidentally, you'll find Wednesdays less crowded and less pricey than Saturdays.) Watch the papers for special catalogue sales. Some great Waddington buys: an Electrohome electric heater, $10; a small pine desk, $20; whole lots of framed prints starting at $5; an upright vacuum cleaner, $10; and a B&W Hitachi that appeared to be new, $45.

Regular auctions Wednesdays and Saturdays at 9:30 a.m. Previews start at 8:30 a.m. on auction days or 4:30 to 5:30 p.m. on the preceding afternoon.
189 Queen St. E. east of Jarvis (362-1678)

Canada Customs Auctions
Ever wonder what happens to stuff that's seized at the border by zealous Canada Customs officers? If it isn't claimed, it's auctioned off at Canada Customs Auctions every few months or whenever 250 commercial shipments have accumulated. Goods and goodies are sold in large lots (try 100 cartons of bikinis on for size) and, according to previous catalogues, you'll find anything from tools, cameras, rugs and tape recorders to garden shovels. The problem is, just how many garden shovels can you use? Six hundred were auctioned off as a lot last year.

Apart from sheer volume, delivery might be a problem because you must arrange your own, and all goods must be picked up within three days of the auction or they are subject to regular storage charges. Catalogues are available.

Watch the papers for dates and times.
Basement of the Queen's Warehouse, 1 Front St. W. (369-4530)

Waddington's

10 Auctions

Metropolitan Toronto Police Auctions
There are as many as eight or nine Metropolitan Toronto Police Auctions annually — they're held whenever enough stolen bikes and unclaimed merchandise accumulates. There's a great selection of bikes: 10-speeds, 5-speeds, 3-speeds and standards. The more exotic imports can go as high as $70; some 10-speeds for less than $40; and standards, from $5 up. Property items are fantastic but they're sold in large lots the average person can't afford to use. Cases of tape recorders, cameras, stereos and record players usually go to dealers, at bargain prices. A word of warning: there's a line-up, sometimes half a block long, so be there early. Auctions start at 6:30 p.m. sharp. All merchandise is sold as is. Sale is on a cash and carry basis only.

No set dates so watch the papers or call for info.
329 Chaplin Cres. (967-2067)

Ontario Ministry of Transportation and Communications Auctions
Ontario Ministry of Transportation and Communications Auctions feature assorted government vehicles: old and recent, *uncertified* OPP cruisers, trucks, motorcycles and snowmobiles. Bids don't include sales tax, and be prepared: a certified cheque or a cash deposit of $100 is required on the spot. After that, you have five days to pay for and pick up your vehicle. And after *that* you have to obtain a certificate of mechanical fitness before you can pick up your license plates. Some sample prices from a recent auction: '72-'75 snowmobiles from $300 to $600; cars '72-'74 GMs, Fords and Plymouths, from $650 to $1600; Ford Econoline Vans from $1,050 to $1,250.

There's about one auction per month, well advertised in the papers. All items are on display from 9 a.m. to 4 p.m. for three days prior to the auctions.

1201 Wilson Ave. at Hwy. 401 and Keele St. (248-3725)

Sheriff's Auctions
They're rare and poorly advertised, but houses, contents of households, stores and cars are auctioned off. In a recent auction, a '71 Cadillac sold for $1,500. (It started perfectly and appeared to be mechanically fit, although all vehicles sold are uncertified.) A deposit of 10% of the bid price (or minimum $200) is required on cars and smaller items, and you have three days to arrange for payment and pick-up; with property, it's 10% of the bid price and 15 days to settle. Cash or certified cheques only. You get a chance to view the merchandise immediately before the sale.

Locations vary, so watch the *Toronto Sun* for ads or call 965-7405 for information.

TTC Auctions
Anything from umbrellas to suitcases full of clothes is auctioned off at TTC Auctions. Pairs of gloves sold in lots of 50 go for around $3 up. But things like cameras, radios and tape recorders are sold individually and you should be able to pick up a tape recorder for from $15 to $20. Only new, lost, unclaimed items are auctioned off — old stuff is discarded. They're advertised in the papers on the Saturday before the sale. No preview.

Twice a year at Waddington's, 189 Queen St. E. on the first Saturday in June and December.
Call TTC Lost and Found (924-2136)

Bazaars & Special Sales

B'Nai Brith Annual Bazaar
It's another blockbuster that features bric-a-brac, clothes, books, records and just plain rummage, and it's crowded. Persist, and you'll find buys like nearly new cords for $1 and an antique match-holder (a collector's item) for an unbelievable $2. To add to the fun, there's a special auction of weekend trips and dinners-for-two, and your $1 admission buys you a chance to win a brand new car.

In Spring, date and time is announced.
At CNE or St. Lawrence Market (783-4694)

Hadassah Bazaar
The Hadassah Bazaar can only be described in superlatives. It's the biggest bazaar of its kind in the world, a fund-raising record (and leg) breaker and an instant immersion course in the subtle and not-so-subtle art of bargain hunting. It's an all-day marathon of boutiques, auctions, gourmet foods, new and used clothing, appliances — and people armed with sharp elbows and determination. But it's worth it, according to one of the most seasoned bargain hunters I know who buys her entire wardrobe there. Her closet's crammed with finds like a Creed's pantsuit for $40, an evening dress from the same exclusive store for $7, and beautifully tailored, lined wool pants, for $8. (You'll find such things in the couturier section upstairs.) People line up for hours but there's a fitting room (public) and a tremendous selection, even late at night. Last year's Hadassah special was a sale of new jeans for $4 each. There's always lots of new

Crowds at the Hadassah Bazaar

merchandise at half-price. So make a day of it — the food's home-cooked. Admission's $1. A new car is raffled as a door prize.

Every fall 9:30 a.m. to 11:30 p.m. Dates announced.
Automotive Building, CNE (789-4373)

ORT Bazaar
This bazaar is a spring fund-raiser for the Organization for Rehabilitation through Training (ORT) and a great place to look for pots and pans, clothes, quilts, toys and books. Edible fare includes candies, homemade baked goods, even patent medicines. There's an evening auction of furniture, antiques and collectibles that you don't want to miss. Admission is a $1 raffle ticket but you'll also have a chance to win a car or its cash value. Dates announced.

St. Lawrence Centre on Front Street E. (630-1946)

Pioneer Women's Annual Bazaar and Auction
A superb combined auction and bazaar with a great deal to offer, from ethnic foods, handcrafted items, special games and free novelties for the kids, new and used clothes. And

you won't want to miss their auction of furniture, appliances and trips-for-two. It's a fall annual and a great place to stock up for Christmas. And besides, it's fun. Dates announced. In 1977, it's held at the International Centre, 6900 Airport Rd. in Mississauga (636-5425)

Flea Markets

Flea markets are one place where haggling pays off. There are two groups of vendors at flea markets: "professionals" who buy at regular auctions and peddle their finds for a profit, and people who are there to recycle their own stuff (also at a profit). My advice to all would-be flea market habitués is to shop around first, then haggle. Go to auctions, visit second-hand stores and antique shops to compare prices and above all, go to other flea markets. I hesitate — not refuse — to recommend one over the other. (They're all unpredictable and as changeable as the weather and each has its own character and prices.) But I will say this much — they make a delightful outing.

Here are a few of the "regulars" in and around Metro:

The Fantastic Flea Market every Saturday and Sunday, 10 a.m. to 5 p.m., Dixie Plaza, Q.E.W. south side at Dixie Rd. (274-9403 days, 275-0203 evenings)

Stouffville Flea Market, every Saturday, 8 a.m. to 4 p.m. Hwy. 47 in Stouffville (640-3813)

Aberfoyle Antique Market and Artisans Village, 1¼ miles north of 401, on Hwy. 6 (Brock Road), exit 37 (274-9403 days, 275-0203 evenings)

The Old Oakville Market, every Saturday and Sunday 9:30 a.m. to 5 p.m., Trafalgar Road and Randall Street, Oakville (844-5500 days, 845-3723 evenings)

Garage Sales

There's a little pack rat in all of us, but even the most avid pack rats are forced to discard their treasures to make room for the new ones — and themselves. Their hoards often show up at neighborhood garage sales at prices you won't believe: a vintage, gunstock walnut end table, $5; a perfectly good Presto pressure cooker, $5; a Sears tape recorder (it worked perfectly), $15; mugs and books, 15¢ to 25¢ each.

Watch the papers or the bulletin board of your favorite supermarket for garage sale ads — it's worth it. And remember cleanups are profitable. Re-cycle *your* junk.

Rummage Sales

Rummage sales have always been a consistent source of funds for churches and charitable institutions and they're always a limitless — if somewhat inconsistent — source of cheap clothing, bric-a-brac, bargains *et al* for you. As the sale draws to a close, items are almost given away. In a frantic effort to clear the counters, shirts and sweaters sell for 15¢ and up; lots of pillowcases for $1 or for 25¢ each; blankets for $2. If you've never attended, don't get your hopes up — some rummage sales are terrific; others are just plain awful. If you feel like taking a chance, they're listed in the paper and often on supermarket bulletin boards.

Goodwill's Annual Antique Sale

The line-up begins to form just after sunrise for this mammoth antique and collectible sale, and when the doors open at 10, you risk being trampled in the rush. Aggressive shoppers, nevertheless, consider this part of the sport and can pick up some fantastic bargains in silver, furniture, dishes, old prints, clothing and curiosities. Admission is $1 before noon and free thereafter.

Annually the second Wednesday in May 10 a.m. till 8 p.m. at Leaside Memorial Gardens.
For information call (362-4711)

Toronto Symphony Annual Rummage Sale
Toronto Symphony Annual Rummage Sale is reputedly the world's largest and it represents a year's hoard of rummage: furniture, antiques, new and used clothes, boutique items, toys, books and plants. It's a traditional stop for seasoned bargain-hunters. We know a family of five that get their entire wardrobe for the year there.) And no wonder. An almost new leather coat, $5; shoes, $1; two turtle-necked sweaters, 50¢; and jeans, $1. During the day there's Bingo and the evening includes an auction of new appliances (refrigerators and stoves etc.) and one sample of their special raffle: a trip for two to Vienna, including return air fare donated by Air Canada and a stay at the posh Intercontinental Hotel. Admission's $1. No charge for kids or senior citizens.

Every May, 10 a.m. to 9 p.m., date announced.
West Annex of the Coliseum (363-7779)

Pawnshops

It used to be that "hock" shops — as they were called — were shady places associated with nefarious characters and "hot" goods. But thanks to Metro's finest, they've changed for the better. Daily police checks and a one-year holding period on all pawned goods have virtually elimi-

Recycling for Profit
Where to sell *your* used clothes, furniture and bric-a-brac

Recycling your old clothes, furniture and bric-a-brac is profitable and practical, once you get used to the idea. Frankly, I never thought of selling my used things (they were always relegated to the Sally Ann or the local rummage sale) until I watched several luxury cars and one limousine disgorging loads of cast-off designers' clothes at one of Toronto's posher clothing establishments. It occurred to me then that charity begins at home, and I've been selling our used stuff ever since, through used clothing outlets, auctions and bargain-type papers. Auctioneers take from 18% to 20% and stores about one-third of your profits. But it's worth it — no phone calls, no — often futile — waiting for the phone to ring.

If it's not practical to transport your stuff, ads in the *Toronto Star's* Little Market at $2 for two lines for two days for things under $75 and ads in the *Bargain Hunter* and *Buy and Sell* are effective — and cheap.

Of the two news sheets, the *Bargain Hunter* is bigger but *Buy and Sell* is cheaper. Rates are based on a sliding scale, according to price. *Buy and Sell* charges 10% of the selling price and has a maximum rate of $30. *Bargain Hunter's* rates are 5% up to $500 and 2% on the balance. *Buy and Sell* commission is based on the actual selling price; the *Hunter's*, on the advertised price.

nated stolen goods and most of what you see is actually "in hock" so to speak. Some of it's brand new, but seldom "hot." The bargains to look for are: old jewelry, charms, watches and musical instruments, notably guitars. As for the rest, be careful — shop around first. And in case you're still leery, you get a full refund if your purchase turns out to be stolen. However, pawnshop proprietors I talked to said, "It never happens."

James McTamney & Company
In keeping with its ripe old age (it was established in 1860), its specialty is antique silver and jewelry, and the front window is filled with old charms (silver charms from $4.50; 10k gold charms from $14.50), charm bracelets (with charms) ($20 and up) and offbeat jewelry. Inside there's a wider selection of jewelry and what must be hundreds of watches ($9 and up) with a one-year guarantee, if you buy one that's more than $20. As for your items, they'll appraise them for a fee: $10 for the first item and then the fee is negotiated on each succeeding item based on time entailed.

Monday to Saturday 9 a.m. to 6 p.m.
139 Church St. (366-9646)

Williams
This is the only shop where haggling pays off. There's an especially fine selection of watches ($10 and up), charms $7 up, and nearly-new and old charm bracelets. Fine, old gold necklaces are from $12 to $900 and guitars from $130.

Monday to Saturday 9 a.m. to 6 p.m.
145 Church St. (368-4861)

Thrift Shops

St. Vincent de Paul
The thing I like best about St.

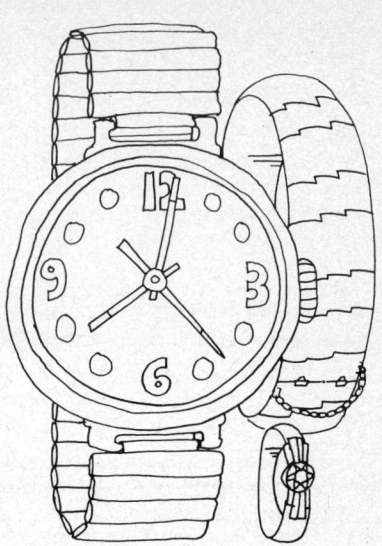

Vincent de Paul is the "Treasures and Bygones" sale at its Church Street store. It's a window sale of everything in the window and beyond, an incredible mixture of unusual bric-a-brac, budget memorabilia and modern funk. Sales are held every three months (on a Wednesday) and items are on display between sales. The window display is neat and prices are clearly marked. Some recent samples: a Polaroid Automatic 100 camera, $5; a genuine office dictaphone, $15; a tankard that looked like pewter, $2.50; assorted silverware for 30¢ and up and an intriguing collection of china figurines for 50¢ and up.

Monday to Friday 9 a.m. to 5 p.m., Saturday 9 a.m. to 4 p.m.
240 Church St. (368-1938)

St. Vincent operates a number of thrift stores around town, but they don't carry furniture and appliances. What they do have — mainly clothes and miscellaneous items — is cheap and strictly "as is."

Monday to Friday, 9:30 a.m. to 6 p.m., Saturday to 5 p.m.
947 Queen St. W. (366-4310)
Tuesday to Friday, 9:30 a.m. to 6 p.m., Saturday to 5 p.m.
348 Broadview Ave. (461-6456)
Tuesday to Saturday, 9:30 a.m. to 5 p.m.
3194 Danforth Ave. (699-5105)
Tuesday to Friday, 10 a.m. to 5:30 p.m., Saturday to 5 p.m.
1102 Queen St. E. (461-7094)
Monday to Saturday, 10 a.m. to 5 p.m.
3436 Lakeshore Blvd. W. (252-1057)

The Gold Shoppe

It's just what's needed to dispel any hangups you may have about buying used jewelry. The Gold Shoppe is so established and respectable that people tend to forget that its fine old — often antique — gold and silver pieces are used. Much of the exquisite collection is gleaned from estate sales.(Estate pieces are priced at 20% below their appraised value and are well below the current price.) Best buys: unusual watch fobs and charms and currently popular fine chains from $20; silver flatware at 20% below the current price; engagement and wedding rings. It also has one of Toronto's finest collections of Victorian silver and jewelry. Watch the papers for The Gold Shoppe's fabulous annual half-price sale. It's usually held in March or April.

Monday to Saturday 9:30 a.m. to 5:30 p.m., Thursday to 9 p.m.
85 Bloor St. W. (923-5565)

The Salvation Army
The first treasure I acquired from the "Sally Ann" was a fine, old oak washstand. It was just $25 and required no refinishing, just a lick of linseed soap and a loving polish with linseed oil to bring out its soft mellow sheen. There are still bargains, surprises and treasures at the Sally Ann's main depot. An early search of their basement provided us with sound, serviceable tires ($6 each for our snows and $3 a piece for summer tires) and a nearly-new bundle buggy, $3, and a later search with a lawnmower and bike, $15 each and a prized antique bob-sled, $5.

The main floor features a better-than-average assortment of used pots and pans, small appliances, bric-a-brac and books, plus a large selection of clothes and toys. Our real "finds" were from the main floor: an old coke cooler for $5, a near-antique calculator, $10 and for just $2, an "original" doll, a replica of the sweetest saddest clown in the world, Emmett Kelly's "Willie."

The third floor used to be an unlimited source of cheap old and antique furniture, but from what I've seen, those days have gone. There are old pieces and used funk, but they're over-priced and of poor quality — $45 for a scratched, warped dresser with a jammed drawer is excessive. And that's just a sample. People never tire of the Sally Ann; it's full of the unexpected but you're sure to come up with something.

Monday to Saturday 8:30 a.m. to 5 p.m., Thursday to 9 p.m.
496 Richmond St. W. (366-4686)
219 Queen St. E. (366-9871)
892 Queen St. E. (461-9721)
3339 Lakeshore Blvd. W. (259-9881)
1490 Dundas St. W. (537-1993)
1181 Weston Rd. (Weston) (767-0848)

The Art of Haggling

Some people are born hagglers. They love to dicker, be it a new car or an old hat at a rummage sale. You can spot a born haggler a mile away — he or she reeks of confidence, refuses to be pressured and is almost sure to end up with the bargain. Any haggler will tell you that it *pays* to haggle. They can't tell you how (they say it's an art) but they will tell you *where;* and that's the secret.

You don't walk into Eaton's or Simpsons and expect to dicker. It just isn't done; their prices are the same for everyone. But there are places like car dealerships, for example, where you can be cheated unless you haggle. There's no law that says a dealer can't sell you a car for $4,500, then sell the same car to a better bargainer for $4,000 five minutes later (see page 113 for more about this.) Haggling's a must: It's up to you — not the salesman — to protect your interests.

Haggling's also part and parcel of buying an older home. Every prospective old-home purchaser bargains; and most offers-to-purchase are substantially less than the inflated asking price. The seller generally asks more than he expects to get.

Generally speaking, the more cash you have, the better your bargaining position, especially with private real estate and car purchases.

Flea markets, rummage sales and garage sales are other hagglers' stamping grounds. Prices are slashed as sales draw to a close.

Haggle — you can't go wrong and it's good experience if you're new at the game. Newspaper ads are another good bet. Always offer less than the asking price when you answer a "for sale" ad in the paper. (The asking price is often deliberately inflated.)

- A successful haggler knows just what to pay, no more, no less. And he'll keep looking until he finds it. Shop around, bone up on prices and know your limitations.
- It helps to know the wholesale price of the item you want. If you don't, figure the dealer or storekeeper paid roughly 55 to 60% of the list price and work from there.
- Small appliance dealers will often match or better "so and so's" price (if you quote it) to get your business.
- Always ask a small dealer or storekeeper if there's a discount for cash. There often is. Some small dealers will order you a specific item at less than mark-up if you pre-pay for the item. (Be sure to get a receipt if you do.)
- Successful hagglers never rush and they can't be pressured — they know there are other comparable bargains and they're prepared to wait till the price is right. So shop around, look for bargains and don't be pressured.

The Jarvis Street Goodwill Services

The Society for Goodwill Services (formerly Crippled Civilians)

The main Jarvis Street store is by far the best used charity outlet in town. Its forte is used appliances and furniture and there's always a large, orderly display on the second floor. Old-to-recent stoves, fridges and freezers are immaculate ($40 and up). The furniture — sofas, chairs, dressers, dining room suites *et al* — is spotlessly clean, and in many cases refinished and/or repainted. (You can pick up a nice used desk for $20 and a dresser from $30 up.) There is also an exceptional selection of working bikes, TVs and radios ($25 and up), and small appliances. (My best find was an Oster stainless steel blender for just $6.) The main floor features beds, carpets and bedding and a wide assortment of men's, women's and kid's clothes, and there are bargains: a handwoven poncho (handcrafted by a Quebec artisan), $2; a hand-crocheted shawl, 60¢; a sable fur piece, $4. Fur coats in winter — and there are lots — are a good buy, too, starting at $30. And then there's the "as is" section downstairs, brimming with just plain junk, kids' toys, household goods and rarities like the air cushion I sat on to write this book.

In the thrift shops the stock varies. The Dundas Street West store also stocks furniture and the King Street West store, unrestored furniture only.

Monday to Saturday 9:30 a.m. to 6 p.m.
91 Jarvis St. (362-4711)

3109 Dundas St. W. (769-2474), 2533 Danforth Ave. (698-6115), 3160 Eglinton Ave. E. (261-7610), 689 King St. W. (366-1434), 2985 Lakeshore Blvd. W. (255-3211), 428 Parliament St. (921-6648), 338 Queen St. W. (363-2827), 755 Queen St. E. (461-2217), 319 Roncesvalles Ave. (534-1686), 1162 Weston Rd. (769-7938)

2. Food

Did you know that every minute you spend in the supermarket beyond the first half-hour costs you an additional 50¢ to 75¢? Or that you buy more when you shop before a meal? Or that much of your food dollar is wasted on attractive packages, processing and advertising? These are just a few of the things you'll find in this chapter along with basic facts about food, price comparison charts and buying and storage tips. You'll discover why food is so expensive; how and what to buy for cheap but nutritious, flavorful meals. And like most of us you'll probably discover that you could be eating better for less. We've included alternatives to supermarket shopping, ways to beat the supermarket game, and a formidable list of marvelous discount food stores with prices you can afford — everything you need to know to stretch your shrinking food dollar.

Supermarket Alternatives

Honest Ed's

Low overhead at Honest Ed's means just that — the ceilings *are* low. And in keeping with Ed's slapstick signs and slogans, the whole store's crazy and remarkably like an old "fun house," with wild neon signs, pitched floors and crowds of people. The real bargains are groceries (on the third floor) and drugs and sundries (on the ground floor). Here's a recent sample of grocery finds: 24 oz. Welch's Grape Jelly, 88¢; Duncan Hines cake mixes, 59¢; two 28-oz. cans peaches, 99¢.

Prescription prices are said to be the best in town. I can vouch for super buys in over-the-counter drugs, cosmetics and sundries. Sunlight dish detergent was just $1.29 for 52.8 oz.; large bottles of Fabergé Organic Honey and Wheat Germ shampoo and conditioner, $1.69; and 150 ml Crest toothpaste, $1.27. If you buy aspirin or other sundry items in bulk, Ed's is the place to go.

Monday to Friday noon to 9 p.m., Saturday 10 a.m. to 6 p.m.
581 Bloor St. W. at Markham St.
(Pharmacy — 534-7668)

Knob Hill Farms

If you believe that bigger is better, you'll go for Knob Hill, with its acres of produce and case lots of canned goods. Of its locations, the Harbor Food Terminal is my favorite — it's neater, better organized, and easier to get around in than the others. Produce is fresh, cheap, and homegrown when possible. Large, firm heads of lettuce are a bargain at three for $1; so are Anjou pears at three pounds for $1, and Ontario carrots at three bags for $1. And the *fresh* meat — often Ontario-raised — is excellent. But I must confess that an incredibly tough, inedible (frozen) duck made me skeptical about their *frozen* meats and poultry. (Either that duck was very old or in the deep freeze for ages — even the cats rejected it.)

Great bargains include *fresh* Ontario pork loin and shoulder for 99¢ and 59¢ a pound respectively, bacon at 99¢ and stewing beef at 99¢ a pound. There's only one small snag: Knob Hill reserves the right to limit quantities. And it often does — usually on the best buys.

Monday to Friday 9 a.m. to mid-

night, Saturday, 8 a.m. to midnight
222 Cherry Street (461-7503)
222 Lansdowne Ave. (534-7901)
Woodbine N. at Hwy. 7, Markham (297-2133)
Hwy. 2 West, Pickering (683-9300)

Olympic Wholesale
Tea grannies and those with a sweet tooth will love Olympic Wholesale. Apart from other non-perishables in giant-sized packs, it stocks boxes of 500 Red Rose tea bags for $3.95 and 100-pound bags of sugar for $17.75. The large assortment of herbs and spices are carefully packaged and labeled by the owner, at bargain prices. Paprika and chili are 65¢ and white pepper's just 85¢. Cereals, rice, nuts, and, for baking, peel and assorted dried fruits and raisins all sell at a substantial discount.

Monday to Saturday 9 a.m. to 7 p.m.
224 Parliament St. (368-2767)

Usher's Surplus Foods Warehouse
"If we have it, it's got to be cheaper," says Usher's. And it usually is — half-price and less. Granted, the merchandise (bankrupt stock, cannery clearance, insurance claims, label changeovers, overproduction) looks different by the time it arrives here. Cans are often a bit dented or rusty, possibly short in weight, and you might find Kleenex boxes with mismatched tissues inside, or oddly shaped or lop-sided soap, even mis-stuffed olives and crazy mislabelled containers — all a pain to the manufacturer but a blessing to you and Dave Usher. You can't match his prices anywhere in town.

Usher's main store on Queen Street West is crammed with bargains, all neatly priced for comparison shoppers. Here's a sample: a four-pack of Listerine toothpaste in 75 ml tubes, $1.69; 48-oz. cans of Del

Olympic Wholesale

Monte pineapple juice, three for $1 (reg. 59¢ each); cases of Romar and Society pet food, 48/15 oz. cans, $13.65 (reg. $16.50); Pamper cat food, $4.05 a case; 2% Carnation milk, two for 63¢ (reg. 37¢); and crusty loaves of bread, two for 39¢ — leftovers from an overproduction run. (All baked goods are day-olds, off-codes or from overproduction.)

Meat is nicely packaged and the produce is fresh, but real bargains are in actual grocery items. Hit Usher's early in the morning or on Thursday afternoon when it's not too busy.

Thursday, 1 p.m. to 9 p.m., Friday, 8:30 a.m. to 9 p.m., Saturday 8:30 a.m. to 6 p.m.
Usher's main store (the one I recommend): 1266 Queen St. W. (531-3514)
169 Queen St. E. (368-1917)
41 Kingston Rd. (284-9231)

Markets

Kensington Market
People tend to rave about Kensington's low prices, old-world charm and colorful atmosphere. And although I offer my comments with some diffidence, I honestly can't see why. I was disappointed in both the prices and the produce, which is generally not of top quality. I don't consider apples at 25¢ a pound a bargain, especially cookers, and poor-quality cookers at that. And most of the not-too-fresh produce is

Eating Better For Less

If you're an average Canadian, you spend no less than 25% of your income on food. But planning ahead, comparison shopping and shopping at different stores can reduce your food bill by at least a quarter. Prices vary from week to week and from store to store. Obviously you can't check every store in town or sit glued to your radio or TV for the latest commodity prices. But there are many practical ways to save. Here are some of them:

- Store brands are usually comparable in quality and cheaper than leading national brands and you can knock at least 20% off a $40 grocery bill by purchasing house brand products.
- Lower-grade foods are more economical and just as nourishing as higher grades like "A" and "Fancy." Look for "Standard" and "Choice" canned fruits and vegetables; Canada Utility-grade poultry for roasting; B-grades for soups and stews.
- Vegetable oils are best buys for cooking — they're cheaper than olive oil and about one-third the price of butter.
- Powdered milk is less than half the price of fresh milk, just as nutritious and excellent for cooking. If your family refuses to drink it, try mixing it with bottled milk in the blender. Chances are they'll never know the difference.
- Most supermarkets offer a rain-check when they run out of advertised specials. Be sure to ask for it. And don't hesitate to return items damaged during delivery or that have gone bad.
- Items marked "exceptional value" or "best buys" generally are. Such explicit advertising is subject to strict government controls.
- It sounds deadly, but planning your week's menu can save you time and money.
- Processed, pre-packaged and convenience foods are high in price and low in nutrition. Your favorite TV dinner, for example, costs you three times more than making it yourself.
- Low-fat protein foods like fish, poultry, legumes and beans are cheaper than beef, lamb and pork and better for you.
- Eat more fresh fruit and vegetables but always buy top-quality produce even it if costs more. If it's bruised or stale you'll end up throwing more than half of it — and your savings — away. Buy fresh fruits and vegetables in season and freeze for later use.
- It pays to buy in bulk. Large unwrapped portions of cheese are cheaper and can be stored; meat specials can be frozen for future use.
- Whole grain cereals are more nutritious and much cheaper than refined or packaged breakfast cereals like Cream of Wheat or Rice Crispies.
- Cheap cuts of meat are succulent and flavorful when cooked in a pressure cooker or clay baker.

sold by the pound, hardly a cheap way to buy unless you're into eggplants — they're light. And the pitiful chickens huddled in crates on the sidewalk are no bargain either. They are tightly crated in all kinds of weather despite the Toronto Humane Society's constant vigilence, and many complaints.

But there are exceptions, notably *European Meats and Sausages* (see page 28) and the *Global Cheese Shop* (page 23). *Daiter's Creamery* at 64 Kensington Ave. (368-8433) with its fresh, thick whipping cream (65¢ for a half pint) and its freshly made cottage cheese ($1.35 a pound), is another. So is *Lottman's Imperial Bakery* at 181 Baldwin St. (368-2688), with its huge assortment of tempting baked goods. (Check the counter for bargain half-priced day-olds.) And if you shop around, there are always fresh eggs for as little as 75¢ a dozen, less if you buy trays.

All of this doesn't mean that *you* won't like Kensington or that you *won't* find bargains — hundreds of people are weekly, even daily attenders. Besides, there's one advantage: it's open every day from dawn till dusk — well, almost.

The St. Lawrence Market

The posh, new St. Lawrence is still a great place for weekly bargains and outings. Most of the produce is farm-fresh — in the North Market anyway — and there's everything from plants and home-baked goodies, to fish, meat and top-quality produce and, in season, fresh-from-the-farm fruits and vegetables, and plants for the garden.

Farm produce is in the North Market along with specialty shops. You'll find garden-sized spider plants for only $6, large jade trees for $9, Jerusalem cherry trees (with inedible cherries) for $2.95, small hanging climbers like Swedish ivy for $2.95 and assorted, tiny plants-in-a-pot for 25¢ and up. They're hung all over the North Market along with baskets of fresh Grade A Large eggs at $4 for five dozen.

And there are wonderful meat stalls (mostly pork), clustered at the north end, all clean, efficient and reasonable. Simon de Groot's ham is just $1.09 a lb. And Roy Maduri, a pleasant young man, will sell you his bacon and ham ends (great for quiche) for 50¢ a pound; his own, delectable smoked hams for $1.19 per pound; and two pounds of liver for just $1.60.

And there are other treats like grain-fed, free range capons, at $1.15 a pound (near the north east entrance); and the sweetest, crispest carrots you've ever tasted, up on the stage, for 50¢ a heaping box or $1 a pony. Crunchy, red eating apples are just $1.25 a basket; cookers, from $2 to $3 a bushel; and boxes of natural vitamins and other natural goodies on special at $1 each, just inside the door of the health food store.

Despite its facelift, the South Market's just the same: busy, crowded and cheap. For sheer variety and reasonable meat and fish prices, you can't beat it. Here are some samples per pound: rib eye steak, $1; peameal bacon, $1.19; roasts of beef, 99¢ on special; sole, $1.99; scallops, $2.99; and cod, $1.69.

Fruit and vegetables are just as reasonable and just as good: Emperor grapes at three lbs. for $1; Sunkist oranges, 99¢; ripe bananas, just 25¢ a pound. And check the various stalls before you buy — there are different specials every week.

If you can afford to splurge and you're willing to wait, the meat auctions in the South Market are well worth it. Prime rump roasts and other succulent cuts go as cheaply as

$1 per pound if you buy several; other commodities are reduced, too. Auctions begin any time between 2 p.m. and 4 p.m.

The North Market's open Saturdays only, from about 6 a.m. to 2 p.m. The South Market is also open weekdays, 8 a.m. to 5 p.m.

Bakeries

Most of the large bakeries operate thrift shops and economy stores where they sell off-code and surplus bread and baked goodies at reduced and half-prices. Most have a good selection and are easily accessible by TTC.

Dad's Cookies
The way the cookie crumbles at Dad's can mean savings for you. A one pound bag of whole unbroken cookies sells for $1.03 in stores but you can buy broken Dad's for as little as 60¢ a pound. The choice depends on what they're making that day: it could be shortcake, chocolate chips or the original oatmeal. And in case you didn't know, Prime Minister Trudeau munches on Dad's cookies every night at bedtime.

Monday to Friday 9 a.m. to 5 p.m.
370 Progress Ave. (291-3713)

Donuts
If you get there early enough, you'll find that your favorite donut haunt sells day-olds for half price. Mixed packages at Mr. Donut are 95¢, Tim Horton's are 85¢. Country Style is most expensive at $1. See phone book for locations.

Hunt's Bakery
It's a huge, bright store featuring fresh off-code and surplus goods at 20% off and day-olds for half price.

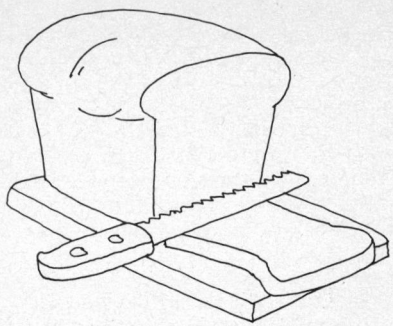

You'll find bread for 25¢ a loaf, butter tarts at six for 49¢ and glazed donuts at six for 49¢. Prices are marked for comparison shoppers. Get there early for best buys.

Monday to Friday 9 a.m. to 9 p.m., Saturday 9 a.m. to 6 p.m., Sunday 9 a.m. to 5 p.m.
66 Alcorn Ave., just above Summerhill

Sara Lee
Sara Lee Thrift Shops are a must if you have a car and a freezer. They carry the usual delicious Sara Lee fare, perhaps a bit lopsided or imperfectly iced, at considerable discounts. In addition, there are weekly specials — packaged deals of several items — for about one-third off.

Monday to Friday, 10 a.m. to 5 p.m., Saturday 9 a.m. to 5 p.m.
379 Orenda Dr., Bramalea (791-2900)

Weston's Thrift Shop
Most baked goods sell at wholesale prices from 24 oz. white bread (33¢) to 16 oz. brown bread (29¢). Get there early and bring your own bag.

Tuesday to Friday 10:30 a.m. to 6 p.m., Saturday 9 a.m. to 4:30 p.m.
652 Dupont St. near Christie (537-2621)

Woman's Bakery

Apart from their usual large selection of bargains, you can look for spectacular clear-out sales. When we were there, bread was five loaves for $1; rolls were 25¢ a bag and five bags for $1; and glazed donuts were five bags for $1. This fresh, clean store is a neighborhood favorite, so get there early for best buys.

Monday to Saturday 9 a.m. to 6 p.m., Friday 9 a.m. to 8 p.m.
792 Queen St. E. at Boulton (465-9912)

Wonder Bread

The shop features reduced items and specials like four loaves of bread for a dollar.

Friday and Saturday 10 a.m. to 4 p.m.
462 Eastern Ave. (No phone, but you can call their main number 465-1161)

Cheese

Global Cheese Shop Ltd.

If you can stand the crowds and disregard the décor, Global will more than meet with your approval. In fact, you'll have a field day, with over 100 kinds of cheeses from all over the world to choose from and what appear to be the best prices in town. In case you're not sure, you get to taste the cheese before you buy it, and prices are clearly marked. Here's a sample of prices per pound: Danish Havarti, 98¢, tangy Canadian cheddar, $1.09, elbo and gruyere, 98¢. Boursin's 75¢ for a half pound and it's their own make; esrom and blue are 25¢ and 49¢ each for 6 oz. pieces.

Monday to Saturday 8 a.m. to 8 p.m.
76 Kensington Ave. (368-0968)

Pasquale Bros. Downtown Ltd.

What makes Pasquale's so special is fine food, low prices and excellent service. Then there's the affable gentleman who presides over the cheese counter. As he proffers his Boursino, he carefully explains how he makes it himself with herbs and garlic — "the chee-sse uf luff" is what he calls it (complete with a knowing smile and raised eyebrows) and he suggests you try it slathered on a French stick just warm from the oven and smothered in butter. How can you resist? You can't, but at $1.29 for 7 oz., it's a bargain — and your guarantee of instant solitude. After all, who dares approach when you've eaten Boursino?

There are other specialties: you can sample Archie's delectable artichoke salad, and over 30 kinds of olives, plus a wild assortment of nuts, herbs and spices, dried fruits and pasta, lots of pasta.

And the prices are reasonable. The wine cheese at $2.49 a pound is excellent; so are the ementhal at $1.99 and the very old cheddar at $2.29 a lb. Olives are 59¢ a pound up, but the best greens and blacks are 99¢. There's only one catch at Pasquale's: you can't sample the cheese and you have to buy at least one pound.

Monday 9 a.m. to 4 p.m., Tuesday to Saturday 8 a.m. to 5 p.m.
145 King St. E. (364-7397)

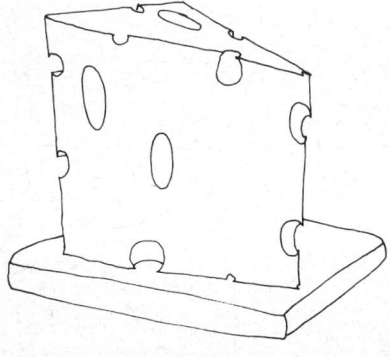

Grocery Price Comparison Chart

Item	"Supermarket" Price	"Milk Store" Price
Meat & Poultry		
(whole)	78¢/lb.	—
Ground beef	84¢/lb.	$1.29/lb.
Bacon	$1.38/lb.	$1.71/lb.
Steak (sirloin)	$1.58/lb.	No steak
Hot dogs	92¢/lb.	$1.12/lb.
Salami	72¢/lb.	$1.12/lb.
Dairy		
Milk homogenized	57¢/quart	59¢/quart
Cheese (Medium Cheddar)	$1.83/lb. (Loblaw's brand)	$2.10/lb. (Becker's brand)
Butter	$1.21/lb.	$1.34/lb.
Bread (sliced)		
whole wheat	47¢/24 oz. loaf	35¢/24 oz. loaf
Detergents		
Laundry powder	81¢/20 oz. box of Tide	91¢/20 oz. box of Tide
Canned Goods		
Tomatoes	63¢/28 fl. oz. (supermarket brand)	75¢/19 oz.
Fruit salad	59¢/19 fl. oz. (supermarket)	65¢/14 oz.
Produce — Vegetables		
Tomatoes	$1.10/lb.	79¢/4
Lettuce: Romaine	59¢/one lb. bunch	—
Mushrooms	$1.78/lb.	—
Produce — Fruit		
Oranges	$1.29/4 lb. bag	$1.39/½ doz.
Apples: Macintosh	$1.39/3 lbs.	$1.39/½ doz.
Coffee	$3.59/lb.	$3.69/lb.
Cereal Special K	71¢/7 oz. box	81¢/7 oz. box
Eggs (large)	94¢/doz. Grade A	98¢/doz. Grade A
Other		
Kraft Mayonnaise	99¢/16 fl. oz.	$1.12/16 fl. oz.
Olives (Manzilla)	89¢/8 oz. jar	89¢/8 oz. jar

Meat for Freezing

"Market" Price
69¢/lb. 3 lb. for $2.00 $1.19/lb. $1.59/lb. 3 lb. for $1.00 59¢/lb.
—
$1.99/lb.
—
(Bakery Thrift Shop) 25¢/loaf
—
65¢/28 fl. oz.
—
79¢-99¢/lb. 45¢ bunch 99¢-$1.09/lb.
99¢/doz. (approx. 4 lb.) $1.25/6 qt. basket
—
—
85¢/doz. Grade A
—

According to the Beef Information Centre in Toronto, around 210 lbs. of a 280 lb. side of beef ends up in your freezer. The rest (about 25%) is waste, a factor to consider when you're buying. Be sure to ask the butcher how much meat he's prepared to guarantee. You should get *at least* 72% of the gross side weight and, if he can't guarantee that, forget it. Find another butcher.

Always check to see if the price of cutting, wrapping and freezing is included in the quoted price per pound. If not, expect to pay from 7¢ to 15¢ more per pound.

Here's how to figure out the price you're actually paying, based on a gross weight of 280 lbs. and a net weight (after trimming etc.) of 210 lbs.:

Price per pound quoted (NOT including cutting & wrapping charges) x side or quarter weight, (Pounds of beef you actually receive) = Price per pound.

e.g. 90¢ (price quoted) x 280 lbs. (gross weight), 210 lbs. (weight after cutting, trimming etc.) = $1.20/lb.

This means that you're actually paying $1.20 a pound for cheap *and* expensive cuts of meat, whether it's Porterhouse steak or hamburger.

Chocolate

Stephanie's Belgian Chocolates
This cozy European-style shop is still selling delectable homemade chocolates and marzipan for just $3.75 per lb. Ask for a sample or two, then pick and choose from a delightful assortment of light and dark chocolates: chocolate shells with creamy fillings, walnut swirls, coconut clusters, chocolate-filled acorns, chocolate-coated ginger and cherries and many others. Candies are hand-packed on the spot — there are no prepacked or stale candies at Stephanie's.

Except for school holidays (Christmas, summer and spring break), it's open Tuesday to Friday 10 a.m. to 5 p.m., Saturday 9:30 a.m. to 5 p.m.
912A Kingston Rd., Pickering (no phone)

Eggs

Balaban's Produce Company
Balaban's devotees come from all corners of the city for the Grade A Pee Wee eggs which are hatched by young chickens before their force-feeding program starts. Pee-Wees are "extra small" and perfect for children's portions, those on low-cholesterol diets, and organic food fanciers. Two and a half dozen cost you only $1, but they're not the only bargain at Balaban's. You'll find standard-sized eggs at about 10¢ a dozen cheaper than in supermarkets, and cracked (but still good) eggs for baking at 70¢ a dozen.

Monday to Saturday 8 a.m. to 6 p.m.
951 Ossington Ave. (533-1104

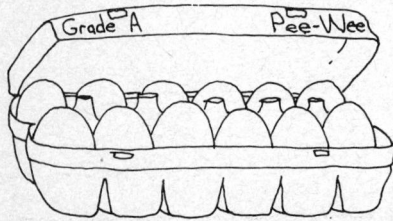

Fruits & Vegetables

Darrigo's Food Markets
At Darrigo's, you'll save 10-20¢ a pound on fruits and vegetables ranging from the everyday to the exotic. Fare includes baby artichokes, kohlrabi, savoy cabbage and lots of other things you might have trouble identifying unless you're a vegetarian gourmet. You can sample 20 varieties of olives while you're selecting your greens and the variety of fresh herbs is unbeatable. The cheese counters are among the most economical in town and you'll find all the standards plus specialty Italian types like Fruilano ($1.59/lb) and guaranteed-fresh Ricotta (99¢/lb).

Tuesday and Wednesday 9 a.m. to 6 p.m., Thursday and Friday 9 a.m. to 9 p.m., Saturday 8:30 a.m. to 6 p.m.
771 Danforth Ave. (461-0349) and seven other locations.

Sunkist Fruit Market
Open round-the-clock everyday in summer and fall (and late even in winter), it's a city-dweller's delight. You're almost sure to find fruits and vegetables you've never tried before, as well as the usual varieties, and all at very reasonable prices. We found endive at three pounds for a dollar, bunches of broccoli for 69¢. There's also a fine selection of specialty items for gourmet cooking.

Winter: Monday to Saturday, 8 a.m. to 10 p.m.
Summer: Daily, 24 hours.
561 Danforth Ave. (463-3727)
7155 Woodbine Ave. (495-1971)

Pick Your Own

We picked our own fruit last year, mostly strawberries, raspberries, peaches and a few apricots. It was a lot of work, but we had lots of fun, got terrific tans — and saved lots of money. And we're still eating frozen strawberries and raspberries and home-made raspberry jam. Strawberries were 35¾ a quart at peak season and raspberries were $1 a quart from peak season on. But prices vary year to year.

It's best to bring your own containers — you save money — and a change of clothes. And be sure to take a lunch. Not all farms have snack bars, they do have picnic tables and washrooms. And a sun hat or scarf's a must.

The Ministry of Agriculture can supply a list of all the pick-your-own places. Contact the Ontario Food Council at the Ontario Ministry of Agriculture at 965-7701, and watch the papers for ads.

Unless you're cursed with a purple thumb or inclement weather, you're bound to save money by growing your own supply of vegetables. All you need is some equipment, spare time and from $15 to $20 to rent a plot from your local borough. They will plow, cultivate and provide water for your garden. You do the rest. Depending on the weather, the season runs from mid-May to the end of October. They're booked well ahead so reserve in advance. For information contact the Parks Department in your borough.

For $30 a season you can rent a 25 x 50 foot plot in Huttonville, and plant, weed and save money to your heart's content. The Metro Garden Club will plow and provide water for your garden; you bring your own equipment and deport your own bugs.

Write Box 1051, Station B, Mississauga or call 270-2522 for information.

Meat & Poultry

A Stork & Sons Ltd.
You can't miss the building — it's the one with the big stork on the wall. Its specialty is fresh daily chicken, duck and turkey. If you've never had fresh chicken before, try it. It's cheap compared to supermarket prices, and it's tastier, juicier and richer than the frozen pre-packaged stuff we all take for granted. You'll find legs, at $1.04 per pound and huge breasts at $1.09 a pound, a bargain.

Tuesday to Friday 8 a.m. to 5:30 p.m., Saturday 8 a.m. to 4 p.m.
238 Queen St. W. (598-3111)

European Meats and Sausage
A store that's packed all day is generally the greatest store of its kind around — or the only store for miles. And this European style meat market is undisputedly "the greatest." The meats are always fresh and of excellent quality, from juicy T-bone steaks ($1.49 per lb.) and lean, ground beef (89¢ per lb.) to chicken legs (89¢) and breasts (99¢). And there's a fine selection of fresh and smoked meats: bacon ($1.19); and ham and liver sausages (79¢). Finally, it's clean, and the service is good, considering the crowds they have to contend with. Be sure to grab a number as soon as you arrive. And whatever you do, get there early and avoid Saturday.

Monday to Saturday 8 a.m. to 7 p.m., Thursday to 8 p.m.
174½ Baldwin St. (364-7591)

Sunnybrook Meat Packers
Here are some of the best bargains in town on bread, milk and meat because, says co-owner Paul Weisberg, "we deal in high volume, low overhead." They process their own meat on the premises, which means they can sell you T-bone steaks at $1.09 per lb. and farmer's sausage for 69¢ per lb. Sliced white bread, fresh, is 25¢ a loaf. Two-percent milk is $1.15 for three quarts — there's a limit of six per customer unless you buy a huge amount of meat — and three quarts of homo is $1.19 compared to $1.53 elsewhere. Sunnybrook's weiners sell at 3 lbs. for $1 and according to a national survey conducted by CBC's Marketplace in 1975, it's the second-best brand in Canada for over-all value.

Monday to Wednesday, 8 a.m. to 6 p.m., Thursday and Friday 8 a.m. to 9 p.m., Saturday 7 a.m. to 6 p.m.
756 Queen St. E. at Broadview (461-8141)

Health Foods

The Full Moon Teahouse and Imports
It's not a Japanese teahouse but a bright, spacious health food store with reasonable prices, more than its share of charm and yes, some offbeat china and tea accessories. There's a complete range of health foods, and prices compare favorably with other budget-minded health food stores. Bowes peanut butter is $19.50 for 25 lb. or 93¢ a lb.; Deaf Smith, $1.36 a lb. Organic wholewheat flour's 25¢ a lb. ($2.08 for 10 lbs.) and unbleached white, 21¢. There are several different granolas and many containers filled with nuts, rice, soup mix (40¢ a lb.), peas, beans and dried fruits. Another attraction is a good selection of incense, custom-made candles, macramé wall hangings, planters and see-through glass jars, great containers for peas, beans and just about anything you care to put in them.

Health Foods

Whole Foods Trading

Monday to Sunday 10 a.m. to 7 p.m. November to April; 10 a.m. to 9 p.m. May to October
2010 Queen St. E. (690-2086)

Whole Foods Trading Company
It's no accident that Whole Foods has all the attributes of a co-op and the assets of a neighborhood store. That's exactly what owner Bruce Brown and partner Sierra, both former Karma Co-op'ers, intended it to be: a self-service, low-priced store with a warm congenial atmosphere. Over a third of their business is wholesale and there are great deals for bulk orders. Pure, untreated crunchy or smooth Bowes peanut butter costs $18.63 (just 75¢ a lb.) for 25 pounds; amber honey, from 58¢ to 60¢ a pound if you buy a 65 to 70 lb. container; and whole wheat flour, just $12.96 per bag. A half bag costs $7.50 ($6.50 plus $1 for rebagging), still a saving when you consider that it's 21¢ a lb. on a per pound basis. But there are savings for non-bulk buyers too. A large 28 oz. jar of Deaf Smith peanut butter is $2.50; amber honey, 70¢ a lb.; their own Cabbagetown crunch or cinnamon sunflower crunch granolas, $1.10; organic vegeroni, $1.03. There are bins filled with flour, grains, nuts, dried fruit, beans of all kinds, split peas and a counter full of dairy products and vitamins. Upstairs on the "mezzanine" overlooking the store, there's a great selection of books and literature, and if you don't find what you want, Bruce is there to give you advice.

Monday, Tuesday, Thursday and Saturday 10 a.m. to 6 p.m., Wednesday, 11 a.m. to 6 p.m., Friday 10 a.m. to 7 p.m.
464 Parliament St. (967-5196)

Alternatives to Supermarket Shopping

Many of the alternatives to supermarket shopping are listed and discussed in this chapter: bakery thrift shops, markets, fish, meat and cheese shops and discount grocery stores like Usher's. Then, too, there are wholesalers who don't like to advertise the fact, but will often sell at wholesale or near-wholesale prices, if you buy bulk orders of canned goods.

Food co-ops are another great alternative if you have some spare time and don't mind pitching in for a few hours each month. At supermarkets, perishable fresh produce has the highest mark-up (32%); packaged goods with the longest shelf life have the lowest (18%). Your biggest savings at a co-op are on fresh fruits and vegetables, cheese and grains — beans, legumes, dried fruit, nuts, honey, peanut butter, flour, meat and pet food. There are basically two kinds of co-ops you can join: large store-type "walk in and buy" co-ops like Karma, with a fixed inventory and a 10%-to-18% mark-up; and smaller "pre-order and pre-pay" co-ops with a 5% to 10% mark-up. (It's much like grocery shopping in the old days when you called in your order and picked it up.) As a member, you're expected to work regularly. At pre-ops, you handle the weekly orders and help distribute the food from a central neighborhood location. Larger co-ops expect you to haul boxes, figure out prices, stock shelves, man the check-out desk and clean up.

There's also a membership fee, but members feel it's worth both the time and the money. Some estimate they save as much as 25% on fruit and vegetables, fresh from the Ontario Food Terminal where co-ops and other merchants buy their produce. And some co-ops have extras like nutrition programs, cooking classes, even meals-on-wheels. Here's a list of food co-ops in Metro, thanks to the Toronto Federation of Food Co-operatives and Clubs. Hours mentioned are those when food is distributed, unless otherwise indicated:

Central Neighborhood House Food Club
(Pre-order and pre-pay)
They sell produce, eggs, cheese, maple syrup, honey and peanut butter. Mark-up: 15%. You work two hours a month.
Food can be ordered Wednesday 2 p.m. to 5 p.m., Thursday, 9:30 a.m. to 1 p.m. It's distributed Friday, noon to 3:30 p.m.
349 Ontario St. (925-4363)

Community Service Grocery
(Walk in and buy) There's a full range of senior citizens' needs at 10% mark-up.
Wednesday 1 p.m. to 4 p.m., Thursday 10:30 a.m. to 9 p.m. and Saturday 10 a.m. to 5 p.m.
136 Main St. (690-2041)

Don Vale Food Club
(Pre-order and pre-pay) There's fruit, vegetables, eggs, cheese and honey. Mark-up: 18%. Members pay $2 a year, plus volunteer labor.
Food's ordered Tuesday 10 a.m. to 5 p.m. and distributed Thursday 10 a.m. to 5 p.m.
20 Spruce St. (922-7391)

Greenwood Food Club
(Pre-order.) Fruit, vegetables and eggs are distributed. Mark-up: 17%. There are no membership requirements.
Thursday 1 p.m. to 7 p.m.
1615 Dundas St. E.
835 Queen St. (461-1168)

Toronto Island Food Co-op
(Walk in and buy.) Mark-up: 10% for working members; 25% for non-working members. Goods sold: flour, nuts, dried fruit, cider, powdered milk and molasses.
Saturday 1 p.m. to 2 p.m. and Wednesday 7 p.m. to 8 p.m.
Co-op house (behind the Ward's Island Club House).
7 3rd St. (368-9384)

St. Jamestown Food Club
(Pre-order and Pre-pay.) Goods sold: fruit, vegetables and baked goods. Mark-up: 10%. Membership requirements: your time.
Food's ordered Tuesday 4 p.m. to 7 p.m. and distributed Thursday 1 p.m. to 4 p.m.
275 Bleeker St., Apt. 501 (923-4402)

Karma Co-op
(Walk in and buy.) Goods sold: Fruits and vegetables, cheese, eggs, grains, flour, honey, oil, peanut butter, spices, vitamins and grocery items. Membership requirements: a $12 loan, an $8 annual fee and a minimum of two volunteer hours a month.
Thursday 4 p.m. to 8 p.m., Friday 12 noon to 8 p.m., Saturday 10 a.m. to 2 p.m.
344 Dupont St. (923-3013)

Karma II
(Walk in and buy.) Goods sold: fruit, vegetables, cheese, eggs, grains, flour, basic grocery items, spices, fresh fruit, nuts, honey, oil and peanut butter. Mark-up: 15%. Members pay $12 a year and work at least two hours a month.
Friday 12 noon to 7 p.m., and Saturday 10 a.m. to 1 p.m.
96 Gerrard St. E.
450 Briar Hill Ave. (483-1409)

Regent Park Food Club
(Pre-order.) Mark-up's 15% on fruit and vegetables and cheese. Members pay $5 a year and work four hours per month.
Pre-order: Wednesday 9 a.m. to 9 p.m. Distribution: Friday 11 a.m. to 6 p.m.
School portable, Oak and River Streets.
42 Blevins Place, Apt. 609 (366-8786)

Woodgreen Produce and Grain Store
(Walk in and buy — for singles only.) Goods sold: fresh produce, grain, dried fruit, nuts and eggs. Mark-up: 15% on produce; 10% on other items. No membership requirements.
Friday 10 a.m. to 2:30 p.m.
835 Queen St. E. (461-1168)

3. Restaurants

Eating out on a limited budget doesn't mean you have to settle for second best or a greasy spoon. Toronto has a fantastic variety of budget-gourmet restaurants and in this chapter we offer our list of great eateries that serve some of the best food in town with prices to match. There is everything from a musical pizzeria, a funky 50s type hamburger joint, pick-your-own, straight-from-the-kitchen Greek restaurants, even a Mediaeval feast. You'll probably find that dining prix fixe has decided advantages. In Places like Old Ed's, Organ Grinder, Spaghetti Factory, a single price buys an appetizer, entrée, dessert, beverage and atmosphere.

The choice is up to you. Here then is our list.

Anthony's Villa

Service with a smile, a song and perhaps even a dance is the rule at this cheerful, informal place where waiters and waitresses double as entertainers. You dine in a grotto-like atmosphere amid crystal, carved wood and red-checked tablecloths, and dinner can be any one of 16 five-course dinners (from $3.95), from Coq au Vin Rosemarie (a generous breast of chicken smothered in onions, mushrooms and wine sauce) to Wiener Schnitzel. "The best of French, Italian and Canadian dishes" is how they put it and you can't argue with the food or the low, all-inclusive prices. Chx, M.C. Licensed.

Daily noon to 2:30 p.m. for lunch and 5 p.m. to 1 a.m. (except Sundays when they close at 10 p.m.) for dinner
146 Dupont St. (924-1886)

Bumpkins

The ultimate budget gourmet restaurant in Toronto is Bumpkin's. The food is so good and the prices so ridiculously low, that there's always a line-up that stretches out to the sidewalk. Hors d'oeuvre, such as avocado stuffed with crab and escargots at $2 tend to make you forget about the strangers seated next to you on the long wooden benches in the noisy front room, or beside you at the tables in the quieter back room.

If you stick to a Bumpkin's special like filet of sole served with tiny roasted potatoes and green beans — plus a salad, cheesecake or pie and tea or coffee, you'll spend under $5 per person — $4.85 actually. If you opt for more exotic exotic fare, the bill may go as high as $8 or $10 per person. To avoid the line-up, be there precisely on the dot of 5:30 p.m. No credit cards. Not licensed.

Monday to Saturday 5:30 p.m. to midnight. Closed Sunday.
No reservations.
557 Parliament St. (922-8655)

Bumpkin's Take-Out

No pennypincher's guide would be complete without Bumpkin's Take-out, the ultimate in cheap, portable potables and gourmet meals-on-wheels (your own) that's an offshoot of the popular, budget-priced restaurant of the same name. A selective Bumpkin's-style menu features unbelievably modest prices and exotic take-out fare, a combination that's impossible to beat. There's a choice of several hot dishes, salads and Dagwood-sized sandwiches made with crusty whole-wheat kaisers. For $2.25 you get a generous portion of delicately seasoned, piping-hot chicken cacciatore or spicy, hot couscous — almost enough for two; delectable crab and avocado salad, a perennial favorite, is just $2.10; and a fresh shrimp salad with crisp, fresh vegetables smothered in shrimp costs $1.50. For potables, you have a choice of herbal teas (30¢) or hot spiced apple cider (30¢). For dessert, there's cheesecake for 60¢ and assorted natural baked delicacies for 35¢ each. One of the best buys is Bumpkin's beef pâté sandwich — an enormous slice of liver pâté garnished with egg, tomato and lettuce and wedged between a generous whole-wheat kaiser — a meal in itself for just $1.15. Order ahead to save time — it's frantic during lunch and dinner hours. No credit cards. Not licensed.

Monday to Friday 11:45 a.m. to 9 p.m., Wednesday and Saturday to 8 p.m.
296 Gerrard St. E. (961-5330)

Country Style
You won't find any frills at this small family-run restaurant specializing in solid eastern European fare like paprikash, schnitzels, stuffed peppers and bean soups. Go when you're really hungry and try the Country Plate. It serves two generously for $7.50, with a variety of meats, rice, potatoes and beets. Top it off with espresso (60¢) and fresh strudel. No credit cards. Not licensed.

Monday to Saturday 11 a.m. to 10 p.m., Sunday noon to 10 p.m.
450 Bloor St. W. (537-1745)

Egerton's
Apart from the Little Red School House décor, the beer and the nightly entertainment the real point about Egerton's is their fast, cheap menu and their breakfast special — two eggs any style, bacon, toast and coffee for $1.25. And it's good! Hearty beef stew, spaghetti, thick roast beef sandwiches and super-cheap daily specials like a double hamburger with French fries and a side salad ($1) are featured for lunch. Am. Ex., Chx., M.C. Beer and wine.

Monday to Saturday 7:30 a.m. to 1 a.m., Sunday noon to 10 p.m.
70 Gerrard St. E. (366-9401)

The Groaning Board
Only chain smokers can resist this airy, spacious health food-type restaurant with its earthy decor, relaxed atmosphere and strict ban on smoking. Non-smoking health food lovers, casual types and penny-pinchers thrive on the clear air, pleasant service, fine food and low prices. Apart from quaint oak church benches, garden-sized plants and gingham lampshades, it's fun to make your own salad at the buffet where you can load up your plate with a nutritious mélange of fresh vegetables, fruits, pickles and garnishes. Then there are those famous Board extras: warm muffins and banana bread and their own delectable fruit-flavored yogurts. For just $3 you can make your own luncheon salad at the buffet and a sandwich (or opt for a casserole). Sample their moist banana muffins and top it off with a warm apple crisp for dessert. For dinner there's a wide selection including old Board favorites like Quiche Lorraine ($3), crêpes filled with combinations of cheese, fruit and/or seafood ($2.50 to $3.50), and special desserts like a huge yogurt parfait ($2), light dessert crêpes topped with frozen yogurt and drizzled with honey or plainer fare of plate-sized oatmeal cookies or date squares (75¢ and up). Nightly enter-

tainment can be anything from a girl who could double for Joan Baez to an old film flick Monday night ($1.50 cover charge). Chx. Beer and wine.

Monday to Thursday 11:30 a.m. to midnight, Friday and Saturday to 1 a.m.
(Note: Monday night — $3 minimum, Tuesday to Thursday — $2 cover, Friday and Saturday — $3 cover.)
1057 Bay St. (922-9876)

Lord Stanley's
Take your kids to Lord Stanley's to show them what lively medieval feasts without knives and forks were like. Unlike Elizabethan times there's no bone throwing but there's a wandering minstrel, lots of singing and food from soup to nuts. Featured is the feast platter (after soup and bread) loaded down with tasty chicken, succulent spare ribs, beef kebobs with onions and mushrooms, and corn-on-the-cob. The finishing touches are grapes, nuts and coffee with a cinnamon stick. The feast costs $8.40 per person with wine; without, $7.40. For kids it's just $5.95. Lunch can be anything from a simple soup, salad and coffee ($1.95) to Quiche Lorraine and salad with black bread ($2.55). Am. Ex., Chx., M.C. Licensed.

Lunch: Monday through Friday, noon to 2:30 p.m. Open for feasting daily, beginning Monday through Friday at 6 p.m., Saturday and Sunday at 5:30 p.m. Reservations not accepted after 9:30 p.m. weeknights, 10 p.m., Friday and Saturday; 8:30 p.m. Sunday.
26 Lombard St. (363-8561)

Mount Pleasant Lunch
A limited menu and gourmet fare at the best prices in town make it a perennial favorite with thrifty gourmands. And in case you haven't been there for a while, the food's still as good, the prices just as low and the service as fast and unobtrusive as ever. In case you've never been, Mount Pleasant Lunch is not at all like the name implies. It's more like a charming French café with its checkered cloths, fresh flowers and tastefully understated décor. Almost any fare on the menu is excellent and in most cases include soup or juice, salad, a main course, beverage and piping hot garlic bread. Dessert's extra at noon, but included with dinner at night. Its daily specials are impossible to resist. Luncheon specials (from $1.65 to $1.85) include old stand-bys like spicy lasagna and wiener schnitzel. But at dinner, expect fare like Rock Cornish Hen, cooked to perfection, or succulent Duckling à l'Orange (from $4.25). (And if you really want to eat on the cheap, try filet of sole for $3.50.) House wines are excellent and reasonably priced at $2 for ¼ litre. There's always a line-up by 12:30 noon and by 5:30 p.m. And don't expect to linger over coffee when they're busy. Dishes are whisked away as you finish your last bite — sometimes sooner if you don't speak up. No credit cards. Wine and beer.

Monday to Friday, 11:30 a.m. to 2:30 p.m. for lunch, and Monday to Thursday 5 p.m. to 10 p.m. for dinner. Friday and Saturday 5 p.m. to 11 p.m. for dinner. Closed Sunday.
604 Mount Pleasant (481-9331)

Lord Stanley's

```
                COCKTAILS
MANHATTAN ..... $1²⁵ COLLINS, RYE, Rum, GIN. $1²⁵
MARTINI ....... $1²⁵ SCREWDRIVER ... $1²⁵
GIMLET ........ $1²⁵ WHISKY SOUR ... $1²⁵
DAIQUIRI ...... $1²⁵ SINGAPORE SLING. $1²⁵
BLOODY MARY ... $1²⁵ OLD FASHIONED. $1²⁵
        IMPORTED RED WINES
YAGO .......BOTTLE ........ $5
CASTELLI Romani ... BOTTLE ... 35oz. .. $6
SZEKSZARDI ... BOTTLE ... 35oz. .. $6
            ROSÉ WINES
MATEUS ROSÉ (IMPORTED) ½ BOTTLE .... $3
MATEUS ROSÉ (IMPORTED) BOTTLE ... $5
JORDAN VALLEY (CRACKLING) ...... $4
    IMPORTED WHITE WINE
LENS MOSER (KREMSER SCHLUCK) BOTTLE. $5
            CHAMPAGNE
BRIGHT'S PRESIDENT ... BOTTLE ... $9
PROVINCIAL SALES TAX NOT INCLUDED.
```
A genuine Honest Ed's menu

Old Ed's
It's not gourmet fare, mind you, but for $3.50 you get a hearty meal and more than your fill of turn-of-the-century décor and decorum — gentlemen *must* wear jackets and ties. Also in keeping with Ed's aesthetic dictates, the awesome 1,000-seat pavilion is packed with antiques and collectibles like old-fashioned barbers' chairs at the bar, impressive stained glass windows, potted ferns, brassware and other nostalgic pieces. Even the prices are reminiscent of a bygone era: $3.50 for your choice of salisbury steak, halibut or Southern fried chicken complete with roll, salad, vegetables, dessert and beverage. Am. Ex., Chx., D.C., M.C. Licensed.

Monday to Friday noon to 2 p.m. and 5 p.m. to 10 p.m., Saturday 5 p.m. to 10 p.m., Sunday 5 p.m. to 9 p.m. 272 King St. W. (863-0087)

Ontario Legislature's Member's Dining Room
It sounds insulting, but the Members' Dining Room at the "Leg", as it's fondly called, is an oxymoron. (No, not Bill Davis, the dining room.) It's delightfully contradictory from the time you enter — whispering over the lavish décor and the garish luxury — to the time you leave, exclaiming over the wildly inexpensive prices. It's a great place to eat, alright, and nobody appreciated it more than I did when I worked there. After all, where else can you have near-gourmet meals, vintage wines and tall drinks (after work) all at prices the average working girl can afford. The answer is nowhere, probably. And things haven't changed that much. There's a new dining room, with thick carpets, soft lights and softer seats that's posher than ever, but the prices are still much the same. Beer's still cheap at 50¢ and so is a Bloody Mary at 75¢. And the food's still as fine and as reasonable as ever — from $2 to $5 a person for meals, like tender, juicy roast lamb or succulent beef stroganoff. And that includes soup or juice, dessert and tea or coffee. You might say it's open to the public in a round-about way — if you've a friend who works there, wangle an invitation to lunch. If you don't, there's no harm in dropping by for lunch or dinner provided it's not between 1 and 2 p.m., or 6 and 7 p.m. (You'll feel as if you've imposed, and you have.) Apart from that, relax and enjoy. After all, it's *your* tax dollar.

8 a.m. to 10 a.m. for breakfast, 11:30 a.m. to 2:30 p.m. for lunch, and 6 p.m. to 8:30 p.m. for dinner when the House is in session.
Basement of the Main Parliament Building, Queen's Park Crescent.

Parkes
At Parkes you can enjoy a complete gourmet meal for about $7 each, without wine. If you stick to the entrées like Chicken Chasseur or

Shrimps Newfoundland (all generous portions) your bill will be around $5. Their Mussels Vinaigrette appetizer is highly recommended ($1.75), delicious homemade soups are 95¢, and for dessert the crème caramel (95¢) is probably the best in town. Am.Ex., Chx. Licensed.

Monday to Saturday noon to 2:30 p.m. and 6 p.m. to 10:30 p.m. (no lunch Saturday)
226 Carlton St. (925-8907)

Peter Pan
Highlights of this 80-year-old restaurant are the original marble topped counters, walnut veneered booths, beautiful stained glass windows and plain, wholesome food. Featured are Depression-type dishes — tangy Welsh rarebit and a green salad ($1.85), a thick juicy 8-ounce hamburger with potato salad and vegetables for $1.95 and evening specials from $3. To top it off there's always apple crumble pie (75¢) or a homemade milkshake ($1.25). No credit cards. Licensed.

Monday to Saturday noon to midnight. (Lunch is served from noon to 2:30 but they're open for coffee, dessert and soup from 2:30 to 6 p.m.)
373 Queen St. W. (364-3669)

Poor Faygees Crêpes
Prices are reasonable, especially for the Yorkville area. For about $4 per person you can enjoy delectable crêpes stuffed with your choice of their 20 fillings. The generous Yorkville Salad ($2.50) loaded with a variety of fresh vegetables, makes a perfect supper on a summer evening when you can eat on the terrace and watch the Yorkville parade. No credit cards. Licensed.

Daily noon to 1 a.m.
113 Yorkville Ave. (961-9339)

Toby's Goodeats
Order a hamburger and a milkshake and you'll think you're back in your old hamburger hang-out or on the set of *Happy Days*. And if your kid thinks of a hamburger joint is McDonald's or the A&W take him along for a glimpse of the past. Featured are '50s-type arborite tables, funky cookie jars, souvenir pennants and straight-from-the-'70s live green plants trailing from the ceiling and natural brick walls. Prominently displayed are Toby's Goodeats T-shirts worn by waitresses.) And the hamburgers? They're *real:* thick, juicy, unprocessed — and they come with real, chunky hand-cut fries and garnishes of tomatoes, onions, pickles, relish, mustard and other condiments. Toby's honest burger, a plain ordinary hamburger, is $2.10. For lighter fare there's a superb spinach salad ($1.25) with bacon bits, cheese, mushrooms and bean sprouts. So order a 95¢ milkshake, eat your heart out and dream about the old days. No credit cards. Not licensed.

Monday to Saturday 11:30 a.m. to 3 a.m., Sunday 10:30 a.m. to 1 a.m.
91 Bloor St. W. (925-2171)

Tramp's
The real attraction of Tramps is high-calibre gourmet food at more than affordable prices. Whether it's their Quiche Maison ($2.50), Coquille de Mer ($3.45) or Paella Valenciana (saffron rice filled with generous amounts of chicken, shrimps and scallops — $3.45) you're sure to approve. Meals come with an excellent salad and warm crusty bread. Am.Ex., Chx., M.C. Licensed.

Monday to Friday noon to 3 p.m., 5 p.m. to 10:30 p.m. Saturday 5 p.m. to 10:30 p.m.
649 Yonge St. (961-8078)

Chinese

Kwong Chow

Sit back and marvel at the menu of hundreds of exotic dishes, from "thousand flower chicken" to squid with snow peas. Or stick with the anti-inflationary — $1.25 to $2.70 — luncheon specials, a real deal when you consider the generous portions of two to three main dishes, rice and tea. And if you're on a fixed budget, their fixed-priced dinners are a bargain. Dinner for four costs $16.95, and includes won ton soup, egg rolls, Cantonese chow mein, shrimps and lobster sauce, honey and garlic spareribs, sweet and sour chicken with pineapple, vegetable fried rice, cookies and tea. Am.Ex., D.C. Licensed.

Monday to Thursday 11:30 a.m. to 1 a.m., Friday and Saturday 11 a.m. to 2 a.m. and Sunday 3:30 p.m. to 11:30 p.m.
126 Elizabeth St. (362-4322)

The Peking Palace

The overall impression of this new Spadina-cum-Chinese restaurant is one of tasteful décor, good service and fine food. The cuisine is Mandarin and the food typically crisp (never soggy) and delicately seasoned — better than it has a right to be at their prices. If you're tired of thick, cardboard-like egg rolls, try theirs — they're paper thin, light and perfectly seasoned. And main dishes like Cantonese-style shrimp chop suey filled with seafood delicacies and crunchy oil-cooked vegetables.

A $2 special lunch includes soup, tea, rice and your choice of main dishes like beef and vegetables, chop suey and several sweet and sour dishes. Under $4 gets you egg rolls, a main course like shrimp chop suey or sweet and sour pork with pineapple and steamed rice and an endless pot of jasmine tea. Chx. Not licensed.

Daily except Wednesday noon to 10 p.m.
296 Spadina Ave. (363-4151)

Sai Woo
If you were a fan of the old Sai Woo, you're bound to like the new one with its original brush paintings, golf-leafed dragons and Oriental splendor. Sai Woo hasn't changed all that much. Granted it's posher and roomier (600 seats) but the food and prices are just as incomparable and the menu as imaginative as ever. For lunch there are still tiny pastry appetizers.

DimSum specialties like cha shiu bow (steamed buns filled with spiced barbecued pork and oyster sauce) and op jak (a delicacy stuffed with shrimps, pork and bamboo shoots and basted with bean curd) for from 25¢ to 85¢ each. Tempting luncheon specials start at 85¢ and dinners-for-two, $9.25. No credit cards. Licensed.

Monday to Saturday 11 a.m. to 3 a.m., Sunday 11 a.m. to 2 a.m.
124-130 Dundas St. W. (366-4988)

Fish

Mr. Oliver's
It took Mr. Oliver months of travel through Europe and the U.S. to develop his concept of "the best reasonably priced lunch in town." His specialty is *fresh* fish and chips and homemade baked goods, including light, airy muffins and flavorful cheesecakes and trifles baked on the premises. You might object to disposable plastic cutlery and paper plates but you won't object to crisp, tasty shrimp and chips ($2.40) or chips and halibut ($2.45). Or a scrumptious homemade chocolate brownie (50¢) or the best rum trifle you ever had for dessert (50¢). The décor is bright and cheery. No credit cards. Not licensed.

Monday to Thursday 11 a.m. to midnight, Friday to 1 a.m., Saturday and Sunday 9 a.m. to 1 a.m.
692 Mount Pleasant Ave. (481-9404)

French

The Bodega
For about $5, you enjoy a simple French country meal with soup or salad, a main course and coffee. For a light supper try Avocado de Desdemona at $2.75. The wine is less than $2 a carafe, the service efficient and the atmosphere cheerful. It's especially nice on a warm summer evening when the terrace is open. All cards. Licensed.

Monday to Saturday 11:30 a.m. to 11 p.m.
197 College St. (979-1287)

German

Cafe May
Their motto is "enjoy an inexpensive meal in a cosy atmosphere". Though the service is efficient you never feel rushed. You'll spend about $5 for soup (45¢ or 85¢), entrée and dessert. Sample their crispy, light Wiener Schnitzel ($3.85) or savory roast pork ($3.85) and, for dessert, an excellent Black Forest cake (85¢) for those who never count calories. No credit cards. Not licensed.

Wednesday to Saturday noon to 11 p.m., Sunday noon to 10 p.m., Monday 5 p.m. to 11 p.m.
396 Roncesvalles Ave. (532-9218)

Griffith's Delicatessen
Behind the bright, busy delicatessen in front lies a cosy, dark Gerham rathskeller — the perfect place for an intimate but inexpensive lunch. Soft lights and a Catholic collection of antiques delight the eye; hearty homemade soups and sandwiches and reasonable prices delight your appetite and your pocketbook.

Homemade soup could be their beef broth thick with vegetables and meat dumplings (85¢); sandwiches, hot Bavarian meat loaf ($1.25) or ham or pastrami on rye ($1.75). Then there's hot chili con carne and rye toast ($1.95) or cabbage rolls with sour cream and home fries ($2.65); and for dessert, black forest cake or an excellent bread pudding. No credit cards. Not licensed.

Monday to Saturday 9 a.m. to 9 p.m.
2086 Queen St. E. in the Beaches (690-4022)

Greek

Mykonos
It's a great place to take the kids for an authentic Greek meal. In true Greek fashion, there's no menu and you get to choose your dishes right from the spotless kitchen. Almost immediately after your arrival the waiter arrives with fresh crusty bread and you're whisked away to the kitchen for a brisk but informative tour of pots full of mousaka, meat balls, eggplant baked in olive oil and spices, chicken, fish, green beans baked in oil and other authentic Greek dishes like spicy Greek salad laced with feta cheese and olives. Then it's back to your table to await the arrival of your food via the waiter. For under $5 you get one meat dish with two to three vegetables, dessert and coffee amid surroundings that can only be described as "unclassic Greek." Licensed. M.C. Chx.

Monday to Saturday noon to 1 a.m., Sunday noon - 10 p.m.
625 Yonge St. (925-8903)

Hungarian

Tarogato
For $5 a person (without wine or beer) you can enjoy a generous portion of their famous cold fruit soup ($1), followed by chicken paprikash or cabbage rolls ($2.90) and, for dessert, home-made strudel (80¢), often still warm from Tarogato's oven. There are more expensive items on the menu, but the bargain fare is just as tasty. Chx. Beer and wine.

Monday to Wednesday, noon to midnight, Thursday to Saturday noon to 1 a.m., and Sunday noon to 10 p.m.
553 Bloor St. W. (536-7566)

Indian

Samina's Tiffin Room
This is an Indian restaurant in a class by itself. Seasonings are used only to enhance the ingredients and the menu is a fascinating assortment of exotica. Main courses are $3 to $4, and the portions are generous. Chicken tikka at $3.75 and Daalcha (beef, eggplant and lentils in a special curry blend) are favorites

with Samina's regulars. Side dishes like cool yogurt with vegetables (25¢), and cardomom and cinnamon rice (70¢) enhance your meal without boosting the tab. Am.Ex., Chx., M.C. Not licensed.

Monday to Friday noon to 2 p.m. and 6 p.m. to 11 p.m., Saturday 6 p.m. to 11 p.m. only.
326 Dundas St. W. (362-0350)

Indonesian

Bali
An Indonesian feast costs about $14, but you can enjoy authentic combination dinners for $5, including refreshing coconut milk drink (75¢) and exotic fruit desserts (50¢ to 75¢). Basic meals like rice, chicken and vegetables ($3.25) or shishkabob with rice and salad ($4) are transformed into exotic fare at Bali. Try their $2.25 luncheon specials if you work in the Lawrence-Avenue Road area. Chx. M.C. Not licensed.

Tuesday to Friday, noon to 2:30 p.m. and 5 p.m. to 9 p.m., Saturday and Sunday noon to 9 p.m.
1554 Avenue Rd. (782-5928)

Italian

Capriccio Dining Room
You can splurge on their antipasto (with secret-recipe marinade) at $3.50 but, for economy, stick to the minestrone and stratiachella ($1.25) to start. The entrées are assorted veal and seafood dishes at about $6 a plate. You'll be full when you've finished but you can split a zabaglione dessert ($2.25) — the classic finish to an Italian meal. The wine list is a pleasant surprise, with Valpolicella Folonari and Colli Romani only $6 a bottle. Chx. M.C. Beer and wine.

Tuesday to Saturday 5 p.m. to 11 p.m., Sunday 5 p.m. to 10 p.m.
580 College St. (535-2229)

Frank Vetere's Pizza
You choose your own toppings and how much of each you want, and Frank's friendly staff will make it up for you on a crust that puts the take-out variety to shame. Two people can eat for as little as $3 or as much as $15 depending on your appetite, and your choice of beer or wine. Chx., M.C. Beer and wine.

Monday to Thursday noon to midnight, Friday and Saturday to 1 a.m., Sunday to 10 p.m.
6 Carlton St. (368-3722)

Old Spaghetti Factory
The spaghetti ain't great but the décor and all-inclusive low prices are irresistible. Adults and kids line up for hours to enjoy the old streetcar, Victorian furniture and fun atmosphere in this huge (600 seats), noisy and ornate restaurant. Featured are hundreds of antiques and collectibles and several kinds of spaghetti with sour-dough bread, salad, dessert and beverage — all for under $3 ($1.95 for kids with parents). There's also more expensive fare like lasagna, chicken cacciatore and veal dishes for those who pass on the spaghetti. There are no reservations

Dining at the Old Spaghetti Factory

for groups under 20 people so go early or be prepared for a lengthy wait on weekends. Am. Ex., Chx., M.C. Licensed.

Monday to Saturday noon to 1 a.m. and Sunday 2 p.m. to 10 p.m.
54 The Esplanade (864-9761)

The Organ Grinder
An enticing combination of Wurlitzer music and pizza attracts a steady stream of music buffs and pizza fans who munch to the tune of the huge 1000-pipe organ and feast their eyes on an array of musical instruments like cathedral chimes, a glockenspiel, player piano and a counter full of smaller ear-teasers. The pizza's not as superb as organist Don Thompson's music but it's cheap ($1.95 to $3.65), *usually* hot and seldom soggy. Your musical knowledge won't help to decipher the menu. There's a host of ingredients from pepperoni, anchovies and shrimp and a medley of musical pizza names like Wurlitzer, piper's delight, marimba, sonata surf, shrimp encore and for those who don't care for pizza there's a watered-down version of Old Spaghetti Factory fare (it's owned by the same enterprising people): Lasagna at $3.95 or Veal Parmagiana at $4.50. Dessert is extra and there's a choice of two: cheesecake ($1.25) and apple pie (85¢). Expect to eat nicely sans vin for under $4. Am.Ex., Chx., M.C. Licensed.

There's entertainment Monday to Thursday 6 p.m. to 11 p.m., Friday 4 p.m. to 12:30 a.m., Saturday 12 p.m. to 12:30 a.m. and Sunday 12 p.m. to 10 p.m.
Monday to Thursday noon to midnight (1 a.m. in summer), Friday and Saturday to 1 a.m., Sunday noon to 10 p.m.
58 The Esplanade (368-1726)

Japanese

Michi
The décor, the food and the service all combine to give you a leisurely evening of Japanese dining. You'll be seated at low bamboo-seat tables by waitresses outfitted in kimonos. The amazing bargains are in the fixed price section — like complete sukiyaki or seafood dinner at $8. You begin with a plate of tiny, palate-clearing appetizers, then await Japanese consommé and a plate of more serious appetizers, like shrimps fried in light batter. Your main course comes with rice and crunchy vegetables and for dessert there's splendid Mandarin orange pie. And if you work in the area, you'll find their lunches just a little more expensive than a take-out ham and cheese with coffee. Even with lots of sâke to wash it down, your bill for two shouldn't exceed $25. Am. Ex., Chx. Licensed.

Monday to Friday noon to 2:30 p.m. and 5 p.m. to 11 p.m., Saturday 5 p.m. to 11 p.m.
459 Church St. (924-1303)

Jewish
The Bagel
For hearty appetites and tight budgets, The Bagel has solid home-cooked fare. Leave your sensitive palate at home and enjoy a generous bowl of meaty cabbage borscht with

black bread (80¢) or the "deluxe items" like huge and spicy cabbage rolls or sweet and sour meatballs, all for under $4 each. The bagels are excellent and lox and cream cheese lovers say The Bagel has the best in town. No credit cards. Not licensed.

Daily 7 a.m. to 11 p.m.
285 College St. (923-0171)

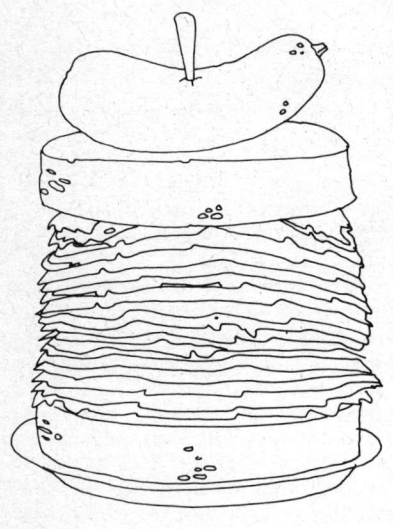

Moishe's Tel-Aviv
As the name implies, the Tel-Aviv features Israeli food, rather than the eastern European cooking you'll find in most Jewish restaurants. Moishe calls himself the Fallafel King, and his regulars come from all over the city for these plate-sized envelopes of pita bread stuffed with spicy meat balls and crunchy salad ($1.10). Fallafels are the best buy at the Tel-Aviv but there's lots more to choose from for less than $3 a person. The place is always crowded and noisy; not recommended for intimate dining. No credit cards. Not licensed.

Daily 10 a.m. to 10 p.m.
440 Spadina Ave. (921-1917)

Vegetarian

Beggar's Banquet
You can feast on fine vegetarian cuisine for less than $5 and, on weekends, enjoy live jazz while you eat. The menu changes daily but each night one national cuisine is featured. The food's all fresh, healthy and imaginatively prepared, like Moroccan couscous with spinach, green pepper and squash. Lunches range from open-faced sandwiches to vegetable stews and you can have a complete noon dinner for about $2.50 each. No credit cards. Not licensed.

Monday to Friday noon to 2:30 p.m., and 6 to 10 p.m. Tuesday dinner only; Saturday noon to 4 p.m. and 6 p.m. to 10 p.m., Sunday brunch noon to 4 p.m.
325 Queen St. W. (366-4147)

Special Occasions

Elinka's
Owners Vera Dimoff and Elinka Petroff are justly proud of their elegant cuisine and comfortable atmosphere. For about $25, two people can enjoy a leisurely meal with wine and all the trimmings. You begin with appetizers like Crab Louis or Oysters Antoine (under $3) and proceed to an entrée like Veal Parmagiano or Pepper Steak Oriental for under $6. Everything, including the bread, is homemade and prepared with care. Daily luncheon specials are $3 to $5. Am. Ex., Chx., D.C., M.C. Licensed.

Monday to Saturday 11 a.m. to 3 p.m. and 5 p.m. to 10 p.m. (no lunch Saturday)
720 Queen St. E. (466-2023)

Nicholas Pearce (left) & David Barrett of Fenton's

Fenton's
Dinner at Fenton's is no bargain if you just want to eat out, but if you want a special treat you can dine here for about $30 per couple on fare that ranks with the best in the city. The menu is uniformly excellent with appetizers like Mussels in curry, lemon and vinaigrette sauce ($2) and Quenelles of Shrimp ($2.75) incredibly reasonable for their quality. The stuffed breast of chicken is probably the best fowl in town and only $6. Reserve several days in advance. Fenton's is as popular as it deserves to be. Am. Ex., Chx., M.C. Licensed.

Luncheon from noon to 2 p.m., dinner 6 p.m. to 9:30 p.m. daily.
12 Gloucester St. (961-8485)

Le Trou Normand
Normandy has its own special cuisine, which is famous for unusual combinations (like rabbit with gooseberries) which come off beautifully. Devotées of Norman cooking consume bracing quantities of Calvados with their meals, but you're advised to opt for wine unless you've a high alcohol tolerance. Appetizers at Le Trou Normand range from $1.85 to $3.20, but two can split a plate of mixed hors d'oeuvres at $2.95. Specialties like rabbit ($7.20) and calve's liver ($6.50) may not appeal to you until you've had them prepared à la Normande. For lunch, they serve standard French dishes with soup, entrée, dessert and coffee for about $3. Reservations are a must for both lunch and dinner. Am. Ex., Chx., D.C., M.C. Licensed.

Tuesday to Saturday noon to 5 p.m., 6 p.m. to 10 p.m., Sunday 6 p.m. to 10 p.m. only.
90 Yorkville Ave. (967-5959)

4. Home

Home is where the heart is and, be it a tiny garret or an elegant Rosedale mansion, we tell you the cheapest ways to find it, furnish it and move into it. You'll discover where to find great appliances and furniture, lush carpets, fine china and kitchen things at more-than-affordable prices. Plus sound equipment for stereo buffs, plants for green thumbers and a do-it-yourself section for handymen (and women). All the information in this chapter, from moving and mortgages to ecology-minded energy-saving tips, is geared to saving you money.

Furniture & Appliances

Auctions, Buy and Sell *and the* Bargain Hunter *are an unlimited source of good used furniture and nearly-new appliances and by far your best bet if you're in the market for either. It's wise to remember that fine old furniture and antiques appreciate in value; new pieces depreciate. A new dining room suite that costs $900 is worth a third of its value in a few years time; an exquisitely crafted vintage suite that sells for a mere $300 today should double, even triple in value in the same length of time. Where furniture and antiques are concerned, it pays to speculate! Shop around, compare prices and talk to dealers before, not after, you buy. Dented, scratched and otherwise damaged appliances are reduced by as much as 40% at many stores and there's generally a large assortment in auctions and newspaper ads at substantial reductions. There are no guarantees and you'll have to shop around but you'll save* money. *And for those on a super-tight budget, the Society of Goodwill Services on Jarvis, second floor, (see page 17) is bargain hunter's paradise. And here's more:*

Aardvark
Contemporary imported furniture and accessories, fabrics from Holland and England, and a small stock

Summer furniture at Aardvark

of very special kids' books and toys are found upstairs in Aardvark, a shop that's just as intriguing as its name. Downstairs it's even more intriguing: a bargain basement, chock full of Aardvark's own goodies at reduced prices, usually half-price and less. To give you an idea, there was a large assortment of kids' toys, books and puzzles for half-price. See-through music boxes — you can actually see how the music's made — were just $3.95 (reg. $8.50). And slick imported lamps (reg. $150) and wall lights (reg. $39) were half-price. There's only one catch: the selection varies from week to week.

Monday to Saturday 10 a.m. to 6 p.m.
61 Front St. E. (368-2697)

Continental Salvage
It's an unlimited but unpredictable source of great bargains — not even the staff knows what's coming next.

Continental Salvage sells new items (almost anything) recovered from insurance claims at up to 50% reductions. Accordingly you might see anything from TVs (Sony color TV, $325) and radios (Panasonic 6-band, $125) to stoves (GE ranges, $185) and refrigerators. Goods are 50% of the marked price except when marked "Net." It's a great place to find appliances, carpets and furniture at bargain prices, but call first to see what's in stock. No delivery.

Monday to Friday 8:30 a.m. to 5 p.m.
43 Front St. E. (364-3441)

Danbury Sales Ltd.
Its specialty is new-and-used office equipment and you can buy it at bargain prices at one of their many auctions, or at their showroom. Used desks, typewriters ($60 and up for a decent one), chairs ($20), stacking shelves and other office "musts" sell for from $2 to $2,000 at the showroom. New desks are $75 and up and if you can't find what you want they'll order it for you. Household furnishings (beautiful brass beds, $300) are available at times. Auctions are held almost anywhere and are advertised in the paper the Friday before the sale. I haven't attended one but they sound promising. Expect anything and everything for the office from typewriters to heavy equipment. It's cash and carry.

Monday to Friday, 9 a.m. to 5 p.m.
1127 Finch Ave., west of Dufferin (650-5241)

Eaton's Warehouse
There are hundreds of appliances in all colors, sizes and descriptions, all at a discount — if you're willing to settle for a few scratches, perhaps a dent or two. And twice a year there are huge annual sales where everything from furniture to clothes,

Annual Sales

Dansk Warehouse Sale
Anyone who appreciates the clean, simple lines of Scandinavian design is sure to appreciate this sale and its prices. You get from 30% to 60% off on everything you see. And that includes your favorite Kobenstyle cookware and serving dishes, fine imported stainless cutlery, glass and china. Most items sell at just over half-price, (a 45% discount, to be exact), and some for as much as 67% — just because they're slight seconds, ends-of-line, closeouts, or a sample from a show or exhibition. Check the papers for spring and fall sales.

60 Horner Ave. (259-1127)

De Boer's Warehouse Sale
We're all familiar with De Boer's. It's the kind of place you look wistfully at from the outside because you can't afford what's on the inside. But take heart. From time to time they have a sale and like their furniture, it can't be surpassed. Just what you'd expect from De Boer's. The trouble is, you can't predict if and when it will take place. It's sometimes once a year, sometimes more, but then as often as not, sometimes less. In fact it can be any time De Boer's sees fit to clear out its huge warehouse. And what a sale! Exquisitely crafted pieces sell at 25% to 70% reductions, sometimes well below cost. So check the papers and wait; you won't be sorry.

620 Supertest Rd., Downsview (661-0512)

Apartment Rental Tips

A suburban apartment is generally less expensive than a comparable unit downtown. But will your savings in rent out-weigh your transportation costs?

Is parking included in your rent or is there an extra charge? If you're forced to park on the street you can be sure of nightly parking tickets in most areas unless parking permits are required.

Ask about rent increases, repairs, general up-keep, heating (in winter), shopping and other neighborhood services. Find out about utilities. If you have to pay for your own, try to get an accurate estimate of costs or see the bills.

Contact the Consumer Protection Bureau and the Landlord and Tenant Advisory Bureau to check for complaints about faulty maintenance or retaining security deposits, etc.

Read your lease carefully — it's binding. All promises your landlord makes should be included. Include a clause that allows you to sublet and make sure you're not responsible for repairs. Note your security deposit on the lease and apply it to your last month's rent.

Many leases have an automatic renewal clause. Make a note of the date and be sure to give one or two months' (or whatever you've agreed to in your lease) notice by registered mail.

Have your lease checked by a lawyer and have a witness there when you sign it.

appliances, linen and carpets goes at up to 75% reductions. There are great "every day" buys too: a new slightly scratched 15 cu. ft. GE frig (reg. $449) for $369; a barely marked 15 cu. ft. Viking frig, just over $399; and a manual defrost, $289. And that's just a small sample — there are rows and rows of other appliances from which to choose.

Monday to Saturday 9:30 a.m. to 5:30 p.m., Thursday and Friday to 9:30 p.m.
2233 Sheppard Ave. W. (744-2111)

Furniture from Henri the 2nd

Henri the 2nd

Saturday is bargain hunter's day at Henri the 2nd, which specializes in beautifully designed home furnishings and accessories at discount prices. Apart from the usual wide selection of overruns, seconds and discontinued lines, there are spectacular flash sales where certain items go at cost. Tables were the big seller at the flash sale we attended. Any table — regardless of price — on the sidewalk in front of the store was $25. Square, chrome and Plexiglass coffee tables had been priced at $85.

And there were factory seconds from the oldest porcelain factory in Taiwan, where any piece painted by an apprentice is classed as a second. Large, hand-painted porcelain steamers sold for $36 to $88; hand-painted porcelain 28" vases, from $36 to $55; and sake cups that make charming bud vases for just $4.95.

And there's much, much more.

Furniture & Appliances

Most of the furniture carried is by Ply Designs and it's sold at 25% less than any other store in Metro because Henri buys up ends-of-lines, overruns and discontinued lines. There's a good selection: a blue denim four-piece sectional sofa, $595; natural birch, upholstered chairs for $149 ($199 elsewhere). Other bargains: Swedish Boda crystal at up to 50% off; Danish Copco cookware seconds are 25% less than anywhere else in the city. The Karelia-type heavy canvas tote bags are $10 and up. It's impossible to speculate as to what Henri will do next. Henri himself doesn't know — he's at the mercy of his suppliers.

Tuesday to Saturday, 10 a.m. to 6 p.m., Friday to 9 p.m.
1541 Bayview Ave., S. of Belsize (488-7763)

Sears' Warehouse
If you're in the market for a new appliance be sure to check their huge display of "Scratch and Dent Clearance" specials, like a 17 cu. ft. Coldspot Frostless refrigerator (reg. $599) for $529 or a Kenmore freezer (reg. $264.98), for $214.98. There's a full warranty and usually a large selection from which to choose. Look for good buys in ends-of-line, scratched and slightly damaged furniture and watch the papers for special sales.

Monday, Tuesday and Saturday 9:30 a.m. to 5:30 p.m., Wednesday to Friday 9:30 a.m. to 9:30 p.m.
2200 Islington Ave. N. (744-4500)

Canadian General Electric Company
Canadian General Electric Co. sells damaged small GE appliances and audio products at about two-thirds to 80% of the retail selling price at three locations. They can't predict what they'll have in stock, so call to make sure they have what you're looking for. Merchandise is guaranteed. All sales final.

Monday to Friday 9 a.m. to 5:30 p.m., Saturday to 5 p.m.
506 Oriole Parkway (481-4710)
Monday to Friday 8 a.m. to 5:30 p.m., Saturday 9 a.m. to 12:30 p.m.
2 Monogram Place, Weston (241-2527)
Monday to Friday 9 a.m. to 6 p.m., Saturday 10 a.m. to 6 p.m.
6101 Yonge St., Willowdale (223-8693)

Philips Consumer Service
If you don't mind slightly battered boxes, reconditioned goods or the odd scratch or two, you'll find many a bargain in small appliances. Everything from 14-speed blenders ($30.95), hand-mixers ($14.95) to shavers ($4 to $10) is under warranty (30 days on labor, 40 days on parts) and well below the distributor's price, at 25% to 40% reductions.

Monday to Friday 9:30 a.m. to 9:30 p.m., Saturday to 6 p.m.
Yonge-Eglinton Centre (489-2022)

Sunbeam Corporation
The Sunbeam Corporation is a bargain-hunter's paradise if you're in the market for appliances. Slightly damaged, marked and end-of-line appliances are on sale at a whopping 30% to 50% discount at Sunbeam's four busy service centres in Metro. We discovered a first-rate toaster for $16, and a blender for $35 (regularly $49.95).

Anything Sunbeam makes from vacuums to lawn mowers is up for grabs. Not even the staff can predict what's coming next, but a quick phone call will tell you what's currently selling and for how much. All merchandise is guaranteed.

Salvage

Teperman & Sons is the Eaton's of the wrecking trade. Like Eaton's, it's the biggest of its kind in Canada. 12¢ a running foot — depending on quality — for 2-by-4, $11.75 a sheet for 4-by-8-by-¾, and $20 to $30 for bathtubs. The booty from Teperman's includes fine oak, brass and marble, mirrors, carpets, desks for $15 and up, plus a complete range of plumbing. Frequently they have restaurant and office equipment.

Monday to Friday 7:30 a.m. to 5 p.m., Saturday to 12 noon. 2478 Eglinton Ave. (651-6161), Dufferin Street at Steeles Ave. (669-2400)

Greenspoon Brothers Ltd. is No. 2 on the wrecking scene.sink. 9¢ a running foot for 2-by-4; $10 a sheet for 4'-by-8-by-¾ plywood; and from $30 up for a fine old, porcelain-castiron bathtub. The largest yard and best selection is the "Highway 7" yard as it's called but there are three others.

Highway 7 store (794-0117): Monday to Friday, 8 a.m. to 4:30 p.m. 1095 Strathy, Port Credit (278-3346): Monday, noon to 5 p.m., Tuesday to Friday, 9 a.m. to 5 p.m., Saturday to 1 p.m. 28 Musgrave (699-7171): Monday to Friday 8 a.m to 5 p.m., Saturday to 1 p.m. Don Mills Road S. of Hwy. 7 (495-6492): Monday to Saturday 8 a.m. to 4:30 p.m.

1808 Avenue Rd., south of Hwy. 401 (781-9389): Tuesday to Saturday, 8:30 a.m. to 5 p.m.
2084A Lawrence Ave. E. at Warden (751-0111): Tuesday to Saturday, 8:30 a.m. to 5 p.m.
2500 Hurontario St., Huron Square, Mississauga (270-0801): Tuesday and Wednesday, 10 a.m. to 6 p.m., Thursday and Friday to 9 p.m., Saturday to 2 p.m.

Art

Art Gallery of Ontario
A $15 yearly membership and as little as $5 a month, rents you one of 900-odd paintings, kinetic works, lithographs and sculptures from the Art Gallery of Ontario's contemporary Canadian rental collection. Pieces and works are acquired on consignment from galleries all over town, so there's always a new selection. Rentals are based on a percentage of the price. A painting or piece valued at $200 or less rents for $5 a month; a $201 to $300 item, for $7 and so on.

Tuesday to Saturday 10 a.m. to 4 p.m., Thursday to 10 p.m.
Lower level of the AGO, 317 Dundas St. W. (361-0414)

Library Art
A 50¢ library card is one of the best investments you can make. Apart from books, cheap entertainment and recreational services, libraries are a great source of free, excellent art. In most cases, all you need is your library card to borrow from their fine collections. Here's a list of what's available:

Cedarbrae Library
Use your library card to borrow Oriental, classical, Renaissance, op and pop art from its extensive collection of framed prints and

reproductions. Canadiana includes the Group of Seven, Eskimo art and old Quebec original prints and some fine AGO and National Gallery reproductions and framed posters. Borrow a series for six weeks *free*.

Monday to Friday 9 a.m. to 8:30 p.m.
28 Fairhill Cresc., Don Mills (431-2222)

Etobicoke
Choose from 60 to 70 ready-to-hang prints, paintings, lithographs, etchings and photographs from promising Metro artists. Cost: $2-$5 per month.

Monday to Friday 10 a.m. to 9 p.m., Saturday 10 a.m. to 5 p.m.
1515 Albion Rd., just west of Kipling (741-7734)

North York
Over 212 mounted prints and reproductions, including some works of Paul Klee and John Constable are available free of charge for four weeks with a library card.

Monday 12:30 p.m. to 8:30 p.m., Tuesday to Friday 9 a.m. to 8:30 p.m., Saturday 9 a.m. to 5 p.m., Sunday 1 p.m. to 5 p.m.
5126 Yonge St., Willowdale (225-8891)

Toronto Libraries
The Group of Seven, Eskimo, Canadian and European artists are featured in its collection of ready-to-hang reproductions. Available free for six weeks with a library card.

Annette: 145 Annette Street (769-5846)
Beaches: 2161 Queen St. E. (691-9298)
City Hall: Nathan Phillip's Square (366-6330)
Danforth: 701 Pape Ave. (465-1221)
Dufferin-St. Clair: 1625 Dufferin St. (652-1460)
Parkdale: 1303 Queen St. W. (532-6548)
Parliament: 406 Parliament St. (924-7246)

U-Frame-It
According to U-Frame-It, you can frame anything — anything, that is, that you can flatten and hang up on the wall. And you'll save from 30% to 50% depending on the kind and style of frame you choose. But whatever your fancy, you're bound to save money by doing the job yourself, and you'll have a first-quality, custom-made frame to show off. There are hundreds to tempt you: square and round, fat and skinny frames in every conceivable style and material.

Costs run from 12¢ to 48¢ an inch and you can frame an 8"-by-10" picture for around $10. You learn by watching at U-Frame-It. Your materials are cut to size and they show you how, by doing a corner of your frame. From then on it's up to you. And if you make a mistake they'll try

U-Frame-It

It's Your Move

The average Canadian family moves every four years, and this "moving" experience costs anywhere from $50 to $5,000, depending on how and where you go. If your company's footing the bill, exorbitant professional moving rates probably won't concern you. But lost or damaged furniture, late deliveries or deliberately deflated estimates should.

In spring and summer — peak season — late deliveries are common. And the moving company's under no obligation to pay your expenses while you and your family wait it out at a motel for two or three weeks. You foot the bill. And what about liability? A mover's liability for loss and damage on a long-distance move is limited to 60¢ a lb. per item; 30¢ on a local move. This isn't much for a treasured 200-year old heirloom weighing 40 lbs.; a mere $24 as a long-distance liability; $12 on local moves. (You can get extra protection through your own insurance agent or the moving company, but you pay extra.)

Long-distance moving costs are based on the weight of your goods, distance and "extras" like packing, unpacking, loading, insurance and storage. No job can be accurately priced until everything has been packed, loaded and weighed. And no matter what they tell you, an estimate is an *estimate* — not a contract; and "low-bill" estimates are hard to resist.

Local movers charge by the hour (if you're lucky they won't get lost en route) and you're charged from the time they leave the office to the time they return. Rates vary.

Whether the moves are short or long, do-it-yourself or professional, there are ways to cut costs.

• Pack as much as you can (everything that's packable) *before* the movers come. You can raid your local supermarket for cartons or buy new ($3.75) or used ($1.25) cartons from moving companies. These may seem expensive but they're strong and built to protect your china and breakables. Packing paper's as cheap as $25 for 100 lbs. at some places.

• Roll up your carpets and get stoves, refrigerators and washing machines ready *before* moving time.

• The less you move, the cheaper it will be. So one idea to consider is to help pay for the move by selling unwanted books, clothes and household goods.

• Get at least three estimates in writing if you're using a moving company. And if one is extremely low, beware. The other two are probably more realistic.

• Be there when the movers weigh your belongings. Was anyone inside the truck when it was weighed? Was the gas tank full or empty? Make sure the weight is accurate — "errors" can mean an extra 400 to 600 lbs. and will cost you money.

• Check out prices and services of independent truckers before you hire a professional moving company. They have terminals in most major cities, they're competitive and their prices are generally lower than moving companies because they only drive with a full load. You can sometimes ask for and get a flat rate and haggle about the asking price. If there's a trailer heading for your destination, make them a low, flat-rate offer — they may accept it. *Be sure to have your stuff insured.*

• If you're a do-it-yourselfer, shop around for the best deal. A local independent mover recently moved a young couple's entire household for $75, a flat fee of $25 plus $50 for two hours' work. The price included two burly men, the truck, ropes and pads etc. and all their items arrived intact. All the couple did was the packing. With a little help from your friends or by hiring students, you can rent a truck, get insurance and move — for a fraction of professional rates. Most moving companies rent trucks including ropes, pads, dollies and other equipment for around $38 a day. (Borisko Bros. price). You pay for gas and mileqge and supply the labor. Rental companies like Avis and U-Haul are generally $30 to $35 a day, excluding ropes and pads, gas and mileage.

• Split the cost of a rental van for long-distance moves with people solicited through newspaper ads or notices on the bulletin board of your local supermarket.

Some extra tips:

• Pack and transport valuable and delicate items yourself.

• Be sure to check out express services (Greyhound, CN, CP and air freight) and rates.

• Be especially careful with china and breakables. Moving companies are not responsible for breakage caused by your "faulty" packing.

• Never lose your bill of lading.

• If you're renting your own truck, a hydraulic tailgate lift is *not* a luxury. It's a necessity for "heavies" like pianos and refrigerators; and it cuts your time and backaches in half.

to fix it. If they can't, you get new materials free of charge. What more can you ask?

Monday to Friday, 9:30 a.m. to 9:30 p.m., Saturday to 6 p.m.
Cloverdale Mall, Dundas St. and Hwy. 427 (239-2445)
Saturday to Wednesday 10 a.m. to 6 p.m., Thursday and Friday to 9 p.m.
5 Hazelton Avenue (967-0500)
Monday to Saturday, 10 a.m. to 6 p.m., Thursday and Friday to 9 p.m.
754 Mount Pleasant Rd. (482-8722)
Tuesday, Wednesday and Saturday, 10 a.m. to 6 p.m., Thursday and Friday to 9 p.m.
5855 Yonge Street (223-4426)

Carpets

The Carpet Shoppe
Need a new rug? Savings are as much as 50% at The Carpet Shoppe. Most of the stock is in the form of clearouts from Burlington Mills and Harding Carpets and there are remnants, long rolls, short rolls and full rugs. Owner Cliff Bell highly recommends assorted 9'-by-12' carpets at $69, and his 24"-by-36" shag mats for $1. Other great buys: 3'-by-5' rugs for $12, 6'-by-9s for $39 and 4'-by-6s for $20. Rugs are cut to size at no cost and estimates are free. And for the do-it-yourselfer, Cliff will rent you a complete box of tools with everything you need, for just $1 a day. Apart from the carpets you see in the shop, there are hundreds more stored within easy walking distance of the store.

Monday to Friday 9 a.m. to 9 p.m., Saturday to 6 p.m.
1640 Bayview Ave. at Manor Road (487-1171)

Elte Carpets Ltd.
Going into Elte's is like entering a textured kaleidoscope of color. There must be an acre of carpets: literally thousands of bolts, samples and remnants. And all the big names are there. There's Harding, Caravelle, Crossley, Bigelow, Celanese and many more, in every possible pattern and texture from your favorite shags to thick sculpted rugs. Prices appear to be about $2 to $3 a yard less than at conventional outlets. Some samples: Bigelow's Royal Star at $12.75 a square yard; and Crossley's Korastan "Chandeau" for around $13 a square yard. And remnants — there's a huge supply — *sometimes*, not always, reduced as much as 50%. Carpets are cut free if it's a straight cut, but there's a charge of 50¢ a foot for tape binding. And if you want your carpet delivered, there's a charge of $25. Shop around first, and be prepared to do a lot of asking; prices generally aren't marked.

Monday to Friday 9 a.m. to 5 p.m., Thursday to 9 p.m. (summer only); Winter, Saturday to 12 noon.
45 Eastern Ave. (362-3723)

The Carpet Shoppe

China

The Stoke-on-Trent China Company
It's no surprise that the Stoke-on-Trent China Company sells fine English china. The name says it all.

Stoke-on-Trent

What *is* surprising are more-than-affordable prices and near-perfect factory seconds with negligible flaws.

Most china shops are stuffy and touristy, but Stoke-on-Trent is a browser's paradise. The walls are lined with irresistible tea chests filled to the brim with china treasures. You're encouraged to dip and dive to your heart's content. Each chest is a surprise package — and just as much fun.

The atmosphere is pleasantly earthy, with natural sunlit walls and "early hay" carpeting (stuffing from the rows and rows of partly unpacked crates and chests). Tea chests and shelves are crammed with a delightful assortment of wares: hand-painted teapots and potties (they make great planters) for $8; pitchers, jugs, sets of dishes, individual pieces, demitasse sets and one-of-a-kind ironstone flow blue pieces. You'll see Enoch Wedgwood, Royal Albert, Aynsley, Pallissy, Johnson Bros., Staffordshire and lesser-known makes, many at one-third of the normal price.

A bone china five-piece place setting sells from $11 to $25, depending on the pattern and make. (The cheapest firsts in other stores are $49 and up.) There are at least 40 patterns in bone china, porcelain and earthenware on display and many, many more upstairs. And the scope's unlimited. You can make up your own version of a place setting or buy individual pieces. If you need assistance, owners Jerry and Kathy Zacks are there to help, and to tell you about Wedgwood's Historical Ports of England sets and what a tot jug is.

Monday to Thursday 10 a.m. to 5:30 p.m., Friday to 9 p.m. and Saturday to 6 p.m.
61 Yorkville Ave. (967-1099)

Dry Goods

David Warsh Textiles
Don't be offended if the service at David Warsh Textiles isn't all that great — he's a very busy wholesaler. But his prices make it worth the wait: soft, 80"-by-100" blankets for $8; soft light polyester comforters for $14, and packages of J.B. Stevens sheets (two sheets and two pillowcases) for only $14. And all his Stevens towels are half-price. Be prepared to do a lot of asking.

Monday to Friday 9 a.m. to 4:30 p.m.
401 Spadina Ave. (979-2263)

Kitchen Things

A.O. White Supply (1963) Ltd.
This restaurant supplier will also supply *you* with all the dishes, pots and pans you need. And there's a huge selection: every conceivable cooking utensil, and a bevy of china

and glassware. Hotel vitrified china comes in four different makes and 17 patterns. And for casual fare or for carefree days at the cottage, the plain white china is a good buy at around $50 for a 60-odd piece set. You can buy half-dozens and dozens to replenish your stock. Cups and saucers are $10.90 and $6.95 a dozen respectively. Plates are $16.50 per dozen. And if you're short of glasses, 8 oz. drinking glasses are just $3.79 a dozen. Heavy cutting boards range from $12.95, depending on the size and there's a superb collection of knives, Henckels and Sabatiers, to name two.

Monday to Friday 9 a.m. to 5:30 p.m., Saturday 10 a.m. to 4 p.m.
318 Queen St. W. (366-6536)

Federal Store Fixtures
If you're tired of pot luck at the Sally Ann and you're not in the market for a particular item, a visit to Federal Store Fixtures is in order. Besides a complete line of new and used restaurant equipment, you'll find many bargains: used cake plates and pans for 25¢ each, heavy 12″ molds for $2.50, spring-form pans for less than $3.50 and a limited number of 10″ high wooden salt and pepper mills for $6.50 a set. Henckel knives sell for 10% less than at other stores and there's a complete line of inexpensive stainless ware.

Monday to Friday 9 a.m. to 5:30 p.m.
475 Queen St. W. (364-3522)

Fortune Housewares and Importing Company
Pennypinchers and gourmet cooks alike tend to rave about Fortune Housewares and Importing Company, a small but select shop that stocks an infinite variety of simple and gourmet cookware. Owners Lily and Paul Menceles import their

Fortune Housewares

wares from all over the world and claim their prices are the best in the city. It's hard to argue. Apart from the prices, what staggers most people is the incredible amount and variety of cookware, flatware, gadgets and utensils neatly displayed on the shelves and rafters: cast ironware, enamelware, pots, pans, crocks, grinders, choppers, kitchen knives, strainers (dozens of them in different sizes), wooden chopping boards and a complete line of wooden kitchen wares, wire egg and garlic baskets. Popular vegetable steamers are $1.25 and up (a Fortune special); chopping boards $2 and up; and woks $3 and up. And that's just a sample.

Monday to Saturday 9 a.m. to 6 p.m.
388 Spadina Ave. (364-6999)

The ½ Price Boutique
There are two floors chock full of housewares, planters, pottery, plants, bric-a-brac and shoes at 50% reductions. The ½ Price Boutique began as a clearance sale that was so successful that owner Bernice Miles decided to continue the practice. You'll find current 8-track tapes, German crystal and a small assortment of plants and much more. (Plants usually come in towards the end of the week.) A large, healthy Pleomele was $7.50; wicker waste baskets that make great planters, $3.50; cutting boards, $1.50 up and pottery seconds from Canada Colony

Landlord & Tenant Disputes

Ministry of Housing
Information Services, Ministry of Housing, 101 Bloor St. W., Toronto, M7A 2N5

Housing Rental Agency
Fifth floor, East Tower, City Hall (367-8570)

Emergency Shelter Information
Dept. of Social Services (367-8608)

The Ontario Condominium Association
84 Castlebury Cresc. (493-7762)

Heat
Minimum heat requirements in rented quarters are enforced by municipal health departments in the city and in each borough.

According to the bylaw, landlords *must* maintain a minimum of 20°C (68°F) during cooler months: Toronto: Sept. 15 to June 1 (367-7466); Etobicoke: Sept. 15 to June 15 (626-4161); North York: Sept. 15 to May 30 (225-4611); York: Oct. 1 to May 31 (midnight) (653-2700); Scarborough: Oct. 1 to May 30 (438-7431); East York: Oct. 1 to May 31 (461-8136)

Office of the Ombudsman
There's a 24-hour answering service.

Monday to Friday 9 a.m. to 5 p.m.
65 Queen St. W., 6th floor (362-7331)

Landlord and Tenant Advisory Bureau
It will help with the landlord problems. It's best to *call*.

Monday to Friday 8:30 a.m. to 4:30 p.m.
67 Adelaide St. E. (367-8572)

Tenant Hotline
For information on the Landlord and Tenant Act, Metro by-laws and rent review legislation write or call. (There's a 24-hour emergency service.)

80 Winchester St., Don Vale Community Centre (922-6544 or 922-6560)

Rent Review Offices, Ontario Ministry of Consumer and Commercial Affairs
They will answer your questions about rent review law or rent hikes.

Monday to Friday 8:30 a.m. to 5:45 p.m.
77 Bloor St. W., Third floor (923-1199)

Other Numbers and Resources

Ministry of Consumer and Commercial Relations
Ontario Consumer, Queen's Park, Toronto (965-3248)

Stoneware from around $2. Merchandise varies from week to week. Prices are half that marked on the label and if you don't see what you want, Bernice will try to get it for you.

Monday to Saturday, 11 a.m. to 6 p.m., Thursday and Friday nights to 9 p.m.
14 Cumberland St. (961-4381)

Plants

Bruce's Green Plants and Flowers
It's a functional little plant shop with no frills — all part of owner Bruce Anson's campaign to keep prices down. To cut cost, he wraps plants himself, forgoes a telephone, deliveries and floral arrangements.

All small plants are 75¢ each or 3 for $2; smaller terrarium plants 50¢ each or 3 for $1. All small hanging plants are just $3 and larger ones, $5. You'll see everything from spiders, ficus, Wandering Jews and begonias to potted geraniums.

Monday to Friday 10 a.m. to 5:30 p.m., Saturday to 3 p.m.
44 Yonge St. at Wellington Street (no phone)

Positively Sunshine
The shop doubles as a resource centre for area teachers who bring kids in to learn about things green and growing, and an informal drop-in centre. There's an incredible selection of familiar and not-so-familiar plants like shy, trailing passion flowers ($13) and what must be the biggest Spider plant ever ($15), but others cost less), a wild assortment of medium-sized potted plants, ($1.25) and hanging plants ($6 and up).

And in case you've got an ailing aspidistra or other sick plants at home, there's a regular clinic on Saturday mornings from 9:30 a.m. to 10:30 a.m.

Monday to Saturday 10 a.m. to 6 p.m.
2184 Queen St. E., Beaches area (690-6588)

Stereo Equipment

Bay Bloor Radio
There's a wide selection of used stereo components and demos on display at all times. According to owner Sol Mandlsohn, here's how you decide what a used unit's worth: if it's a year old, expect to pay from 40% to 50% of its original value; at two years, from 40% to 50%; and at three, only 30% to 40%. A 30-day warranty is given on all used models and a full year on demos which are sold at a 25% to 30% reduction. Trade-ins on new and used are accepted and evaluated free of charge. They're held intact for two weeks, in case you change your mind. And there's a money-back guarantee within 14 days of purchase; returns are accepted within 42 days.

Monday to Saturday 10 a.m. to 7 p.m., Thursday and Friday 10 a.m. to 9 p.m.
Manulife Centre, 55 Bloor St. W. at Bay (967-1122)

Fairview Electronics
Fairview sells nearly new and used components at its Weston Road store. (The Albion stores accepts trades but only sells new stuff.)

Because of Fairview's own plan for new stock purchasers, many trade-ins are less than a year old. Customers often take advantage of the plan which allows them to trade in Fairview-bought equipment within a year with hardly any loss of money

— a Concord receiver, $80; a BSR turntable with magnetic cartridge, $100; and two Avant speakers $30 — a definite incentive to buy new — and from Fairview. But it's hard to resist the used bargains: a compact RCA package, including receiver, turntable and two speakers, for $200; and Fairfax 500 receivers at about $95.

Monday to Friday, 10 a.m. to 9 p.m., Saturday 9 a.m. to 6 p.m.
1812 Weston Rd. south of Lawrence (249-6363)
1038 Albion Rd. (741-6164)

Kelly's Stereo Mart
It generally pays to buy in bulk and Kelly's does just that, with 86 stores across Canada. They claim their prices to be "the best in Canada" and have new component systems from $300 to $5,000 and a wide variety of used ones. Bargains in used components range from 40% to 80% off the price of new equipment and they're sold with a 90-day minimum warranty. The best selection of used equipment appears to be at their Yonge Street stores, notably at numbers 356 and 784 respectively.

10 a.m. to 6 p.m. Monday to Saturday, Thursday and Friday to 9 p.m.
784 Yonge St. (961-8226)
Monday to Friday 9:30 a.m. to 10 p.m., Saturday 9 a.m. to 6 p.m.
356 Yonge St. (595-1115)
Monday, Thursday and Friday 9:30 a.m. to 9 p.m., Tuesday, Wednesday and Saturday, 9:30 a.m. to 6 p.m.
322 Yonge St. (597-0450)
Monday to Saturday 10 a.m. to 6 p.m., Thursday and Friday 10 a.m. to 9 p.m.
508D Lawrence Ave. W. (783-1149)

National Sound
Few people would rent an abandoned funeral home, haul out the coffins, install some sound equipment, set up shop and expect to survive. But that's exactly what Paul Jilek did several years ago when he successfully opened his first discount audio equipment store on Queen Street West. And he's more than survived. He now has four established National Sound stores across Metro.

To the delight of his customers, Jilek continues to sell such brands as Kenwood, Empire, Toshiba and Sony at a minimum of 20% below the suggested list price — one reason why you can pick up a Kenwood package deal (receiver, turntable and two speakers) for $395. And that's not all. Toshiba 20" color TVs that normally sell for $599 are $499 at National Sound, with the usual 30-month warranty on parts and labor. There's a complete range of new and used sound equipment, plus tape recorders, radios (clock and otherwise) and TVs. Trade-ins are accepted, so some good used stuff is available. The best bargains are at the original Queen Street location, fast becoming the bargain and used-stereo centre.

Monday to Wednesday 10 a.m. to 7 p.m., Thursday and Friday to 9 p.m., Saturday to 6 p.m.
1894 Lawrence Ave. E. (755-5297
730 Yonge St. (961-4101)
402 Queen St. W. (863-1939)
Monday to Friday 10 a.m. to 9:30 p.m., Saturday to 6 p.m.
1011 Albion Rd. (745-6866)

Wicker

Wicker World Inc.
For inexpensive baskets, trays, bric-a-brac and pottery, drop in at Wicker World Inc. shops, filled with an unusual assortment of wickerware, baskets and artifacts from around the

world. The large baskets ($4.99 up) make great clothes hampers and toy boxes; smaller sizes (99¢-$2.98) can become attractive planters and wastebaskets. Colorful Mexican pottery and bric-a-brac sell for $2.98 up; cosy Mexican ponchos for less than $25; and snug, double-knit Mexican sweaters for less than $40. Damaged merchandise clears for just a fraction of the original cost. Sample prices: chairs for $9.95, king-sized baskets for $1.99.

Monday to Saturday 10 a.m. to 6 p.m., Friday to 7 p.m.
1378 Yonge St. (924-6101)

Wing On Company
According to the Chinese, crickets are good luck and fun to have around. (They sing and eat just about anything.) You'll have to catch your own cricket, but you can buy a real cricket cage at Wing On Company. Their selection of Chinese basketware is probably the best in the city, as are the prices. You'll find sampan hats (99¢ to $3.25) that make great catch-alls; assorted baskets and containers ($1.15 to $1.95) — ideal planters and hangers, bamboo and rattan cases ($7.95 to $13.95), great tote bags and lightweight brief cases.

Monday to Saturday 10 a.m. to 7 p.m.
356 Spadina Ave. (366-1284)

Household Rentals

Chair-Man Mills
If you're having your yearly bash or family get-together, Chair-Man Mills will rent you anything you need to carry it off in style — it's more convenient, and cheaper than buying glasses and dishes you'll never use again. Chairs are just 75¢ each, a table for 10, $3.75, Dinnerware (Rogers silverplate) and respectable china rent for 12¢ a piece and his very best — Rosenthal china that nobody else rents — 20¢ a piece. All rates are

by the day. Minimum delivery charge is $25 and there is a handling charge of $5 on all orders.

Monday to Friday 9 a.m. to 5 p.m.
300 Consumer's Rd. (492-0400)

For Do-It-Yourselfers

Cashway Lumber Company
If you don't mind a run-of-the-pile selection, with limited quantities on best sales, Cashway is a good place to buy new lumber and building supplies of all kinds at low prices. In many cases, there is no sorting and you take what you get — mahogany 4'-by-8' panels at $3.98 each and 2-by 4 by 8's economy spruce, 59¢ each - but at those prices it's hard to argue. There is a wide range of items on display at discount prices: flooring, light fixtures, paint, shelving, mahogany bi-fold doors ($17.75 and up), pine louvered doors (from $29.95) and much more. At a recent insulation winter clear-out sale truckloads of batts were $5.99 to $6.99 a carton and special Zonolite pouring insulation, $2.27 to $2.49 a bag. Cash and carry. Delivery can be arranged if necessary, but there is a charge.

Monday to Wednesday 8:30 a.m. to 6 p.m., Thursday and Friday to 9 p.m., Saturday to 5 p.m.
Bramalea Rd. and Steeles Ave. (677-4265)
Yonge St. and Oak Ridges (773-4381)

Cashway Lumber Company

4896 Steeles Ave. E. (297-4462)
Out of town locations — see your telephone book

Furniture Revival Centre
It provides the do-it-yourselfer with everything that is needed to refinish furniture, from grandmother's platform rocker to your favorite oak washstand. For just $2.50 an hour you get to use their tools, chemicals and space and this includes things like expensive stripper and lacquer, and friendly advice. If all goes well, an oak washstand can be refinished in eight hours at a cost of $20. It's a combined learning and money-saving experience and it's fun to discover the vintage woods lurking under all that paint.

Monday to Friday, 9 a.m. to 4 p.m.
11 Glencameron Rd., Unit 14, Thornhill (889-0657)

The Paint Centre
Don't be fooled by the name — its specialty is low-priced wallpaper, floor covering and carpets. Owner Darrell Day keeps about 100,000 rolls of paper in stock — mostly discontinued lines and a few seconds — all brand names like Sunworthy, Mesonyl and Flexor, and all sold at a 50% to 80% discount. Look for prepasted vinyl for $3 a double roll and up, and fabric-type for $4 a single roll. Brand-name cushioned vinyl floor covering seconds sell from $3 to $4 a square yard (regular $12).

We've found a great selection of quality carpets from a bankrupt sale at about "50% off Eaton's prices and 40% off Factory Carpet's." Shags were from $5 a square yard; hardtwist broadloom from $4 to $10. And yes, paint (Selectone mostly) at reduced prices and a good selection of painting "musts."

Monday to Friday, 9:30 a.m. to 6

p.m., Saturday to 5 p.m.
86 Parliament St. (at King) (368-8714)

Plumbing Mart
Plumbing is one of the things we take for granted until a pipe bursts or the toilet backs up. If you can't afford a $15-and-up visit from your friendly plumber (who wouldn't be friendly at those prices?), take your problems to any one of the Plumbing Mart's five stores. Apart from an overwhelming selection of plumbing fixtures, tools and materials, they have free advice to offer. And that's probably what you need most. (What's the point of buying a "snake" to unclog a drain if you don't know how to use it?) They'll advise and equip you for anything you want to take on, from installing new taps and drainage pipes, to major installations, like a pressure system.

Monday to Friday 9 a.m. to 9 p.m., Saturday to 5 p.m.
2047 Avenue Rd. (481-7555), 24 Arrow Rd. (745-1444), 299 Danforth Rd. (694-2320), 4133 Dundas St. W. (233-0838), 2210 Queen St. E. (690-2623)

Handyman Rentals

Rent-alls are often the cheapest, easiest way to cope with major cleanups and home repairs. After all, who can afford a chain hoist or a chain block? According to our own informal poll, here are what seem to be the cheapest rent-alls in town:

G&W Rent-All Ltd.
They rent anything from a tree cutter to a metal detector and more conventional fare: equipment for cleanups, painting, plumbing, gardening and a complete range of power tools. Daily rates for floor sanders are $17 a day ($12 for 4 hours); and for industrial vacuums, $10 a day ($7 for four hours). On the auto scene, steering wheel pullers are $2.50 a day, and a large gear puller, $5.

Monday to Friday 7 a.m. to 6 p.m., Saturday 8 a.m. to 5 p.m.
1595 Ellesmere Rd. at McCowan (438-9787)

Kennedy Rent-All Ltd.
There's a complete range of both functional and specialized equipment for just about anything you want to tackle, from home repairs to car repairs. And the prices are reasonable — $10 a day for an industrial vacuum, $16 a day for a floor sander and edger and from $3 to $5 a day for a combination steering wheel/gear puller ($8 a day for a hydraulic one).

Monday to Friday, 7:30 a.m. to 6 p.m., Saturday 8 a.m. to 5 p.m.
1415 Bathurst St., S. of St. Clair (532-1161)
80 Laird Dr. (429-4432)

Mortgages

If you're buying a new house, chances are you won't have to shop around for a mortgage. Most builders make prior arrangements with banks and other reputable lenders, and qualifying for the mortgage loan will be your main concern.

Financing the purchase of an older home is up to you, your lawyer or your realtor. You'll find that rates vary immensely, depending on the lender and the type of mortgage. Rates on a first mortgage are generally from 10¼% to 10½%; 13¼% and up on a second. (If you borrow from a private lender rates can be as high as 15% to 18%.)

Conventional first mortgages are available for most new and older homes which means you can borrow up to 75% of the appraised value for 25 years, but a minimum down payment of 25% is required. Although there's no legal maximum the most you can reasonably hope to borrow (from conventional sources) is $50,000.

A high ratio mortgage means you can borrow up to 95% of the value of a house that costs up to $40,000 (if it costs more than that you can't borrow a full 95%) for up to 30 years. Your down payment's from 5% to 10% less than a conventional mortgage, but there's a 1% to 2% life insurance premium and interest rates are slightly higher.

Twenty-five year NHA mortgages are available through most banks and financial institutions, according to terms set out in the National Housing Act (NHA). The lender sets the mortgage rate — bank and trust company rates are *generally* lower than mortgage companies — and there's an insurance premium of up to 1% of the amount of your loan added on. If you're buying an older home you might be slapped with an additional 1% charge for repair hold-backs.

Never consider a high-interest rate second mortgage unless you can manage the down payment. (A high ratio first is your best bet.) Rates are usually 2.5% more and up, over prime first mortgage rates and they're generally short-term three- to ten-year loans. (Some lenders may go to 25 years.)

Before you're mortgaged to the hilt, here's the general rule followed by most banks and financiers: Mortgage payments should *never* exceed 30% of your gross salary. (If two of you work be sure to include both incomes.) If you gross $1,200 a month, your gross debt service, including principle, interest and taxes (your mortgage payment) should not exceed $360 — or 30% at most; better still, $334 or 27%. Your total debt service — mortgage payments plus all other debts including car loans, Chargex, Eaton's, Simpsons's accounts etc. — should never exceed 37% or $444 (based on $1,200 a month).

Saving Energy & Dollars

There are hundreds of ways to save energy and money in your home. And when you consider the alternative — oil, gas and electricity costing almost 18% more each year — you can't afford to ignore them. Some, like insulation and regular furnace maintenance cost money, but they soon pay for themselves with reduced heating bills. Others, like turning down your thermostat, wearing warmer clothes around the house in winter, turning out lights, and showers instead of baths, are free and can save you up to $100 a year — as much as $200 if you're a big energy waster.

The biggest energy and dollar savers are insulation, regular furnace maintenance and thermostat setbacks (lower temperatures). According to the Ministry of Energy, they can reduce an annual $300 fuel bill to $165, a saving of $135. (See our chart.) You may not notice it, but a steady flow of money often escapes from the tightest of household budgets in the form of wasted energy costs. These tips gleaned from experts can help you reclaim some of your hard-earned dollars.

• Next to your furnace your hot-water heater is the largest energy user in your home. A good insulating jacket can reduce heat loss from the tank by as much as 80%. Set the thermostat at 110° (60°C) and 140° (43°C) if you have a dishwasher.

• Insulating your hot water pipes saves you money and heat. By wrapping a 10-foot pipe you save enough energy in one month to wash three full loads of dishes in your dishwasher.

• Short hot water pipes are more economical than long ones. For example, 10-foot rather than 30-foot pipes can mean 10 showers a month in terms of savings.

• Dripping hot water taps can mean as much as $18 a year down the drain. It's cheaper to repair them.

• You pay more for hot soaks in the tub. The average bath takes 10 gallons of water; the average shower, six. The next time you take a bath, measure the water with a yardstick and compare the amount with your next shower (keeping the plug in while you shower).

• Keeping your furnace thermostat at 68°F (20°C) during the day and 63°F (3°C) at night can save as much as 15% on your fuel bill — $45 if your annual bill's $300. When you're away, set the thermostat at 60°F (16°C) — your pipes and plants won't freeze and you'll save money.

• Heating and cooling appliances use more energy than all your other appliances — and lights — put together.

• Read your electric and gas meters on the last day of your

billing period and when the meter man comes. Compare your readings with your bill. Everyone — including the computer — makes mistakes.

• Use fluorescent lights in bathrooms and kitchens — they're cheaper and more efficient than incandescent bulbs. And use bright lights only where they're really needed, in the study or sewing room, for example.

• Instant-on TV sets use electricity 24 hours a day unless you turn off the mainswitch.

• Choose an air conditioner with an energy efficiency ratio of at least seven, if you must buy one. Adequate insulation also helps to keep your home cool.

In the Kitchen

• When you use your oven, plan complete "oven" meals and cook enough to freeze and use another day. Incidentally, preheating's not necessary except for baked goodies, and peeking's expensive — you lose 20% of your heat every time you open the door.

• Turn off your dishwasher after the final rinse cycle — the hot dishes will dry themselves. (And wash only full loads.)

• Make sure you have a full load when you use your washer or dryer. Putting one pair of jeans through a complete wash and dry cycle is expensive — and

Energy-Saving Measure	Fuel Bill Before Energy-Saving Measures	Saving	Reduced Fuel Bill
Semi-annual furnace service (oil furnace)	$300	10%	$270
Insulation: Additional insulation to ceiling and basement walls, plus storm windows and doors, weather-stripping and caulking.	$270	20%	$216
Lower Temps. Lowering daytime temperature from 72°F to 68°F (22°C to 20°C) and to 63°F (17°C) at night.	$194.40	15%	$165.24

***Based on chart from *100 Ways to Save Energy in the Home*.

Saving Energy (cont.)

wasteful. And ye olde clothes line will save you money in the nice weather.

- Electric frying pans, broilers, toasters and other small appliances are more efficient than your stove. (Toasting in the oven uses three times as much energy as a pop-up toaster.) And efficient glass and ceramic baking dishes will bake at 25°F (14°C) lower than metal pans.

- A $25 pressure cooker's one of the best fuel savers around. Vegetables cook in seconds or a very few minutes — and retain their nutritional value — and meats, even whole chickens and roasts cook in minutes as compared to hours.

Average Wattage and Annual Consumption in Kilowatt Hours (KWh) of Common Household Appliances

It's wise to find out how much energy an appliance uses before — not after — you buy. Check the small plate on the side or bottom of the appliance for the wattage rate: the higher the rate, the more electricity it uses and the more it costs to operate. See the chart below for the average wattage and yearly consumption of everyday appliances. You'll be surprised at the findings.

Appliance	Average Wattage	Est. Annual Kwh Consumption
Air conditioner	860	500
Clothes dryer	4,850	900
Dehumidifier	260	400
Electric kettle	1,500	150
Electric stove	12,200	1,200
Electric water heater	4,800	4,000
Humidifier	177	200
Iron	1,100	120
Mixmaster	150	15
Refrigerator (12 cu. ft.)	240	850
Refrigerator (12 cu. ft. frost-free)	320	1,200
Freezer (14 cu. ft.)	400	1,200
Freezer (14 cu. ft. frost-free)	540	1,600
TV (B&W tube)	160	400
TV (B&W solid state)	55	350
Toaster (pop-up)	1,100	40
Vacuum cleaner	630	40
Automatic washer (not including hot water)	520	90

Cutting Your Heating Bill

INSULATION
Your furnace is the biggest energy guzzler in your home — heating accounts for over 50% of your energy budget — and with fuel costs rising a steady 17.9% a year, you can't afford to waste your energy dollar or your heat. Poor insulation is the biggest single cause of wasted heat in most homes. Heat escapes through ceilings, walls and floors and filters through minute cracks in windows and doors causing cold walls, drafts and snarky remarks about your innocent furnace and the weatherman. By completely insulating your home you'll be warm and comfortable in winter, cooler in summer — and you can cut your present fuel bill by as much as 50%! A more modest improvement can save you 20% to 30% annually. And the insulation pays for itself in five years. Consider a $150 or $210 fuel bill instead of your usual $300 and you'll see that it's worth it. (See our chart for estimated savings.)

Here are some basic facts about heat loss and insulation:

• An uninsulated ceiling loses more than 10 times as much heat as an insulated one.

• Insulation's rated according to "resistance value" (R-value) and the higher the R-value, the better the insulating qualities. Some brands may be thicker than others; but if the R-value's the same, they're equally effective. You should find the R-value stamped in large letters on the cover, but if it isn't there, check with the dealer.

• If you're attic's uninsulated, 40% of the overall heat loss is through your roof. (That's why R28 insulation's needed.)

• Walls are the second biggest offender and R12 insulation can cut heat loss by as much as two-thirds.

• A single glass pane window loses 12 times as much heat as a properly insulated wall. Adding storms and double panes will cut the loss in half.

• Sealing cracks around windows and doors with weather stripping and caulking can save as much as 20% of your fuel bill.

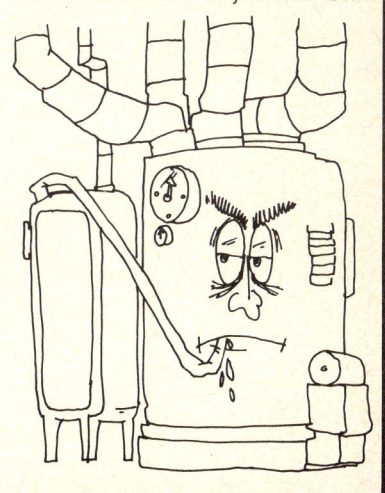

Cutting Your Heating Bill
(cont.)

Savings Chart (Based on a CMHC two-storey house, at least 20 years old, with 2½" insulation in the ceiling only and basement walls 1/3 above the ground.

Present Annual Fuel Bill	$500	$400	$300	$200
Ceiling (R7)				
Adding 2½" R-7 batts	save $30	$24	$18	$12
Adding 6" loose wool R-14	save $40	32	24	16
Walls Insulated After Ceiling				
Blowing 3½" R-7 wool	save $137	$109	$82	$55
Blowing 3½" R-15 UF foam	save 170	136	102	68
Styrofoam 1" plus drywall R-5	save 92	74	55	37
Basement Walls				
Adding 2" R-6 Foamboard	save $21	$17	$12	$8
Adding 3½" R-10 batts	save 25	20	15	10
Minimum Annual Fuel Bill	**$265**	**$212**	**$159**	**$106**

Material Adapted from *100 Ways to Save Energy and Money in the Home* published by Energy, Mines and Resources, Canada.

There are many types of insulation from traditional batt and blanket types, loose fill and rigid panels; but fibreglass is generally considered to be the cheapest and the most effective. And for do-it-yourselfers there are free books available to tell you everything you need to know to insulate your home, from how to, R-values, materials and cost.

100 Ways to Save Energy and Money in the Home is put out by Energy, Mines and Resources Canada and it's full of advice and "tips on how you can stretch energy and put money in your pocket."

Write: 100 Ways, Box 3500, Station C, Ottawa, Ont. K1Y 4G1.

Pick up a copy of Ontario Hydro's do-it-yourself guide to *Insulating Your Own Home* at the Hydro's Public Reference Centre. There's a study area where you can browse through a wide range of reference and resource material, hundreds of books, brochures, reports and papers. The staff is helpful and you can get copies of any material for a nominal charge.

Monday to Friday 9:30 a.m. to 5:30 p.m.,
700 University Ave., Mezzanine Floor, Hydro Place (592-3311)

Central Mortgage and Housing Corporation (CMHC) has a complete information kit on home insulation.

For info write 650 Lawrence Ave. W. (781-2451)

Free Firewood

Everyone from MPPs to conservationists are telling us to turn down the heat and wear sweaters. If you want to comply but can't stand the cold, there's usually free firewood at the Unwin Dump. It's usually well-stocked, as Metro's tree-trimmers operate all year round. You're welcome to whatever's there and it's free for the taking.

Monday to Friday, 8:30 a.m. to 3:30 p.m., Cherry and Commissioner Streets (367-7742)

5. Clothing

There are a growing number of alternative clothing stores around town to save you money: if you don't mind recycled clothing, there are unlimited savings at used clothing stores, and shoppers who prefer to buy new can choose among wholesalers who sell to the public, and a number of discount stores with seconds, irregulars, close-outs and ends-of-lines. These alternatives offer used or new clothing at fantastic reductions.

A word of explanation might help here! Discontinued lines are simply that and they're cleared at discount prices; irregulars and seconds have slight flaws — usually nothing that affects the overall wear and quality — but they should be carefully checked for major flaws; samples are items from displays and fashion shows; surplus and over-runs are simple "goofs" — there are too many of them and they must be disposed of, usually in a hurry. Be sure to compare prices before you shop. Stick to name brands you know and buy for quality. Cheap clothes aren't bargains if they don't stand up to wear and tear.

Clearance Outlets

Benny's Denim and Leather Boutique

Everyone's wearing denim these days and one place to get it cheap is Benny's. Everything he sells is reduced by 15% or more: jump suits, jeans, three-piece denim suits, skirts, painter's pants and much much more. Name-brand jeans like Lee's, Levis and Wranglers are $10 and up; Carhart overalls, $19.95; Canadian-made shirts, $5 and men's suits (reg. $150), $65. There's a complete size range from 23 to 36. Clothes are neatly organized and priced. And you'll find owner Benny D'Amico friendly and helpful.

Monday to Saturday 10 a.m. to 9 p.m.
272 Church St. (864-1532)

Benny's

Black Whiskers Fashion

Just as chic as the name suggests, Black Whiskers Fashion is a small, select boutique that features low-priced, top-quality imports and domestic apparel. You'll discover gorgeous St. Clair shirts and Jousse skirts and pants for half the retail price: there are 200 to 300 shirts and sweaters; plus evening dresses, overalls, jumpers, jeans and cords. Owner Albert Mamann's smooth Parisian accent, French charm, and impeccably tailored French imports are a combination you can't resist. And why should you? Jousse pants, regularly $70 are $36. Jousse skirts $36, shirts $14.98; on the homefront, Landlubbers and HIS slacks $10. Albert buys whole lots of close-outs, overruns and ends-of-lines which is why she can offer such low prices.

Monday to Saturday 9 a.m. to 6 p.m.
418 Spadina Ave. (366-1018)

Boo Boo's
Boo Boo's specialty is jeans, jeans and more jeans — Levis and GWGs in all sizes and at cut-rate prices. Seconds, yes, but there are no serious or obvious flaws, just the odd off-centre or slightly crooked seam, or a pulled thread or two. All Boo Boo's jeans and cords are the same price, regardless of make. You'll pay $10.48 for cords, around $12 for regular jeans and just over $15 for pre-faded jeans. You'll find some great extras; shirts, overalls, long and short denim skirts and scarves, for about 30% to 40% off.

Monday to Friday 10 a.m. to 9 p.m., Saturday to 6 p.m.
3038 Danforth Ave. (690-3406)
Hours same as above.
2629 Islington Ave. at Albion (745-4646)
Monday to Friday, 9 a.m. to 9 p.m., Saturday to 6 p.m.
3070 Don Mills Rd. at Sheppard (496-0432)
Monday to Friday, 10 a.m. to 10 p.m., Saturday to 6 p.m.
Rockwood Mall, Dixie and Burnhamthorpe (625-7676)

Central Hosiery
Cheaper by the dozen is the way you get panty hose at Central Hosiery. The brand recommended by the owner sells for $9 a dozen or 75¢ a pair — in average, tall and queen sizes. You'll also find stacks of fine quality lingerie, (nightgowns and housecoats) at half the retail price. Socks, children's clothes, sheets and tablecloths are all unpriced, so be prepared to do a lot of asking.

Monday to Friday 9 a.m. to 5:30 p.m., Sunday to 2 p.m. Closed Saturday.
413 Spadina Ave. (924-4898)

Lawrence Emporium
It's generally true that stores that advertise a lot have to write the cost into their selling prices. But there are exceptions, notably, Lawrence Emporium and its five stores in Metro, all clearing houses for factory samples, irregulars, clearances, ends-of-lines, seconds, and overruns. The stock varies according to what's available, but you'll find that men's, women's and children's clothing (largely Canadian brand names) sell from 40% to 60% of the regular retail price. The Emporium recently purchased over 1,000 Joseph Ribcoff dresses (samples and slight irregulars) that sold for from $29 to $60 in stores and cleared them for $6.99 and $7.99.

If you head for the basement, you'll save on toiletries and kitchen essentials. Special Kitchen Bags (32 oz. Palmolive dishwashing detergent, 12 J-cloths, 22 oz. Ajax cleanser, 22 oz. 409 spray, 2 lbs. ABC detergent, 50 baggies and 100 ft. of Stretch & Seal) sold for a petty $5 on a recent bargain day.

All stores open Monday to Friday 9:30 a.m. to 9:30 p.m., Saturday 9 a.m. to 6 p.m.
5576 Yonge St. at Finch (221-9319)
Sheridan Mall, Erin Mills Parkway (823-5758)
1973 Lawrence Ave. E. at Warden (752-1660)
Shopper's World in the Albion Mall (745-8750)
28 Dundas St. E. at Hwys. 5 and 10, Mississauga (270-7262)

Pennington's Wearhouse
If you've emerged a loser in your battle of the bulge, or you're just plain big, you're probably well acquainted with Pennington's, a women's clothing outlet specializing in larger sizes from 14½ to 52. What may have escaped your notice is that Pennington's has its own clearance house. You'll find favorite clothes and appropriate sizes at 20% to 50% less than you normally pay at other Pennington stores. They're not seconds — just ends-of-lines or ends-of-season. To accommodate its customers, the "wearhouse" is ample, with bright, neat fitting rooms.

Monday to Friday 11 a.m. to 9 p.m., Saturday 10 a.m. to 5 p.m.
3711 Keele St. (630-3302)

St. Lawrence Sales and Wellington Sales
These neighbors both have a large assortment of jeans, cords and overalls — some at less than half price. They're mostly seconds and overruns. Look for TeeKays, U.S. Top, Levis, HIS and other brand names. Wellington carries a full range of sizes from kids' through to adults', St. Lawrence, just adults, specializing in second-hand clothes.

Monday to Saturday 10 a.m. to 6 p.m.
St. Lawrence Sales, 40 Yonge St. (366-8950)
Wellington Sales, 42 Yonge St. (363-7740)

The Wholesale House
These three busy outlets are a shambles, but you won't mind — they're chock full of bargains, all brand name merchandise at reduced prices. The stock varies according to store; so here's a rundown on each:

The biggest and undisputedly best store is at Wilson Avenue. There's a super selection of children's clothes, from 40% to 60% off, as well as women's clothes. Don't be surprised to see $200 dresses for $60; 3-piece pantsuits worth $90 for $30, and tailored shirts (reg. $17) for $4 and $5. The Finch Avenue store is much the same, but the selection's not as large, so if in doubt, go to the Wilson Avenue store.

You'll find lots of denim and women's sportswear only, at the Merton Street branch, the smallest and newest location where denims sell at 50% reductions across the board. Jeans here are from $9.95, overalls, $16.75 and jumpers, $15.75 and you're sure to see your favorite brand.

The stores are casual and the staff is friendly. Be prepared for casual comments from other shoppers, like "take if off, it looks terrible" and don't be shy about asking for information. The rule is: if you don't see it on the floor, *ask*. It could be in a stack of boxes in the rear.

Monday to Saturday 10 a.m. to 6 p.m.
928 Wilson Ave., Downsview (635-8401)
652 Finch Ave. E., Willowdale (223-7671)
Monday to Wednesday 10 a.m. to 6 p.m., Thursday and Friday, noon to 6 p.m., Saturday 11 a.m. to 4 p.m.
232 Merton St. (489-4286)

Mostly Recycled

Big Sister Thrift Shop
Here's a source of funds for the Big Sister Association and Huntley Youth Services, and of better used clothing for you. Big Sister's specialty is women's and children's (notably babies') clothing, with a very limited selection of men's suits and coats. Prices are reasonable: a boy's imported velour shirt with a Holt Renfrew label, $1.50; a lambswool sweater,

Free Haircuts

Toronto's leading salons need models for aspiring stylists and you can be one! Your haircut is free. The only hitch is that you might not be chosen. In which case you'll have to resort to the bargain haircutting on the next page.

Vidal Sassoon
Student hairdressers choose the heads and the hair they need for haircuts (with blow-dry). No appointments needed but it's always best to call first. And if you're the nervous type, a more advanced hair snipper will cut your locks free, but by appointment only.

Monday and Friday at 5:30 p.m. and Tuesday at 6:30 p.m., 37 Avenue Rd. (920-1333)

Bruce of Crescendo
You may not make it at Bruce of Crescendo's posh salon, where students carefully select the hair they want to work with. But it's worth a try.

Wednesdays at 4 p.m., Toronto-Dominion Centre (362-1068)

Malcolm's
If you're chosen by a student, you'll make it at Malcolm's.

Tuesday or Wednesday, 6:15 p.m. (You take your chances.) 132 Cumberland St. (925-2891)

Robin Barker Hairloom
Men and women get equal treatment at this pleasant salon where free cuts, styling, a wash and a blow-dry are available.

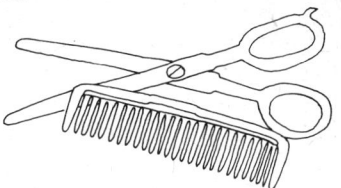

Thursdays 9 a.m. to 11 a.m., 651 Church St. (961-8121)

Van Fike Advanced School of Hair Design
Treat yourself to one of the best freebies in town at the Van Fike Advanced School of Hair Design. Its "students" — all licensed hairdressers — are there to learn the latest men's and women's cuts and styles. They always select a style that meets with your approval and suits your hair, a compromise and a learning experience for you and your stylist. You'll learn a lot about your hair that you probably don't know, things such as thickness, texture and special problems. And they'll teach you the proper way to use a blow-dryer, perhaps even a curling iron. A shampoo, cut and blow-dry takes about 1½ hours. (Permanents and highlighting Wednesday only, before noon.) Models for 16 students are needed every day but Monday.

Tuesday 11 a.m. and 3 p.m., Wednesday 2:30 p.m., Thursday 11 a.m., 1:30 p.m. and 3 p.m., and Friday 10 a.m. 750a Yonge St. (921-9239)

Bargain Haircuts

Just in case you didn't know, George Brown College has an efficient, superbly equipped hairdressing school where you can treat yourself to a new hairdo for less than $1. Students get to use your head, but it's worth the risk at 75¢ for a shampoo, 50¢ for a haircut, and as little as $3 for coldwaves or coloring. And there's a discount for students and senior citizens (50¢ for a shampoo and set, and 25¢ for a cut). All work is strictly supervised and by appointment only.

Thursday 1:30 p.m. to 3:30 p.m., Friday 9 a.m. to 1 p.m.
Nassau and Baldwin Streets
(967-1212)

Marvel Beauty School
Marvel offers a complete range of hairdressing services at very reasonable rates. For example, a straight shampoo and set is just $1.50; with a cut, just $3. They charge $6 for a tint retouch, including shampoo and set. However, prices for a full coloring job depend on a variety of factors, such as length of hair and degree of color change. All work is carefully supervised and you get to pick your own style.

Monday to Friday 9 a.m. to 3 p.m.
33 Bloor St. E. (923-0991)
282 Dundas St. E. (967-1800)

Toronto Barber College
Contrary to popular belief, the Toronto Barber College doesn't specialize in rudimentary beard shaves. What it does do — and well — is to teach aspiring hair stylists the fine art of perfect scissoring, shaping and current men's and women's hair styling. Apprentices, deftly cut and style your hair under the supervision of professionals. A testimony to their expertise is the fact that they've built up an established clientele — a steady stream of satisfied, modish regulars.
Cost for a cut, shampoo and styling is $3.50. They're busy, so be sure to call first.

Monday to Friday 9 a.m. to 5:30 p.m., Tuesday and Thursday to 7 p.m.

just $5, and a brown cord, blanket-lined Sysser raincoat, an unbelievable $12. Look for good buys in books, dishes, silverware, and bric-a-brac. And be sure to watch the papers for Big Sister's special monthly events, such as the annual December Anniversary sale where collectibles, antiques, giftware and toys go at bargain prices. Consignments are taken but must be clean, in good condition and up to date. You get 50% of the selling price.

Monday to Friday 10 a.m. to 4 p.m., Thursday 7 p.m. to 9 p.m., Saturday (winter only) 11 a.m. to 3 p.m.
1743 Avenue Rd., just north of Lawrence (782-9065)

L'Elégante Ltd.
L'Elégante is probably the most elegant used clothing establishment in town. After all, who can argue with such haute couturiers as Yves St. Laurent, Valentino, Dior, Pucci, Missoni, Geoffrey Beene, Tiktiner, Givenchy and Pierre Cardin? And they're all there. Not all the chic selections are originals, but they're all haute couture, in vogue (less than 18 months old) and immaculate. L'Elégante has an established clientele of customers and consignees who do most of their buying in Europe. Clothes brought in on consignment sell for one-third (or less) of the original price. L'Elégante gets 30%, you get 70%. You'll be dazzled by the clothes and the prices.

A beautiful fully tailored St. Laurent coat, originally $895, for $295; a $1,500 leather and sable coat for $250 because it's a bit on the short side (perhaps not for you); short stylish hip-length mink jackets for $300; Gucci shoes currently worth $125 can sell for less than $40 and nearly new cashmere sweaters, for $39.

Browsers aren't hassled; they're handled with care in this beautifully appointed store with its plush carpets, comfortable chairs and relaxed atmosphere. Owners Mary Gauvreau and Mary Ann Ryan and staff are friendly and helpful. If you're in the market for something special, they'll call you if it comes in.

Monday to Saturday 9:30 a.m. to 5:30 p.m., Thursday to 7 p.m.
130A Yorkville Ave. (923-3220)

L'Elegante Ltd.

Extoggery Limited
Undoubtedly the Eaton's of the used clothing trade, this chain is established, reliable and consistent, with six thriving outlets offering a dazzling array of goods. There's sports equipment, clothes for the entire family, china, silverware, paintings, bric-a-brac, books and small appliances. All six locations are bright immaculate, and accessible. You'll find that each one has its strong points.

The Merton Street store is the largest and has the best overall selection; the Beaches store is a great all-round store with what seems to be the best men's selection; the two Yonge Street stores have terrific women's fashions and fur coats. But any Extoggery store adds up to bargains you can't resist: a Holt, Renfrew Italian sweater at just $7; an immaculate, crisply tailored suede coat with a raccoon collar, $95; a hip-length muskrat jacket, $23.95; a warm black seal in the fashionable longer length, $49. And that's not all. A special this year was warm, rugged sheepskin mittens made from remnants for $3.95. Jeans and cords are around $7, children's, $4.95, and a pile-lined men's GWG jacket, just $7.95.

Clothes and other goodies are taken on consignment but they must be scrupulously clean, in perfect condition and seasonal. Make an appointment to bring things in — they're booked weeks ahead, especially in the fall. Items are displayed for three months, with a slight reduction in price after one month if they don't sell. They're sold for about one-third of their original value. Be sure to remember your pick-up date if you want your things back, otherwise they go to charity.

Hours vary with each store, so call first.

115 Merton St. (488-5393)
634 St. Clair Ave. W. (653-0282)
3250 Yonge St. (482-2811)
2425 Yonge St. (482-5335)
2221 Queen St. E. (698-0400)
269 Ellesmere Rd. (449-0399)

The Fashion Mine

From the outside, it's just another Yorkville boutique. Inside, it's anything but. Fashion Mine offers a profusion of exquisite, nearly-new designers' clothes of recent vintage at prices you can afford. Reductions are up to 75%, with a full range of sportswear, coats, shoes, evening wear and some samples, and a wide selection of sizes and styles. The Mine has an established clientele and caters to women only. You can take your cast-offs in on consignment any day but Saturday, but they must be of top quality, flawless (no ripped seams, cigarette burns or stains, please), and reflect the current fashion scene. You receive 70% of the selling price.

Monday to Saturday 10 a.m. to 6 p.m., Thursday to 8 p.m.
113 Yorkville Ave. (923-3332)

Flying Down to Rio

Flying down to Rio could be a profitable excursion if you take the time to drop in on one of Rio's three stores. And if you're in the market for jeans, army pants, a heavy sweater or even a soft 30s type dress (the kind Carole Lombard used to slink around in), chances are, you won't be disappointed. Rio's forte is new and recycled clothing and accessories up to the 1950s.

Wellesley Rio is more functional than its Yorkville counterpart. And the new Baldwin Street store is modeled after the Wellesley one. Its racks and shelves are neatly stocked with a wide assortment of children's and adults' jeans and cords from $4 to $18. Cosy quilts go for $12 and up; jean jackets, from $8 to $12; old fur coats (there's a large assortment) from $25; overalls from $8, and jean shorts from $3 to $8. Some Rio finds: a pair of broken-in immaculate Levi cords, $7; a great Irish fisherman's knit woolen sweater, $10; a lovely old, very large quilt, $20.

Rio features a complete range of kids' and adult sizes, so bring your child along. They'll love the juke box in the Wellesley Street store. By the way, if you prefer functional clothing, shop at Wellesley. If you're in the market for antique shoes, jewelry or offbeat oldies, try Yorkville. *Bon Voyage!*

Monday to Wednesday and Saturday 10 a.m. to 6 p.m., Thursday and Friday to 9 p.m.
10 Wellesley St. W. (922-7591)
107 Yorkville Ave. (961-1646)
Monday to Friday noon to 6 p.m. and Saturday 10 a.m. to 6 p.m.
39 Baldwin St. (no phone)

The Junior League Opportunity Shop
Here's another fund-raiser that doubles as a neighborhood thrift shop. It's just across the road from the Mount Pleasant Lunch and just up the street from Second Nature Boutique, a three-way stop you won't want to miss. Best buys are in women's, children's and baby clothes. Cashmere and lambswool sweaters are $2 to $20; long skirts, $8 and up; babies' sweaters and bonnets, $1 and up. There's a counter full of silverware, antiques, china and bric-a-brac and shelves lined with books.

Be sure to watch for their special sales in the papers, especially the annual toy sale (late November — early December) of new and nearly-new toys at one-half to one-third the regular price, from Fisher-Price and Playskool toys to dolls, books, puzzles and current favorites like *Sesame Street* characters. Also watch for the annual book sale and a cruisewear sale where items like Stearnes life jackets are up for grabs for $10 or less.

Monday to Friday 10 a.m. to 3:30 p.m., Thursday 7:30 p.m. to 9:30 p.m., Saturday 10 a.m. to 1 p.m. Closed on all school holidays.
539 Mount Pleasant Rd. (488-7217)

Miranda's Second Time Around
The specialty here is samples. Popular makes like Bagatelle, Charade and Wendy — to name a few — are available at reduced prices and in all sizes up to 14. Prices are usually 35% off the retail price, sometimes less. Fashionable cowl-necked sweaters are $8; denim skirts and jeans, $11 and up. You'll find most of the current favorites — overalls, jumpers, blazers and dresses. The stock is gathered from fashion shows across the country and there's a big turnover, so check the shop regularly.

Monday to Saturday 10:30 a.m. to 6 p.m., Thursday and Friday to 9 p.m.
12 Hazelton Ave. (923-7604)

Second Nature Boutique
A charming "neighborhood" salon of "used" clothing with antique bric-a-brac, jewelry and objets d'art so reasonable that even dealers shop there, according to owner Ruth Silverberg. Another bonus is sample imported (French and Italian) shirts for two-thirds or one-half the retail price — shirts retailing for $20 — and there are two full racks of fashionable maternity wear. Try on some of the fine shoes and boots — Frye boots go for $20.

A Joan Crawford-era skunk jacket with wide, padded shoulders sold for $30 recently and a flawless full-length muskrat coat was $250. There's also a good selection of

Second Nature Boutique

men's wear, including Lou Myers and Harry Rosen suits, and kids' clothes in the basement, plus a bargain section where *everything* is half-price.

Second Nature will take your cast-offs on consignment provided they're cleaned, up-to-date and of good quality. Then they're priced at about one-third of the original value and the split is 60/40 in your favor. If they're not sold in 60 days, and you fail to pick them up, they go to charity. It's a treat to shop at Second Nature — it's bright, cheerful and reasonable — just what Ruth Silverberg intended.

Monday to Saturday 10 a.m. to 6 p.m., Thursday to 9 p.m.
514 Mount Pleasant Rd. at Millwood (481-4924)

The Shoppe D'Or
Look for a fine selection of "better" used ladies' clothing and new sample pieces here, at substantial savings. All the merchandise is less than a year old and some of it is brand new. Used articles sell for roughly one-half of their original cost, sometimes less, and new items such as showroom samples sell at half price. There are some great buys: several stylish showroom-sample coats in a variety of sizes, styles and colors were selling for $69 and up, when we visited, and a nearly-new two-piece ski suit selling for close to $200 in sports stores was $60. Clothes taken on consignment must be of top quality, not more than a year old, seasonal and spotless. You collect two-thirds of the selling price.

Monday to Saturday 9:30 a.m. to 5:30 p.m., Thursday to 6:45 p.m.
119 Yorkville Ave. (923-2384)

Tribe
Although Tribe offers a unique collection of memorabilia (clothing, accessories and jewelry from the Twenties to Forties), there is more practical fare in the form of recycled clothes at reasonable prices. Jeans at $4 to $6 and overalls at $6 to $10 are enough to warrant a visit. But there's more: quilts at $30 up; and sweaters, skirts, jackets and shirts. Often featured is a rack of assorted items for $5.

To make it easy, clothes are neatly arranged in order of size and there's usually a pretty fair range of men's, women's and children's sizes in practical clothing. Tribe can even make you a fitted, Western-style shirt from recycled fabric.

Wednesday and Saturday 12:30 p.m. to 6 p.m., Thursday and Friday 12:30 p.m. to 6 p.m. Closed Sunday to Tuesday.
2 Phipps St. at St. Nicholas (921-7871)

Children's Clothing
New & Used

I.O.D.E. Second Appearance Shop
They're noted for a small selection of quality children's clothes, toys and books. Kids' overalls sell for 50¢ to $1, girls' party dresses for around $1.50. Toys like old dolls and cars are usually 5¢, and nearly new quality toys like Fisher-Price sell at 1/3 of the retail value; children's and adults' books, 35¢ for hard cover and 25¢ for paperback.

If you live in North York, Second Appearance should be your Sally Ann. All profits go to local hospitals and educational funds, like scholarships for North York Schools.

Monday to Thursday 10:30 a.m. to 5 p.m., Saturday 10 a.m. to 1 p.m.
1119 Avenue Rd. (781-5966)

Second Childhood
A select shop that features nearly-new designer clothes for kids. You'll see names like Cacharel, Absorba and Ellen Henderson, and you'll find pint-sized Cardin suits, Harrod's coats and Saks Fifth Avenue fashions at less than half the original price. You get 40% of the selling price for your child's hand-me-downs but owners Jill and Leslie Crossland are selective. All items must be clean, in tip-top shape and of top quality.

Monday to Saturday 10 a.m. to 5 p.m.
158 Cumberland St. (924-3385)

Toby's Discount Children's Wear
Toby's prices may not be as low as other discount outlets, but all the merchandise is retail quality (no substandards or ends-of-lines) and Canadian-made. You'll find brand names like Teacher's Pet, Honey Child, and Robin Sportswear all at 15-35% off in sizes from infants to 14. We saw UFO overalls at $12.65 (regularly $19), and top-quality infant sleepers for $7.49. Boys' dress suits that sell for $35 to $40 in department and specialty shops were $26 at Toby's where children's party clothes are always featured.

Monday to Saturday 10 a.m. to 6 p.m.
3899 Bathurst St. (638-2869)

Willie's
For new clothes at bargain prices you can't beat Willie Fleischer's Children's Wear (better known as "Willie's".) Your only problem will be finding your way through the mounds and mounds of men's, women's and especially children's clothes. Willie's is *always* busy — and for good reason. All of Willie's clothes are brand names at wholesale prices or less. There are no substandards or seconds, and Willie stands behind his merchandise. Look for TeeKay's, Teacher's Pet, HIS, Tam O'Shanter, and Mr. Leonard, among others. A successful search at Willie's produced a pair of children's jeans (TeeKay's), $6; two Teacher's Pet T-shirts, $6; a set of boys' Fruit of the Loom thermal underwear, $2. A word of warning: hit Willie's during off-hours, between 9 and 11 a.m., and 2:30 to 4 p.m. Otherwise, it's hard to get near the counters, and you'll be caught in the long line at the cash register.

Monday to Saturday 9 a.m. to 6 p.m.
44 Stafford St. at King St. W. (363-9595)

For more sources of Recycled Children's clothes see:
Big Sister Thrift Shop (page 70)
Ex-Toggery (page 73)
Flying Down to Rio (page 74)
and Junior League Opportunity Shop (page 75)

Furs

Avon Furs
New fur coats are expensive, one reason to think "used." And if you don't mind styles that are a bit dated there are many good and not-so-good used furs at Avon. What makes Avon so special is owner Harry Cornblum, whose family has been in the business for 53 years. He sells them "as is" and he'll take the time to point out a coat's good and bad points — he's honest. Prices on used coats are $60 up. There's a reasonable selection of Persian lamb and seal (from $60), beaver ($100 and up), a few long, stylish muskrats ($100 and up), and mink stoles and jackets (from $200). Newly remodelled coats that have been discarded by their owners in favor of something new are great bargains and come with full warranty. Avon also features new leathers (jackets from $89 and coats from $189) and light, warm, synthetic furs ($39 and up). And in case you opt for a new fur coat, up to $50 is allowed on trade-ins.

Monday to Friday 9 a.m. to 5 p.m., Thursday 9 a.m. to 2 p.m., Saturday 9 a.m. to 3 p.m.
686 Bathurst St. (534-7565)

Paul Magder Furs
If this is the year you've promised yourself a fur coat, you're in luck. Thanks to the racks and racks of used but immaculate fur pieces (more than 1,000) that line this store's walls, there's bound to be a coat to suit you and your budget. They offer a wide range of sizes, too, from 5 to 40. The rear of the store is festooned with men's and women's used furs: coats, stoles, jackets and accessories such as the tiny fox chokers that were popular in the 1920s and 1930s. Muskrat, raccoon and Japanese rabbit are all big sellers this year and you'll find them more expensive than black-dyed muskrat or rabbit, Persian lamb and other less popular furs. A fashionable, good-quality long muskrat coat costs $250 to $300; a fair-to-middling one, around $150; $195 will get you a stylish, nearly-new dyed muskrat fun fur; $300 buys a warm, durable, ever-popular raccoon coat. And Japanese rabbit? Who knows? The cheapest furs from $10 to $60 are in the basement. There are about 500 great buys, but be on the lookout for loose hems and tears. Caveat emptor: There are exchanges on gifts only.

Monday to Saturday 9:30 a.m. to 6 p.m., Thursday and Friday to 9 p.m.
202 Spadina Ave. (363-6077)

Shoes

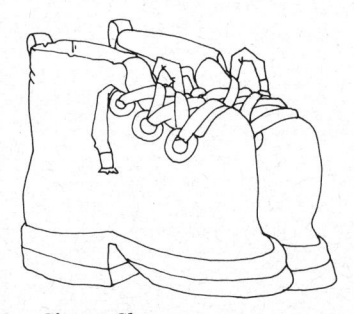

Joe Singer Shoes
Joe Singer Shoes is a traditional shop for seasoned bargain hunters. And why not, when you can pick up high-fashion top-quality footwear at a 30%-to-70% discount? There are some seconds but the main sources of Singer's vast selections and bargain prices are closeouts, cancellation, overruns and double-runs. Accordingly, imported winter boots sell for $45, and most Canadian makes are substantially less. There's a complete

Shoes 79

range of men's and women's sizes and what Joe considers to be the largest collection in town of leather handbags for around $25. You'll find Singer's a pleasant place to shop — it's roomy, with lots of viewing mirrors and most of the stock is on display.

Toronto locations, Monday to Saturday 9 a.m. to 6 p.m., Thursday and Friday to 9 p.m.
903 Bloor St. W. (533-3559)
915 Danforth Ave. (461-6045)
Monday, noon to 6 p.m., Tuesday, Wednesday and Saturday 9 a.m. to 6 p.m., Thursday and Friday to 9 p.m.
10341-A Yonge St., Richmond Hill (884-0360)

Lori's Shoes
Old-world craftsmanship and modern technology combine to make Lori's shoes and boots one of the best buys in town. Actually, they're made by John and Helen Denich who, by making their own rubber soles and molding them to the leather uppers, have come up with a solid but comfortable vulcanized shoe at rock-bottom prices. Roots-type shoes are just $14, a far cry from the real thing at $35.50; and shoes similar in style to ever-popular Wallabies, just $10. Kids' fleece-lined boots are $5; unlined, only $4. Shoes and boots are made-to-measure or you can choose from their factory stock of styles and colors.

Monday to Friday, 8 a.m. to 6 p.m., Saturday to 4 p.m.
99 River St. (366-7046)

Maher Shoes Warehouse Outlet
If you're a Maher fan, you'll be more than pleased with the wide assortment of men's, women's and children's shoes at, at least 30% reductions. There are many Maher favorites: Root-type suede shoes in assorted colors from $9.75 to $15; fashionable leather and suede espadrilles, $13; men's shoes for $15 and assorted boots for $5 and up. Shoes are mostly ends-of-season and discontinued lines, and there's a complete range of men's, women's and kid's sizes. The store is neat and the service is good.

Monday to Saturday 9 a.m. to 6 p.m., Thursday and Friday to 9 p.m.
Northtown Plaza, Yonge Street near Finch (221-2892)

Savage Shoe Factory
If you're addicted to weekend outings, you'd be wise to include Preston on your itinerary. Savage has its own retail outlet for factory seconds, store rejects and returns. Check your choice carefully because some defects could affect the wear. All men's, women's and kid's shoes and boots are greatly reduced and there's a complete range of sizes. The factory is self-service, large and always packed, so be prepared for a lot of looking and trying on.

Tuesday to Friday 10 a.m. to 9 p.m., Monday and Saturday to 5 p.m.
250 Dolph St., Preston (519-653-1262)

The Shoe Bin
You won't believe your eyes or the prices at The Shoe Bin, a new Greb outlet in Mississauga. The top price for a pair of insulated, water-proofed and lined Kodiak boots is $29.95. They're factory seconds with minor flaws — crooked eyelets, perhaps, or a mark or two — but nothing that affects the wear and over-all quality for which Greb is noted. The Bin stocks a complete line of Kodiaks, both soft and steel-toe types. The smallest size is a men's 6 (a woman's 8).

The shoes are mostly discontinued

lines and overruns. You can expect to pick up your favorite sandals — even Hush Puppies — for $10 to $15. Bauer Supreme skates are $40. Another bonus: no boot at The Shoe Bin costs more than $29.95, and only shoes costing $30 or more are taxable.

10 a.m. to 6 p.m., Thursday and Friday to 9 p.m., Saturday 9 a.m. to 4 p.m.
1911 Dundas St. E., west of Hwy. 427, Mississauga (624-9712)
Tuesday and Wednesday 11 a.m. to 5:30 p.m., Thursday and Friday to 8 p.m., Saturday 10 a.m. to 4 p.m.
5 Michael St. off Victoria, Kitchener (Toronto no. 362-1939), ext. 150)

Sunbeam Shoe Company
There's a great assortment of men's, women's and kid's shoes and boots: ever-so-slight seconds, ends-of-lines and discontinued lines. You pay up to $15 for first-line women's shoes, and $17 for your favorite BeeJays. Try to get there early; they're busy.

Saturday only, 8:30 a.m. to 5 p.m.
750 Elm St., Port Colborne (1-834-4531)

Walkin Shoes Ltd.
An aptly named wholesale-retail outlet that buys up job lots, case goods, closeouts and complete shoe stocks and sells them at bargain prices at its new family footwear store, Walkin Shoes Ltd. The Walkin family has been in the shoe business since 1918 and Irv Walkin has achieved a delightful combination of low prices, personal service and a wide selection. You'll see names like Gamin, Clarke, Savage and Florsheim, and you'll find shoes that are $30 elsewhere are $10 at Walkin's; leather joggers, from $8 to $10; and stylish Italian imported dress shoes, $10. Irv plans a special sale each and every week of the year. When we were there, any shoe on the rack was just $5. Buster Brown shoes for kids (limited sizes) were $6, and men's slippers (a wide assortment of leathers — some with sheepskin linings), from $4 to $5.

Monday to Saturday, 9 a.m. to 5 p.m.
246 Parliament St. (363-2582)

The Warehouse Shoe Mart
The shoes are all from $1 to $12, but the thing to look for is men's, women's and children's jogging shoes. They're mostly North Stars and Cougars in a wide range of styles and colors and a complete range of sizes. Name brand suede athletic shoes often sell for as low as $9.99, and less for kids. There's also a fair-to-middling selection of clogs for $7.99 and up. A word of warning: the stock varies from week to week.

Monday, Tuesday and Wednesday 10 a.m. to 7 p.m., Thursday, Friday and Saturday to 9 p.m.
720 Bathurst St. (534-2255)
260 Spadina Ave. (368-5034)

6. Leisure

It's almost impossible to be bored in our fair city with its miles of waterfront, the Island, and more libraries, theatres, recreational and educational facilities than anywhere else in Canada. In this chapter you'll learn all about the places to enjoy your favorite sport or hobby, take in a play or an old movie, learn a new skill or polish up an old one — at prices you can afford. And you'll also discover where to buy cheap books and records, hobby supplies, toys, sporting goods and much more.

Cheap Movies

"Going to the show," as it was called in the old days, meant attending a reputable theatre or going to "the cockroach palace." Today, moviegoers can watch their favorite flicks at several excellent, but cheap, movie houses. Both veteran movie buffs and pennypinchers will be delighted by the fare and the prices. Prices are from $1.99 — some are freebies — and there is everything from classics to current Oscar winners.

Here's what's available:

The Cinema Archives: Admission $2.50, children's show Sunday at 6:30 p.m. $1.
560 Palmerston above Bloor (536-7382)

The Roxy: Admission $1.99, senior citizens and children 75¢
1215 Danforth at Greenwood (461-2401)

New Yorker: Admission $2.75, $1.50 for the late film
651 Yonge St. (925-6400)

OISE: Admission $2 every Wednesday and Thursday evening at 7:30 p.m. and $1.25 at 9:30 p.m.
252 Bloor St. W. (961-3035)

Poor Alex Theatre: Friday and Saturday admission $1.50
296 Brunswick Ave. at Bloor (920-8373)

The Centre: Admission $1.99 for adults, $1.49 for students, 99¢ for children
772 Dundas St. near Bathurst (368-9555)

Kingsway Theatre: Admission $2.
3030 Bloor St. W. at Royal York Rd. (236-2437)

The Screening Room: The Kingsway Theatre: Admission $1.99
3030 Bloor St. W. (236-2437)

Cinema Lumière: Admission $2.50 (Mon. to Thurs. $2 for the second feature), Senior citizens and children $2.
290 College St. (925-9938)

Revue Repertory: Admission $2.
400 Roncesvalles Ave. (531-9959)

Poor Alex Theatre

Free Movies

Dawes Rd. Library
Films every Tuesday at 2 p.m.
416 Dawes Rd. (757-8649)

Bloor and Gladstone Library
Films every Wednesday at 7:30 p.m.
1101 Bloor St. W. (536-3402)

The Sanderson Library
Films every Thursday at 6:30 p.m.
725 Dundas St. W. (366-1741)

Library House
Movies every Friday at 7:30 p.m.
265 Gerrard St. E. (921-8674)

Harbourfront
Movies every Wednesday at 7:30 p.m.
Harbourfront York Quay (369-4951)

York
Every Thursday through Sunday
Curtis Lecture Hall, York U., 4700 Keele St. (667-2100)

"Home" Movies

If family and guests alike cringe when you mention home movies, it's time for a new approach. Why not a real movie, say a W.C. Fields classic or a toe-twister like Phantom of the Opera? They're free and readily available (for overnight borrowing) along with a projector, at your nearest film library. There's a great selection of shorts, documentaries and full-length features and they're all listed in the library catalogue. And it's one sure way to beat the high cost of movies. Here's a list:

East York Film Library
A course in projector operation's a must. They don't offer one but they accept your credit in a course from another branch. Library card and ID (with your current address) required as well. Projectors: $3; films, free.

Monday to Friday 9 a.m. to 8:30 p.m., Saturday 9 a.m. to 5 p.m.
Sir Walter Stewart Library, 170 Memorial Park Ave., Leaside (425-8222)

Etobicoke Film Library
There's a proficiency test and a course, if you fail (both by appointment only). Bring your library card and ID with your current address. It's $3 for a projector; the film's free.

Monday to Friday 10 a.m. to 9 p.m., Saturday 10 a.m. to 5 p.m.
1806 Islington Ave. (248-5681)

National Film Board
"North of Superior" is probably the best-known NFB film. But there are other greats, hundreds of them, and most are available to you *free*. There's no catch and no deposit and you can take two hours running time of film. There is a free catalogue to choose from but there are no projectors. Book at least two days in advance and be sure to name some substitutions in case one of your choices isn't available.

Monday to Friday, 8 a.m. to 5 p.m.
1 Lombard St. (369-4093)

North York Film Library
There's no proficiency test — they take your word — but you must be 18, a library member, and supply another piece of identification with your current address. Films are free; 16 mm projectors, $3, 8 or super-8 $2. Catalogue orders only.

Monday to Friday 9 a.m. to 8:30 p.m., Saturday 9 a.m. to 5 p.m.
35 Fairview Mall Dr. (492-0121)

Scarborough Film Library
If you're over 18 and have a library card, you can rent a projector, provided you can pass their profi-

ciency test. Rentals are $3 and films are free. Choose from their stock or order from the catalogue. Book well ahead, especially on week-ends, and allow five working days for catalogue orders.

Monday to Friday 9 a.m. to 8:30 p.m., Saturday 9 a.m. to 5 p.m.
496 Birchmount Rd. (698-1191)

The Toronto Film Library

It costs $3 to rent a projector and films are free for people with library cards. There are ten projectors, all heavily booked, and a wide selection of film features, shorts and documentaries. You can order from the catalogue (available in all Metro library branches). Book well in advance, especially for weekends.

Monday to Friday 9 a.m. to 8:30 p.m., and Saturday 9 a.m. to 5 p.m.
40 Orchardview Blvd. (484-8250)

Recreation, Cheap & Free

For those who like to play 'n learn there's a host of cheap, often free facilities all across Metro at schools, libraries, community colleges and centres and the Y. It would take a volume to list them all but the scope is tremendous and defies description. There are free films, workshops, free entertainment for kids and adults and hundreds of recreational and educational activities.

And there's less conventional fare. For 35¢ a session — baby sitting's free — your library can tell you how to be a group leader or how to get along with your child. And from $15 up, depending on the course and the college, you can learn just about anything imaginable, like creative welding, script writing or yoga. Or if you're an aspiring, long-winded musician or swimmer, the Board of Education will see that you get a crack at swimming, scuba diving or the bagpipes. Free brochures listing courses, prices and free fare are available on request.

Contact your local library, community college and/or centre or Y for info and special events.

Boards of Education

Schools are an unlimited source of adult education, recreation, arts and crafts. Brochures are available from your local Board of Education. Write or call:

Toronto
Monday to Friday 8:45 a.m. to 4:45 p.m.
155 College St. (598-4931)

East York
Monday to Friday 8:30 a.m. to 4:30 p.m.
840 Coxwell Ave. (465-4631)

Etobicoke
Monday to Friday 8:30 a.m. to 4:30 p.m.
Etobicoke Civic Centre (626-4360)

North York
Monday to Friday 9 a.m. to 5:30 p.m.
5050 Yonge St. (225-4661)

Scarborough
Monday to Friday 8:30 a.m. to 4:30 p.m.
140 Borough Dr. (438-7541)

York
Monday to Friday 8:30 a.m. to 4:30 p.m.
2 Trethewey Dr. (653-2270)

Colleges

There are literally hundreds of unusual and no-so-unusual fun and educational courses to choose from including sports, technical and academic courses, arts, crafts, yoga and many more. Brochures are available on request. Write or call:

Centennial College of Applied Arts and Technology
Warden Woods Campus, 651 Warden Ave., Scarborough (694-3241)

George Brown College
P.O. Box 1015, Station B, Toronto (967-1212)

Humber College of Applied Arts and Technology
P.O. Box 1900, Rexdale (675-3111)

Seneca College of Applied Arts and Technology
1750 Finch Ave. E., Willowdale (491-5050)

Ryerson Polytechnical Institute
50 Gould St., Toronto (595-5000)

Public Libraries
Libraries provide all kinds of free recreation and entertainment. In addition to films to borrow and cheap movies, there are programs for senior citizens, adults and kids, workshops, lessons in arts, crafts, music and dancing and many other popular pastimes. Call or write for brochures.

East York
Monday to Friday 9 a.m. to 5 p.m.
Unit 34, Thorncliffe Park Dr., Toronto (423-6218)

Etobicoke
Monday to Friday 8:30 a.m. to 9 p.m., Saturday 9 a.m. to 5 p.m.
1806 Islington Ave., or Box 501, Etobicoke P.O. (248-5681)

North York
Monday to Friday 8:45 a.m. to 5 p.m.
35 Fairview Mall Dr., Willowdale (494-6838)

Scarborough
Monday to Friday 9 a.m. to 5 p.m.
1076 Ellesmere Ave., Scarborough (291-1991)

Toronto
Monday to Friday 9 a.m. to 5 p.m.
40 Orchard View Blvd., Toronto (484-8015)

York
Monday to Thursday noon to 8:30 p.m., Friday noon to 6 p.m., Saturday 10 a.m. to 5 p.m.
1745 Eglinton Ave. W., Toronto (781-5208)

Metro Toronto Library
Monday to Friday 9 a.m. to 9 p.m., Saturday 9 a.m. to 5 p.m.
789 Yonge St., Toronto

Music Library —
Audio-visual Service
Monday to Friday 9 a.m. to 5 p.m.
789 Yonge St., Toronto (962-3901)

Municipal Reference Library
Monday to Friday 8:30 a.m. to 8:30 p.m.
City Hall (366-6431)

YMCA, YWCA, YMHA & YWHA
Ys offer a wide range of low-cost and free activities and services, including day camps, music, dance and art lessons, swimming and phys-ed programs, counselling, fitness programs, creative classes and workshops, drop-in centres and take-a-break groups for mothers with youngsters.

Metropolitan Toronto Young Men's Christian Association (YMCA)
Monday to Friday 8:30 a.m. to 9 p.m., Saturday 9 a.m. to 6 p.m., Sunday 12:45 p.m. to 3:30 p.m.
40 College St., Toronto (921-5171)

Regions:
Central Unit, 40 College St. (921-5171)

St. Jamestown Unit, 260 Wellesley St. E. (964-8775)
West End Unit, 931 College St. (536-1166)
High Park Unit, 2665 Dundas St. W. (763-1193)
York Centre Unit, 2547 Eglinton Ave. W. (653-7401)
Harriet Tubman Centre, 15 Robina Ave. (654-4203)
Etobicoke Unit, 3226 Bloor St. W. (231-2297)
Action Service Contact Centre (255-5322)
North York Unit, 567 Sheppard Ave. E. (225-7773)
Scarborough Region, 3150 Eglinton Ave. E., Scarborough (266-7797)

Young Women's Christian Association of Canada (YWCA)
Monday to Friday 9 a.m. to 5 p.m.
571 Jarvis St. (921-2117)

Metropolitan Toronto YWCA
Monday to Sunday, switchboard open 24 hours
80 Woodlawn Ave. E. (923-8454)

North Program Centre
Monday to Friday 9 a.m. to 10 p.m.
2532 Yonge St. (487-7151)

East Program Centre
Monday to Friday 9 a.m. to 5 p.m.
1152 Gerrard St. E. (466-9878)

Young Men's and Young Women's Hebrew Association (YM-YWHA)
Sunday to Thursday 9 a.m. to 9:30 p.m., Friday 9 a.m. to 5:30 p.m.
4588 Bathurst St., Willowdale (636-1880) and 750 Spadina Ave. at Bloor St. (924-6211)

Recreation Departments
Toronto's boroughs offer a wide range of recreational facilities including arenas, swimming pools and instruction, recreation centres, parks, playgrounds, rinks, gymnasia and community centres. Brochures are free on request. For information, contact:

Toronto Department of Parks and Recreation
8:30 a.m. to 4:30 p.m.
East 21 City Hall (367-7251)

East York Recreation Department
8:30 a.m. to 4:30 p.m.
550 Mortimer Ave., Toronto (461-9451, ext. 31)

Etobicoke Parks and Recreation Services
8:30 a.m. to 4:30 p.m.
Etobicoke Civic Centre (626-4557)

North York Recreation and Parks Department
8:30 a.m. to 4:30 p.m.
5145 Yonge St., Willowdale (225-4611)

Scarborough Parks and Recreation Department
8:30 a.m. to 4:30 p.m.
150 Borough Drive, Scarborough (438-7411)

York Parks and Recreation Department
8:30 a.m. to 4:30 p.m.
2700 Eglinton Ave. W. (653-2700)

Metropolitan Toronto Regional Conservation Authority
8:40 a.m. to 4:30 p.m.
5 Shoreham Dr., Downsview (661-6600)

Harbourfront
Harbourfront features special ethnic festivals plus free movies, rock concerts and regular Sunday night jazz concerts at 7:30 p.m., and they're expanding this year to accommodate the crowds. An extra bonus is their fine, almost free summer sailing program. This year they offer basic sailing lessons to youngsters from 12-16 at $25 for 15 hours. Everything is supplied, even life jackets. They

Kids playing at Harbourfront

sail around Toronto Bay in 20-foot luggers (lee boards) for three hours a day, Monday to Friday in a series of five scheduled lessons.

207 Queen's Quay W. (369-4951)

Sporting Goods

Collegiate Sports
Weekly specials, hard-to-match prices and sheer variety are reasons why the sporty set flocks to Collegiate for equipment and attire. In a recent spectacular "tennis" sale, racquets sold for $3 to $10 less than the regular Collegiate discount price. Another recent special was a Toronto Bluejay's sale with all baseball equipment drastically reduced. Louisville Slugger gloves (reg. $36.98) were $32.88, other gloves were up to $10 off the regular price, and everything from bats, balls, T-shirts and helmets were knocked down. Watch the papers for their super record-breakers where off-season stuff goes from 30% to 50% off.

Daily 9:30 a.m. to 9:30 p.m., Saturday to 6 p.m.
Yorkdale Plaza (781-9127)
Monday to Friday 9:30 a.m. to 9:30 p.m., Saturday 9:30 a.m. to 6 p.m.
1255 The Queensway (255-2391)
Daily 10 a.m. to 9 p.m., Saturday to 6 p.m.
1510 Warden Ave. (447-9115)
Daily 10 a.m. to 6 p.m., Thursday and Friday to 9 p.m.
116 Wellington St. (363-9095)
Daily 10 a.m. to 9 p.m., Saturday to 6 p.m.
7171 Yonge St. (889-8800)

King Sol Outdoor Store
Outdoor types and those why just want to look the part will find everything they need here, at discount prices. Two huge rooms are crammed (neatly) with every conceivable kind of outdoor gear and camping equipment and apart from the selection, the prices will dazzle you. There are rubber rafts suspended from the ceiling, backpacks

galore, army wear, blankets and sleeping bags, pots and pans and a wide assortment of clothes and much more. And the prices? Yucca-brand backpacks (we saw them in other stores for $9) were $6.99; sturdy, light, Made-in-China downfilled jackets, $24.95. Heavy canvas army coats with thick pile lining — the kind that never wear out — were selling for $39.95; Canadian-made T-shirts, for $2.50. And the day's special: HIS brushed denim men's suits, $19.95.

Monday to Saturday 9:30 a.m. to 6 p.m., Thursday and Friday to 9 p.m.
639 Queen St. W. (363-9944)

King Sol Outdoor Store

Liftlock Fibreglass Company
For a sturdy factory-second canoe, try Liftlock Fibreglass in Peterborough. Flaws are minor, no scratches, dents or cracks, just a few inoffensive bubbles. All seconds are guaranteed to be structurally sound and are under full warranty. Liftlock's single-unit, chopped fibreglass construction makes for a strong but light canoe. The 14-footers sell for $169 (regularly $199) and 16-footers for $199 (regularly $239). They're available in ten colors.

Monday to Friday 8 a.m. to 5 p.m.
615 The Kingsway, Peterborough (705-742-4344)

National Gym Clothing and Sporting Goods
It features sports clothes for the armchair sports enthusiast and sporting goods for the sports person. With two floors of every conceivable type of sports equipment from water skis and tennis, golf, skiing and hockey essentials, to sportswear and just plain clothes, you're sure to find what you want at bargain prices. There are specials on Cooper, CCM and Louisville hockey sticks, at two for $8.95 — "Buy one and get one free." Adidas track suits, $16.95, Levi shirts and jeans, $9.95 and $13.88 respectively. When we were there, all ski-wear was on sale at 25% off. And there's a fantastic sale every September: they're open for 60 hours straight and everything in the store is reduced.

Monday to Friday 9 a.m. to 10 p.m., Saturday to 6 p.m.
4938 Yonge St., Willowdale (222-6506)

The Outdoor Stores
There's everything you need for the great outdoors and more at Outdoor Stores' "feature" prices: camping equipment, fishing equipment and tackle, knives, guns, canoes, motors, tennis, baseball and sports equipment, sleeping bags, backpacks — you name it, they've got it. Watch for special sales with super discounts.

Monday to Friday 9 a.m. to 9:30 p.m., Saturday 9 a.m. to 6 p.m.
1205 Finch Ave. W., Downsview (638-2325)
2958 Danforth Ave. (699-9792)
Dixie Plaza, Mississauga (274-3471)
134 Temperance St. (364-8335)

Sports Repair Services
Owner Bruce Smith, who has extensive experience in the sports equipment trade, intends to cover the sports repair market within a 30-mile radius of Metro. Broken but still usable sports equipment can have another go-around thanks to this

new, comprehensive repair shop. Either you personally take your battered skis, unstrung tennis racquets or coming-apart footwear to the location in the Victoria Park and Steeles area or, for no extra charge, you leave the item at your local sporting goods store and pick it up a few days later. Prices for some of the work: new bases for skis, from $35-$38; ski-edge sharpening from $10 per pair; new palm and preservative for goalie mitts, $18; fitting new blades for hockey skates, $6.50 plus blade; and replacing brake cables and blocks in bikes, $12.

Monday to Friday 8:30 a.m. to 5 p.m., Saturday 9 a.m. to 1 p.m.
596 Gordon Baker Rd., Willowdale (497-3400)

Sport Swap
Making it on the slopes can be hard on your legs and your pocketbook. One way to alleviate the financial strain is to drop in at Sport Swap; you'll not only save money, you'll make the slopes in style. They sell used skis for half-price and sometimes less, depending on the length and condition. And they'll take trade-ins if you want to get new stuff or update your equipment. Or, if you decide to pack it in they'll sell your cast-offs or arrange a swap. Their specialty is installations, hot waxing and general repairs. And you're virtually assured of proper equipment and fit, an essential for beginners. If skiing's not your bag, there is always a wide assortment of better quality new-and-used bikes for half-price or less, waterskis and camping equipment. A word of warning: don't go in looking for skis in the summer or bikes in the winter. Stock at Sport Swap changes with the seasons, as do the hours.

Winter, Monday to Friday 10 a.m. to 9 p.m., Saturday 9 a.m. to 6 p.m. Summer, Monday, Wednesday and Saturday 10 a.m. to 6 p.m., Thursday and Friday to 9 p.m.
579 Mount Pleasant Rd. (481-0249)

Books & Records

Albert Britnell Bookshop
Britnell's is one of the best bookstores around for rare and recently published books. But in case you didn't know, it's also a great place for bargains. They run a continuous sale of first-rate closeouts and publishers' overruns, at 25% to 50% reductions that you won't want to miss. There's a tremendous selection (about seven long tables' worth) and a fast turnover.

Monday to Saturday 9:30 a.m. to 6 p.m., Thursday to 9 p.m.
765 Yonge St. (924-3321)

Around Again
Remember The Yardbirds or Little Caesar and the Consuls? If you do, chances are you'll rave about Around Again, a funny little shop with over 6,000 used records and a limited selection of books in stock. The bulk of the store's collection is rock from the sixties and seventies — oddball and vintage Beatles albums, out-of-prints and disbanded groups. And if you can't find your all-time favorite there, owner Barbara Eisenstat keeps your name on file and calls you when — and if — it comes in. Records are in good shape — they're carefully checked and tested when they arrive. But if in doubt, check your purchase on their testing facilities. All used records sell for about $2.50 and for every record you bring in, you generally get $1 cash or $1.25 credit towards the purchase of other records in the store. Your paperbacks are worth 25% of the original price.

Monday to Saturday noon to 6 p.m.
18 Baldwin St. (979-2822)

Classic Bookshop #55
Whether you're into cooking, history or just plain books, join the bookworms in the basement of the downtown store. It's Classic's bargain basement and, in Classic style, its large tables and long shelves are lined with reams of contemporary and classic paperbacks, hardcovers and book sets, in an on-going, continuous sale of closeouts, overruns and out-of-prints. There's literally every conceivable category, topic and book, all at half-price to 75% off.

Monday to Saturday 10 a.m. to 10 p.m., Friday to 11 p.m.
285 Yonge St. south of Dundas Street (366-1912)

Cole's
They're "the book people" and there's a fine selection of books in all categories — fat and thin, hard and soft — at over 30 locations in Metro — plus half-price publishers' sales, reduced-price clearance sales and 99¢ specials. Their biggest store at Yonge and Charles features a better-than-average range of self-help, do-it-yourself and reference books. Hours vary. Over 30 Metro locations. Check your phone book for the location nearest you.

Don's Discs
Don's discs are records and owner Don Keele says he's the only dealer around who sells *used* 45s (about 20,000 in stock, mostly from the fifties and sixties). Most of them sell at 5 for $1 and other records range from 10¢ to $15 for collector's items. He has one Elvis Presley record on a Sun label that's worth $50 to collectors. His stock originates from as far

If You can Stand the Crush, Sam's Got 'Em
or The Great Boxing Day Sale

Sam The Record Man's annual Boxing Day Sale is a seasonal tradition that's so popular it's almost frightening. It's the one time of the year when Sam sells everything in the store at cost or near cost, and the event is just too huge, too awful to describe.

Sam Sniderman added 600 square feet of extra space and seven extra cash registers one year, in a valiant attempt to accommodate the thundering hordes. You guessed it, he couldn't. His determined fans were lined up for hours, smack in front of Sam's competitors, refusing to be distracted from their mission (a situation Sam finds a trifle amusing and embarrassing). He can't understand it, can't explain it and admittedly can't cope with it. He even tried a two-day sale one year, but it just didn't work. On Boxing Day it was the usual chaos; the next day, it was zilch. Sam never tried it again.

Sam's opens at 8:30 a.m. but some people arrive at 6 p.m. armed with formidable "Wanted" lists. From the time the store opens its doors until midnight, it's "hairy," to quote Sam. So save your money, make your list and get in shape. You'll need to.
Sam's is on Yonge Street, just north of Dundas.

away as Detroit, but you can take your oldies in too. You get half the selling price (which varies) if you take cash, and 65% to 70% if you trade them in.

Tuesday to Friday 12:30 p.m. to 6 p.m., Saturday 11 a.m. to 5 p.m.
1452 Queen St. W. (531-1288)

The Nth Hand
The shop features a wide range of near perfect, used books and records at prices "cheaper than any place but the Sally Ann." Records are rated "crummy", "soft", "medium," "hard" and "harder rock" and there's a good selection of classical, folk and soul music. Because owner Paul Steuwe is very particular about the records he takes on trade-ins, his stock — except for those clearly marked "crummy" (10¢) — is flawless. Albums like Jim Croce's "Photographs and Memories," Tchaikovsky's "Pathétique" and the Beatles' "Magical Mystery Tour" sell for $2 to $2.50; records with surface noise (no scratches) for $1.50. Floor-to-ceiling shelves are lined with virtually unmarked books on health, sci-fi, the occult, art, poetry and other topics. Paperbacks are in the 50¢ to 75¢ range; hardcovers vary. Trades are welcome if records and books are in near perfect condition, and two of your oldies will get you one of Paul's on a straight trade. Cash for records ranges from 75¢ to $1 and he'll give 20% retail price for books.

Tuesday to Saturday noon to 6 p.m.
102 Harbord St. (921-2381)

Old Favorites Bookshop
It's favored by thrifty bookworms and Coke drinkers alike, and for a valid reason: there are over 200,000 used books in stock, including many classics and some current, and a vintage Coke machine that still dispenses an ice-cold bottle of Coke for just a dime. And if some of your books are just gathering dust, take them to Old Favorites. You can take cash or choose other books. Bookworms will probably opt for books — the selection is too tempting to resist.

Tuesday to Saturday 10 a.m. to 9 p.m.
250 Adelaide St. W. (363-0944)

Other Books and the 50¢ Bookstore
Other Books has thousands of new and used books — so many, in fact, that you need the map inside the door to guide you through the rows of floor-to-ceiling shelves. Used books mostly sell for a third to half price and there are always three or four sale counters of new books at incredibly low prices.

The 50¢ Bookstore owned by Other Books, is another cheap book outlet

Books and records at the Nth Hand

that not only sells second-hand hardcovers and paperbacks for 50¢, but also takes exchanges. The stock varies but they try to maintain a wide selection of foreign language books.

Other Books:
Monday to Saturday 10:30 a.m. to 10:30 p.m., Sunday 2:30-10:30 p.m.
491 Bloor St. W. (961-5227)

The 50¢ Bookstore:
Tuesday to Saturday noon to 6 p.m.
499 Bloor Street West (922-7662)

W.H. Smith
There's always a counter of sale books in any number of categories. Largest stores are at T-D Centre and 1500 Yonge St.

Daily 9:30 a.m. to 6 p.m., Thursday and Friday to 9 p.m.

Paperback and Record Exchange
If your records and books are gathering dust, trade them in at the Paperback and Record Exchange. You receive one half of the Exchange's selling price for your rejected records. Most records are priced up to $2.90, so if you bring in two in good condition you might get one free. There's a big turnover (300 to 400 every week) and a wide selection of oldies but goodies, 1950s albums, plus folk, blues, rock and classical albums. About all that's missing is the current rock scene except after the Christmas gift trade-ins in January. All records are visually inspected for scratches and flaws. There's no surefire guarantee but you can play your selections in the store before purchasing. Your old paperbacks are worth 25% of the cover price if you buy another, 10% if you don't. You'll find many old favorites, classics and current bestsellers.

Tuesday to Thursday 11 a.m. to 6 p.m., Friday to 8 p.m., Saturday 10 a.m. to 6 p.m.
3402 Yonge St., two blocks north of Fairlawn (487-9311)

Records-on-Wheels
They're probably the cheapest retail and wholesale record outlet in Canada and their everyday prices for records are the best in town. Current "top ten" albums sell for $4.99 to $5.59 regular and from $3.97 to $4.44 on sale and there's a selection of over 10,000 from which to choose. (Their 4,000 square foot warehouse is literally stacked with records.) Trade-ins are accepted and you get one new album for four oldies.

Monday to Thursday 10 a.m. to 10 p.m., Friday and Saturday to midnight.
629 Yonge St. (961-3319)
Monday to Wednesday 9 a.m. to 6 p.m., Thursday to Saturday to 9 p.m.
Newtonbrook Plaza (221-8321)

* * *

If you don't mind a limited selection, Records-on-Wheels has a small outlet at the Harbour Square Tuck Shop. Current favorites are $5.98, not-so-current ones, $4.99 and popular doubles are $6.98. If you don't see what you want they'll order it from the warehouse.

Monday to Friday 9:30 a.m. to 9 p.m., Saturday 9:30 a.m. to 7 p.m., Sunday 9:30 a.m. to 6 p.m.
Harbour Square, second floor, southeast side

Round Records
If you make regular trips across the border you've probably found that you can buy records there at half the Canadian price. Better still, drop in at Round Records. Apart from a complete selection of new records at prices comparable to Sam's and

A&A, they have a good assortment of nearly-new and used albums for $2.35 to $3.35 — everything from old to recent rock, folk, classical, plus vintage albums. Recent finds: Rod Stewart's "Sing It Again, Rod" and Joplin's "Pearl," both $2.35. And in case you want to gather up your oldies and dust collectors and trade them in on something new, you're allowed $1 to $1.25 on trades, depending on the record and its condition. All records are visually inspected and spot-tested.

Monday to Wednesday 10:30 a.m. to 9 p.m., Thursday and Friday 10:30 a.m. to 10 p.m., Saturday 10 a.m. to 7 p.m.
46 Bloor St. W., 2nd floor (921-6555)

*For Sound Equipment see p. 56.

Toys

The Children's Own Storefront
Neighborhood kids, many of them pupils of owner-teacher Elaine Sherman, are free to roam around this bright, select toy shop with its handcrafted toys, books and puzzles. There is always bubble gum, balloons and assorted knick-knacks the kids can afford and a good supply of recycled toys at reasonable prices. Used books, mostly kids' picture books, cost 50¢ each, and recycled toys like a Playskool work bench (complete), 75¢.

What really makes the store a standout is the exquisite handcrafted toys, dolls and puppets you see. A 5' high pine rocking giraffe that no child could resist (I know this one couldn't) was $85. Handmade Raggedy Anns were $10 and up. Custom-made dolls' rockers with rattan seats cost just $3.95; and an assortment of hand puppets (the Lambchop kind) were $1.95. A word of warning: don't make a special trip. Store hours are irregular, to say the least, and adjusted to meet Ms. Sherman's teaching schedule. But if you're in the neighborhood drop by.

Hours are posted on the door.
599 Queen St. W. (no phone)

Horizon Stores
A quick survey shows their regular prices are more modest than those of other discount stores (even Honest Ed's) and more than equal the sale prices of neighboring toy stores. As you'd expect with Eaton's there's a huge selection of toys in every Horizon store, from virtually indestructible Fisher-Price favorites to Sesame Street characters. But that's not all, they also carry housewares, shelf appliances and a large assortment of basic family clothing needs. Apart from everyday bargains, special features like Boxing Day and post-Xmas week sales mean even greater savings.

Yonge-Eglinton Centre (Yonge and Eglinton), (489-2131)

Horizon store

Victoria Park and Sheppard, (493-6801)
Gerrard Square (Pape and Gerrard), (461-0485)
Rockwood Mall (Dixie Rd.), (625-2760)
Dufferin Mall, (531-5708)
Rexdale Plaza (Rexdale and Islington), (745-6171)

Toyerama
The stock varies but there's usually a good selection of name-brand toys. Mattel, Marx, Hasbro and Fisher-Price are just a few of the names to look for plus books and records. Everything is half-price — sometimes less — and a bargain at one of their two stores is a sure thing. For example, childrens' books are priced at four for $1.

Monday, Tuesday and Wednesday 10 a.m. to 6 p.m., Thursday and Friday 10 a.m. to 9 p.m., Saturday 9 a.m. to 6 p.m.
Dundas St. W. and Hwy. 427 (233-2121)
3701 Keele St. (636-4972)

Hobby Supplies

Gwartzman's Canvas and Art Supplies
Owner Paul Gwartzman of Gwartzman's Canvas and Art Supplies is unabashedly and justifiably immodest as he talks about the bargains in his shop. "Everything we have is the best deal in town" he says. "If we find that we're being undersold we cut our prices." It's that simple. A best buy is jute for macramé plant hangers and wall hangings at $6.50 for 5 lbs. of 8-ply jute (the usual price is $8.98). And $13 for 10 lbs. of 12-ply jute, which is almost unheard of. He also stocks educational art supplies of all kinds — paper, crayons and

Paul Gwartzman of Gwartzman's

paints — and a complete line of fine art supplies, all at substantial savings.

Monday to Saturday 9 a.m. to 6:30 p.m.
448 Spadina Ave. (922-5429)

Other Art Supplies
Other Art Supplies carries a complete range of artists' materials, from paints and brushes to framing equipment for the finished product. Students and members of Three Schools get 10% off the already reasonable prices.

If your own crafts are beginning to look marketable, Other Delights, in the same building, will be happy to appraise them. Other Delights sells assorted knick-knackery, specializing in handcrafted pottery, toys, jewelry and greeting cards. They take work by local craftspeople and Three Schools instructors on consignment. It's open 11 a.m. to 6 p.m. Monday to Saturday.

Monday to Thursday 9:30 a.m. to 8 p.m., Saturday 9:30 a.m. to 6 p.m.
302 Brunswick Ave. (961-5226)

Hobby Supplies

The Kite Store
If someone tells you to go fly a kite, you can do it in style at $1.49 and up, with almost any kite imaginable, from a bright silk grasshopper kite to a monstrous 45-foot long "mylar" dragon kite. There are hundreds, in every conceivable shape and material: traditional English cloth kites, hand-made Oriental rice-paper kites — even a Japanese carp wind sock.

Monday to Wednesday and Saturday 10:30 a.m. to 6 p.m., Thursday and Friday to 9 p.m.
848A Yonge St. (964-0434)

Fabric and Drapery Mill Outlet
Most people I know who sew do it because they like it, or to save money, rarely both. Regardless of which category you're in, you'll find it hard to resist the prices and the goods at this busy outlet. There are remnants, ends-of-bolt, seconds and first quality materials of all kinds. Much of the stuff you see is half-price, and if you shop around you'll find it almost impossible to beat their prices. Terry velour is $3 a yard up, and popular denim fabrics just $1.99 a yard and up.

Monday to Friday 9:30 a.m. to 9:30 p.m., Saturday 9 a.m. to 6 p.m.
1310 Dundas St. E., Mississauga (275-0442)
2160 Hwy. 7, Concord, Ontario (669-2251)
8401 Woodbine Ave. (495-6919)

The Original Stitsky's
Stitsky's has three full floors, crammed (in neat fashion) with an incredible selection of dry goods, from special Holly Hobbie cotton prints to heavy, woven Indian bedspreads. My advice is to head for the basement — if you can tear yourself away from the first floor — where the real bargains are. Some material is

Fabric at Stitsky's

20% off but most is half-price. You'll see cotton chambray in muted blues that make perfect jean shirts for $1.98; fine-wale corduroy for tops and pants, $2.77; and decorator-type burlap, $1.19 to $1.59.

Upstairs on the third floor — the drapery floor — a special treat: drapery closeouts at 98¢ a yard, pillows (regular $12.98) for $9.98 and some ready-made draperies from 20% off. There is also a great assortment of sewing notions.

Monday, Tuesday and Wednesday 9 a.m. to 7 p.m., Thursday and Friday to 9 p.m., Saturday to 6 p.m.
754 Bathurst St. (537-2633)
5385 Yonge St. (Northtown Plaza) (226-3636)

Wine Art
Wine Art owner Mike Arthur estimates that you can make your own fine, mellow wines for from 35¢ to 65¢ a bottle! All you need is some special equipment, concentrates, some spare time and a great deal of patience (you'll need this while

you're waiting for your wine to mature). The store is stocked with everything you need to start you on your own reds, whites and rosés. There are books to guide you, spigots, syphons, strainers, even hops and malt if you're into beer. Your equipment will cost less than $25, and concentrates from $3.95, depending on what kind and how much you want to make.

To give you an idea, 32 oz. of Spanish red, white or Rosada concentrate makes a full two gallons of wine and costs $4.95; and 140 oz. of French white or rosé concentrate makes 5½ gallons and costs $13.95. And they're not just any old concentrates: they're the product of the finest vineyards in the world, from France, Italy, Spain, Austria and California. (The advantage of the concentrates is that you can make wine all year.) There's free appraisal service at any Wine Art store and if you really get carried away there are more than 30 winemaking clubs in Ontario.

Avenue Road and Bloor Street West stores, Tuesday to Friday, 9 a.m. to 6 p.m., Saturday to 5 p.m. All other stores, Tuesday to Friday 10 a.m. to 6 p.m., Saturday 9 a.m. to 5 p.m.
2046 Avenue Rd. (487-7124)
3891 Bloor St. W. (233-8226)
7600 Yonge St. (889-8832)
889 Millwood Rd. (421-7134)
Dorset Park Plaza, Kennedy Road (755-8311)

7. Of Consuming Interest

This chapter's all about money: Where the cheapest loans are, the subtle art of chargemanship, how to make the most of your savings and basic facts about credit. We won't presume to tell you how to spend your money or how much you should save. It's your money and your budget must be tailored to suit your life-style. Here then, is our Dollars and Sense guide:

Special Information Directory

Information centres and multi-service centres provide a host of free services from legal assistance, day care, home help, emergency driving, debt, budget and credit counselling to medical care as well as up-to-date information on resources and activities in your area. Here's a list of information centres (hours vary).

Municipal Government Information

Main switchboard numbers and departments providing information and direction are listed.

City of Toronto: 367-9111; Information Office 367-7341
East York: 461-9451 to Clerk's Dept.
Etobicoke: 626-4161; Borough Clerk's Dept. 626-4270
North York: 225-4611 to Public Information Office
Scarborough: 438-7111; Communications Section 438-7212
York: 653-2700
Metro Toronto: 367-9111; Metro Chairman's Office 367-8011

Information Centres

City of Toronto
Bloor Bathurst Information Centre
They provide legal assistance, special services including emergency interpreters for Spanish and Portuguese speaking people, a neighborhood housing registry and income tax clinic and form filling.

1006 Bathurst St., Toronto (531-4613)

Neighbourhood Information Post (N.I.P.)
There's a registry for sitters and home day care. They'll locate transportation when needed, have an odd jobs registry, provide information of Ward 7 activities, and they offer an income tax clinic.

265 Gerrard St. E., Toronto (924-2543)

East York
Neighbourhood Information Centre (N.I.C.)
They offer legal aid, day care and home help. There's a paperback library, room registry, and help in various languages. A special consumer help office and an income tax clinic.

81 Barrington Ave., Toronto (698-1626)

Thorncliffe Information Post (T.I.P.)
For those who need emergency driving in the Thorncliffe area. There's also a cleaning registry, a registry for sitters and locating of private day care.

45 Overlea Blvd., Toronto (423-3322)

Action Service Contact Centre
Counselling is available regarding legal aid; debt, budget and credit counselling; a baby-sitting and child care registry are also available. An income tax service for seniors and the under-$6,000 bracket is provided and they operate the Birmingham Drop-in Centre for teens, 11 to 17. They serve the area south of Queensway.

185-5th St., Toronto (255-5322)

Etobicoke Central Information and Referral
Available are a rooms registry, friendly visiting and a Special Needs Assistance Program for the handicapped. Central-van takes senior citizens shopping and there's an income tax service for seniors. Legal aid is referred to Bloordale School. The area served is between the Queensway and Highway 401, Mississauga and the Humber region.

3828 Bloor St. W., Islington (236-1886)

Rexdale Community Information Directory
Information is available on legal aid, credit and debt counselling, counselling for East Indian immigrants, an Italian and Slavic language Outreach and Canada Pension counselling. They serve the area north of Highway 401.

1530 Albion Rd. (Albion Shoppers World), Rexdale (741-1553)

Community Information — Fairview
Legal aid is available Wednesday and Thursday evenings.

Box 2273, 1800 Sheppard Ave. E., Willowdale (493-0752)

Downsview West Information Post
They offer general information services and referrals for the Dufferin-west area at the boundary of North York from Hwy. 401 to Steeles.

20 Yorkwoods Gate Blvd., Downsview
P.O. Box 2278, Station C, Downsview (635-1827)

Scarborough
Information Scarborough
There's advice on legal aid and a family doctor referral service.

545 Markham Rd., Scarborough (431-2244)

Information Agincourt
2240 Birchmount Rd., Agincourt (293-1818) (293-2427)

Dufferin-Eglinton Information Centre (York)
The emphasis is on helping the Italian and West Indian communities.

636 Glenholme Ave., Toronto (789-4394) (789-4395)

Community Information Centre of Metropolitan Toronto

This Metro-wide information and referral service can't solve your problems for you but they can direct you to someone who can help, possibly through one of the hundreds of free community services and resources in Metro. They provide up-to-date information about all the highly specialized services at your disposal like legal aid, health, recreational and educational facilities and financial counselling and a host of others. So if you need a free

When Things Go Wrong

Even the soundest credit risks can be hit by unforeseen disasters like sickness and unemployment. And if you're ill or jobless for a long time, chances are you won't be able to make your loan payments on time — if at all. The results can be disastrous and more than a little frightening and embarrassing. Before things reach this state, it's best to call and write your creditor(s) and explain what's happened. If your credit record's unblemished (so far) they'll probably be understanding. Some lenders may offer to defer the debt, others will accept reduced interim payments. But some will demand the full amount and turn your account over to a collection agency. (Unfortunately public utilities are included in this group except they don't use collection agencies — they just cut off your service.) If you can't come to equitable terms with your creditors and you're burdened with excessive debts, take heart. There are people and agencies who can help. Here's a list:

Federal Trustee, Bankruptcy Branch, Canada Department of Consumer and Corporate Affairs
If the trustee agrees that bankruptcy is the best solution to your problems and you have little or no income, he'll provide a bankruptcy service for a nominal fee. You're assessed on a personal basis and not everyone qualifies for bankruptcy. Incidentally, you can keep anything that can't be deemed an asset: household furnishings valued at under $2000, your clothes (excepting your mink coat and other luxuries) and a few tools of your trade. The only debts that are not dischargeable are alimony and child support and any fines levied by the courts such as parking fines et al.
Monday to Friday 8:15 a.m. to 5 p.m.
241 Jarvis St. (369-2341)

Credit Counselling Service of Metropolitan Toronto
This agency will help you solve your debt problems and prevent future ones. They'll act as a mediator between you and your creditors, and pro-rate debts. Serves the Judicial District of York.
Monday to Friday 8:30 a.m. to 4:30 p.m.
74 Victoria St., Ste. 618 (366-5251)

Referee, Small Claims Court, Ontario Ministry of the Attorney-General
If you've inadvertently signed a loan contract containing a wage assignment clause, the court referee's the man to see. You need an appointment and be sure to take all documents relevant to your income, expenses, debts and creditors with you.
Monday to Friday 8:30 a.m. to 4:30 p.m.
425 University Ave., Rm. 201 (965-5591)

day camp or subsidized day nursery for your child, legal assistance, financial advice or a cheap place to live, drop in or give them a call. Service is available in 12 languages and there's a 24-hour service for emergency calls. Their Directory of Community Services, a complete compendium with hundreds of problem-solving agencies costs $4.

Monday to Friday, 8:30 a.m. to 8 p.m. Metro branch, 110 Adelaide St. E. (863-0505)
They provide immediate call-back answering service, so that service is provided 24 hours a day, seven days a week.

Community Information Directory
Monday to Friday 9 a.m. to 5 p.m.
1530 Albion Rd. (Shopper's World Plaza) Rexdale (741-1553)

Action Service Contact Centre
185-5th St., South, Etobicoke (Lakeshore area) (252-6471)

Etobicoke Central Information and Referral
3828 Bloor St. W., Etobicoke (236-1886)

Volunteer Service Centres

Volunteer Service Centres, like CARE-RING groups provide services including a drive to your doctor or dentist appointment, emergency baby sitting, friendly visiting, shopping and tutoring. Here's a list which also describes the areas of the city they serve.

Care-Ring Armour
Area: Yonge St. to Spadina Expressway; Lawrence to Sheppard Ave.
Monday to Friday 9 a.m. to 4:30 p.m.
63 Dunblaine Ave., Toronto (486-8558)

Care-Ring Bayview
Area: Leslie to Yonge; Lawrence Ave. to Finch Ave.
Monday to Friday 9 a.m. to 5 p.m.
Trinity Presbyterian Church (489-4494)

Care-Ring Don Mills
Area: Victoria Park to Leslie St.; Eglinton Ave. to Hwy. 401
Monday to Friday 9 a.m. to noon; 1 p.m. to 4 p.m.
33 Overland Dr., Don Mills (441-1077)

Care-Ring Downtown
Area: Downtown
Monday to Friday 9 a.m. to 5 p.m.
Trinity Square, Toronto (598-4521)

Care-Ring East Scarborough
Area: Scarborough south of Hwy. 401, Midland Ave. to Port Union
Monday to Friday 9 a.m. to noon
Knob Hill United Church, 23 Gage Ave., Scarborough (431-5072)

Care-Ring Flemingdon
Area: Flemingdon
Monday to Friday 9 a.m. to noon, 1 p.m. to 4 p.m.
150 Grenoble Dr., Don Mills (429-1016)

Care-Ring Lakeshore
Area: South of the Queensway between Etobicoke and the Humber River
Monday to Friday 9:30 a.m. to 4 p.m.
185 5th St., Toronto (255-3335)

Care-Ring North Toronto
Area: Bayview Ave. to Bathurst St.; CPR tracks south of St. Clair Ave. to Lawrence Avenue.
Daily, 24 hours
1066 Avenue Road, Toronto (486-0620)

Care-Ring Northwest
Area: Yonge St. to Dufferin St.; Sheppard Ave. to Steeles Ave.; also Yonge to Bathurst; Hwy. 401 to

Credit

- Comparison shop for the lowest interest rates. By law, banks, trust companies and other money-lending institutions are required to tell you their standard annual percentage rates (APR). There's no minimum but they range from the legal maximum of 24% per annum charged by finance companies to standard 13½% bank rates. Credit unions and trust companies are often lower.

- Be sure to ask for preferred rates — they can be as low as 10½% on a collateral bank loan — "if the bank's fully protected" with adequate collateral.

- Read your loan contract carefully. Check for wage assignment and right of offset clauses that give the lender the right to have money deducted from your wages or from other bank accounts.

- If you're a first-time borrower, don't take the fastest, easiest route to your nearest finance company. Granted, you'll probably get your loan but it's an expensive proposition at 24% a year. Start with the cheapest lender and work your way up: Some bank or trust company may consider you a good money-manager and a good risk because you've never borrowed before. And if one bank or trust company turns you down, try another.

- Keep your credit period as short as you can realistically afford. The longer your term, the more it will cost you.

- Always put down the largest downpayment you can manage: the more you can apply, the smaller your credit charges and the sooner you'll be out of debt.

- Never sign a blank contract. And always get a copy of verbal agreements in writing before accepting money (or merchandise). The agreement should be complete in every detail including principal amount of loan, finance charges and other add-ons, total amount of debt, the amount, due dates and frequency of installment payments, plus penalties if you default on payments.

Interest-free Loans

The Toronto Hebrew Re-Establishment Services grants interest-free loans as it sees fit, to "temporarily needy" Ontario residents over 21, irrespective of race, color or creed. You need two acceptable guarantors and you'll be interviewed by a Board member. If you're accepted, you get an interest-free loan of $1,000. (They'll sometimes lend you $2,000 for business purposes only).

Monday to Thursday 9 a.m. to 5 p.m., Friday 9 a.m. to 4 p.m., 152 Beverley St. (869-3811)

Sheppard Ave.
Monday to Friday 9 a.m. to 5 p.m.
4003 Bayview Ave., Apt. 1008, Willowdale (961-0447)

Care-Ring Rexdale
Area: Rexdale north of Hwy. 401 (Ward 4, Etobicoke)
Monday to Friday 9 a.m. to 5 p.m.
Messages: Monday to Friday noon to 5 p.m., Rexdale C.I.D. (741-1553)
Thistletown United Church, 1030 Albion Rd., Rexdale (745-4472)

Downsview Volunteers
For the elderly in Downsview (Keele St. to Jane St., Hwy 401 to Steeles Ave.) They offer friendly visiting, transportation and have cleaning and agency referral.
Tuesday to Wednesday, Friday 9 a.m. to 2 p.m.
c/o Family Service Association, 1315 Finch Ave. W., Downsview (638-3892)

Parkdale Golden Age Foundation
They'll find someone to do shopping, light cleaning, laundry or provide transportation to the doctor for the elderly in the Bathurst St. to Parkside Dr., Lakeshore-Bloor St. area.
Monday to Friday 9 a.m. to 4 p.m.
100 Close Avenue, Toronto (536-5534)

Share
Share serves senior citizens in Ward 4 (Bathurst St. to Dufferin St.; Lakeshore to Bloor St.) They offer home services, friendly visits, shopping, transportation to medical appointments.
Monday to Friday 9:30 a.m. to 4:30 p.m.; 24 hour answering service
40 Westmoreland Ave., Toronto (535-7232)

Ward Nine Senior Link
This is a service for the elderly in Ward 9 (Victoria Park to Coxwell Ave.; Lakefront to Danforth Ave.) They will find transportation to the doctor, for social activities, and emergencies, or shopping; and will locate people to do light housekeeping and odd jobs.
Monday to Friday 9 a.m. to 5 p.m.
907 Kingston Rd., Toronto (691-7407)

West Metro Senior Citizens' Services Inc.
The elderly in Ward 3 (Ossington Ave. to Old Weston Rd., Bloor St. to Rogers Rd.) can find transportation to medical appointments, receive friendly visiting and get help with shopping and banking errands, odd jobs, and general cleaning.
Monday to Friday 9 a.m. to 5 p.m.; 24 hour telephone service.
21 Blackthorn Ave., Toronto (656-3101)

York Services to Seniors
Home services for the elderly in York borough are offered, including housework, odd jobs, visiting, shopping and a telephone check.
Monday to Friday 9 a.m. to 4:30 p.m.
1695 Keele St., Toronto (651-7833)

Multi-Service Centres

They're centres where you'll find government agencies and several organizations and church groups working together to provide a complete range of social services, almost always free.

Agincourt Community Services Association
Counselling, legal advice, volunteer services (emergency driving, homemakers, visiting and shopping) are all available here.

Monday to Friday 9 a.m. to 4:30 p.m.

2240 Birchmount Rd., Agincourt (293-1818) (293-4084)
Area: Hwy. 401 to Steeles, Victoria Park to Markham Rd.

Lakeshore Area Multi-Services Project (L.A.M.P.)
Services to Lakeshore residents are co-ordinated here, including a community health centre, day care centre, seniors' lounge and seniors' foot care clinic, information and referral and borough dental service.
Monday to Thursday 8:30 a.m. to 8:30 p.m., Friday to 5 p.m.
185 5th St., Toronto (252-6471)

Regent Park Community Services Unit
This multi-service, self-help unit was set up and directed by the tenants of Regent Park. There's a variety of social services including counselling, referral and resource information, material aid, a drop-in centre and legal assistance.
Monday to Friday 9 a.m. to 5 p.m. Evenings by appointment.
63 Belshaw Pl., Apt. 101, Toronto (863-1768)

Thistletown Community Services Unit
Serves northern Rexdale.
Monday to Friday 9 a.m. to 5 p.m.
Unit 1: 244 Jamestown Cres., Rexdale (745-2822)
Monday to Friday 9 a.m. to 5 p.m.
Unit 2: 1621 Albion Rd., Rexdale (743-4869)

Warden Woods Community Services
This social service centre features children's aid, public health, legal aid, and activities for all ages.
Monday to Friday 9 a.m. to 5 p.m.
74 Firvalley Court, Scarborough (694-1138)

West Hill Community Services
Available are counselling, legal advice, health information, mothercraft and discussion groups. A year-round playschool for pre-schoolers is open as well as a meals-on-wheels service by referral from doctor or public health nurse.
Monday to Friday 9 a.m. to 5 p.m., Wednesday 6 p.m. to 8 p.m.
4301 Kingston Rd., Scarborough (284-5931)

York Community Services
Available are counselling to Borough of York residents for social problems, legal aid, a medical clinic and information services. Italian is spoken.
Monday to Friday 9 a.m. to 5 p.m., Monday to Wednesday to 9 p.m.
1651 Keele St., Toronto (653-5400)

Children's Storefront

There's great coffee, a clothing exchange, toys to borrow and people to talk to at this bright, friendly drop-in centre. It's for parents and kids under six, and almost everything from the toy library to the paints and games they supply is *free*. The only charges are $3 for a yearly membership, and a fee for limited day-care. (They'll baby-sit members' kids, but it's by appointment only and the fee's on a sliding scale to suit your budget.) The centre is staffed by people trained in child development but it's not strictly for kids — separated dads are encouraged to visit with their kids there on week-ends, and you can drop in for coffee anytime.

Monday to Thursday 10 a.m. to 4 p.m., Friday 10 a.m. to 1 p.m.,
994 Bathurst St. (531-8151)

Tips for Borrowers

Canadians are big spenders and big borrowers. Believe it or not, statistics show that we owe about $28 billion in consumer credit. About $9 billion of this amount is to banks in the form of personal or consumer loans at 13.5%. The bank's prime lending rate is 8.25% — a rate reserved for a few select low-risk "blue chip" borrowers. And it's generally true interest rates reflect the risk involved: high risk means high interest; low risk, low interest.

- It's easy to get a loan if you're an established professional man with a secure position and an excellent credit rating. Lenders don't like to take chances. They prefer people who don't move around a lot — it's a sign of stability — with a regular, preferably high income and collateral like stocks, bonds and savings. However, women (established or otherwise) and people without a credit rating or an "acceptable" occupation, especially those who move around a lot may find it hard to get a loan. Like them, you may be turned down for reasons you don't understand. Perhaps you're a bartender (an "unacceptable" occupation in most cases) or a freelance writer or artist with no regular income. Or perhaps you're new on the job or new in town. (You could be unstable). Or you've never borrowed money or used credit cards before. (How do they know you'll pay them back?) And last but not least, you're a woman. It's difficult for a married woman to maintain an independent credit history, the reason why a close friend of mine in a high-paying professional position was refused a loan without her husband's signature. And single women are generally considered poor risks because of limited earning power and a tendency to move around and quit to get married and have children.
- The fastest way to establish a credit rating is with credit cards and regular deposits in your savings account. Your savings can be used as collateral for a loan and if you use — not abuse — your credit cards, you should be home free. Married women should maintain their own personal chequing and savings accounts and assume responsibility for credit cards. Apply for the card in *your* name — without your husband's signature — and make sure your name is on the card. And once you've established a sound credit rating, your husband's signature should not be required on a loan.
- And if you're refused a loan? Ask why. Under the terms of the Credit Reporting Act you're entitled to know the reasons, provided you ask within two months of the date of your loan application. And if you suspect your credit history may be inaccurate, ask for the name of the credit reporting agency they used — you're entitled to know this too, thanks to the same Act.

Cheap Credit:
The Subtle Art of Chargemanship

Credit cards are convenient, but they tend to be pernicious. They make it too easy to buy things you don't really need, and they charge interest rates that are higher than — in many cases — you really need to pay. Chargex, for instance, charges 18% per annum (1½% per month) on the unpaid balance. But most banks charge around 13½% per annum for consumer loans. The moral: with credit, as with anything else, it pays to shop around.

- To demonstrate this proposition, we shopped around for a $300 loan to buy a home freezer. We found that some banks discourage small personal loans for amounts under $500. Instead, they encourage you — even pressure you — to use your Chargex card. They tell you it's faster and more convenient. It also happens to be much more profitable for them. In some cases, it's cheaper to use Chargex, but only on small, short-term loans of about $100 for one month. With Chargex, this would only cost you $1.50; with a personal loan, there's a $5 handling charge at most banks.
- But remember: there is *no* minimum for a personal loan. Any bank can and will process one. And regardless of what they tell you, you're better off to borrow $300 at 13½% with a personal loan — even if it takes longer to get — than to borrow at 18% with your convenient Chargex card.
- Be sure to check with your bank for preferred rates. When we inquired at the Commerce, interest rates and terms were spelled out in a straightforward manner. And nobody suggested Chargex as an alternative. Also, Commerce has a preferred rate of 12% for its Key Account holders. (Key accounts cost $2.50 per month and offer many other services, such as a reduction on the first year's charge on safe deposit boxes.)
- The Bank of Montreal's attitude towards loans is spelled out in its slogan: "Let's Sit Down and Talk About It." That's precisely what you do, and you're assessed on a personal basis. The Bank of Montreal offers "Full Service Package" accounts (similar to Key Accounts at the Commerce) with a preferred 13% interest rate on consumer loans. Again, nobody suggested that there's a minimum for personal loans, or that we use Chargex.
- The Royal admitted that there's no minimum on personal loans, but strongly urged the use of Chargex for all the usual reasons. Among the services Royal provides (for a monthly $2.50 fee) is "Royal Certified Services," a plan which, among other things, provides a $300 overdraft protection. In other words, if you don't have sufficient funds in your account, the bank will make good for amounts up to $300. All Royal Certified Services card holders are entitled to a

preferred rate of 13% on consumer loans.
• Toronto-Dominion prefers you to use Chargex because it's simply not worth their while to process and handle a $300 personal loan at 13½%, they say.
• The Bank of Nova Scotia also suggested Chargex.
• To borrow $300 for one year from the banks costs about $23. Monthly payments: $27 per month. Interest: 13½% on the unpaid balance (less at some banks, more at others). Compared to finance companies, it's still a bargain. Household Finance charges $42.57 to borrow the same amount for the same period of time. Monthly payments: $30. Effective interest rate: 23.92%, almost 2% per month.
• Eaton's and Simpsons aren't far behind. Their interest rate: 1.75% per month, or 21% a year.
• At Canadian Tire, you lose your Canadian Tire discount coupons if you charge, and you pay 24% in interest per year. There's no interest charged for 25 days — but you still lose your coupons.

• **Better pay cash or get a bank loan.**

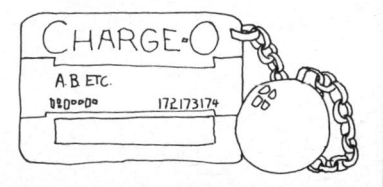

Legal & Bankruptcy Counselling

York Judicial District
Credit Counselling Service of Metropolitan Toronto
They help prevent and (if it's not too late) resolve financial problems with creditors. They pro-rate debts, act as intermediary between debtors and creditors, and teach you all about credit.

Monday to Friday 8:30 a.m. to 4:30 p.m.
74 Victoria St., Toronto (366-5251)

Referee, Small Claims Court, Ontario Ministry of the Attorney General
He assists people with debt problems, particularly with summonses and garnishees (before and after judgments). You need all information relating to income, expenses, debts and creditors.

Call for appointment.
425 University Ave., Rm. 201, Toronto (965-5591)

Federal Trustee, Bankruptcy Branch, Canada Department of Consumer and Corporate Affairs

Monday to Friday 8:30 a.m. to 4:30 p.m.
241 Jarvis St., 4th Fl., Toronto (369-2341)

Toronto Hebrew Re-Establishment Services
They grant interest-free loans up to $1,000 to Ontario residents over the age of 21, irrespective of race, color or creed. Your reasons for borrowing must be acceptable and $1,000 is tops. (In special cases it *may* be increased to $2,000 for business purposes.) You need two acceptable guarantors and you'll be interviewed

Where the Cheapest Loans Are

- Borrowing directly from an insurance company against the cash surrender value of your policy is by far the cheapest loan you can get. The amount of your insurance is lowered until your loan is paid, but terms are extremely flexible and the interest can be as low as 6% a year.

- A collateral loan with your stocks, bonds, term deposit(s) or savings as security is the cheapest bank loan you can get. The interest rate's low — usually 10% to 13% a year — and your savings or term deposit continue to accumulate interest.

- Low-interest Home Improvement Loans through Canada Mortgage and Housing Corporation at 11.63% per annum are available through any chartered bank for home improvements. And financing over a 10-year period means small monthly payments.

- Provided you're a member, credit unions are an excellent source of low-interest loans with flexible terms. Each branch has its own interest rates but they're generally less than bank rates (usually 1% per month or 12% per year on the unpaid balance) and members can borrow a fixed amount according to the amount of money invested. (Sometimes there's a set maximum amount regardless of your investment and ability to pay.)

This chart shows rates and charges based on a $3,000 loan for 36 months.

Type	Annual Percentage Rate	Monthly Payments	Total Charges
Demand Collateral Bank Loan	10.5	$97.51	$510.36
Credit Union**	12	99.65	587.40
Bank Loan (Preferred Rate)	13	101.09	639.24
Personal or Consumer Loan	13.5	101.80	664.80
Auto Dealer	16.8	— —	730.00
Finance Company	24	115.96	1174.20

- Borrowing against the cash surrender value of your insurance policy is the cheapest, sometimes as low as 6%.
- The maximum in some cases is 27 months. Total charges over 27 months: $438.00. Payments: $30 per *week*.

by board members. And you must be employed.

Monday to Thursday 9 a.m. to 5 p.m., Friday 9 a.m. to 4 p.m.
152 Beverley St., Toronto (869-3811, Ext. 278)

Legal, Consumer & Human Rights Services

Legal Services
Ontario Legal Aid Plan
York County Area Office
Monday to Friday 9 a.m. to 3:30 p.m.
204A Richmond St. W., Toronto (Civil Matters) (598-0200)

Old City Hall
Monday to Friday 8:30 a.m. to 3 p.m.
*Tuesday and Thursday evening by appointment.
Rm. 303, 60 Queen St. W., Toronto (Criminal Matters)

Legal services are provided with fees on a sliding scale in all Provincial courts, including Criminal and Family divisions, County, Supreme and Appeal courts. Apply direct to Legal Aid office. Eligibility for full or partial assistance is determined by the Ontario Ministry of Community and Social Services. Minor cases may be referred to law students.

You can obtain advice or file an application at the following locations:

Toronto
Dixon Hall Neighbourhood Social and Family Service Centre, 58 Sumach St., Toronto (863-0498)

Problem Central, 151 Rosemount Ave., Toronto (656-1252)

Italian Immigrant Aid Society, 1215 St. Clair Avenue W., Toronto (652-1033)

East York
Neighbourhood Information Centre, 81 Barrington Ave., Toronto (698-1626)

Etobicoke

Bloordale Community School, 10 Toledo Rd., Etobicoke (626-4229)

Humber College Rexdale, 205 Humber College Blvd., Rexdale (675-6251)

Rexdale Community Information Directory, 1530 Albion Rd., Rexdale (741-1553)

North York
Community Information-Fairview, Fairview Mall, 1800 Sheppard Ave. E., Willowdale (493-0752)

Downsview Legal Aid, Downsview Public Library, 2793 Keele St., Downsview (630-3419)

Link Information and Referral, 5126 Yonge Street, Willowdale (223-9727)

York Finch General Hospital, 2111 Finch Ave. W., Downsview (744-2538)

Scarborough
Information Scarborough, Cedarbrae District Library, 545 Markham Rd., Scarborough (431-2244)

Provincial Court Office, 2222 Eglinton Ave. E., Scarborough (757-8421)

Warden Woods Church and Community Centre, 74 Firvalley Ct., Scarborough (694-1138)

York
York Community Services, 1651 Keele St., Toronto (653-5400)

Lawyer Referral Service
Sponsored by the Law Society of Upper Canada, they'll help you find

a lawyer. Referrals will provide a half-hour interview with a lawyer at a cost of $10 for legal advice or direction. If you exceed the allotted half-hour interview you pay whatever you and the lawyer agree on. Available to anyone on legal aid. There are also referrals to lawyers who speak other languages than English.

Monday to Friday 10 a.m. to 5 p.m.
Osgoode Hall, 120 Queen St. W., Toronto (362-4741)

Neighbourhood Legal Services
Here's free legal advice and help with problems concerning welfare, tenants' rights and unemployment insurance. Serves the Don district.

Monday to Friday 10 a.m. to 5 p.m.
316 Ontario St., Toronto (928-0110)

Parkdale Community Legal Services
Free legal assistance is available to individuals and groups in Parkdale who can't afford legal costs or obtain legal aid. There's referral to other community services as needed. The staff includes lawyers, law students and a director.

Monday to Friday (except Thursday) 9 a.m. to 7:30 p.m., Saturday 10 a.m. to 2 p.m.
1267 Queen St. W., Toronto (531-2411)

Woodgreen Community Centre
Legal clinic Monday and Wednesday after 5 p.m.

835 Queen St. E. (461-1168)

Church Street Community Centre
Legal clinic Wednesdays 6:30 p.m. to 9 p.m. on a first-come, first service basis.

519 Church St. (923-2778)

Student Legal Services
Law students, supervised by lawyers, provide legal service and advice (within prescribed limits) to anyone who can't afford a lawyer and is not eligible for Ontario Legal Aid. Service includes Small Claims Court, Summary Convictions, Highway Traffic Act, Workmen's Compensation, immigration matters, landlord-tenant disputes, advice on divorce procedures and drafting certain documents. Located in neighborhood centres throughout Metro Toronto. Contact:

Community Legal Aid Service Program (C.L.A.S.P.)
Monday to Friday 9 a.m. to 5 p.m.
Osgoode Hall Law School, 4700 Keele St., Rm. 123, Downsview (667-3143)

Campus Legal Assistance Centre (C.L.A.C.)
Monday to Thursday 10 a.m. to 6 p.m., Friday 10 a.m. to 4 p.m.
University of Toronto Law School, 44 St. George St., 2nd Floor, Toronto (978-6447)

Lawline
Monday to Friday 10 a.m. to 6 p.m.
Telephone information and referral (978-7293)

Medical & Dental

This section's for families who need dental and medical assistance, from how to locate a doctor or dentist in Toronto to a list of various medical clinics and low-cost dental services. Some clinics are geared to meet the needs of a specific area but almost all of them will treat non-residents in emergencies or if you're prepared to wait for an appointment.

Academy of Dentistry
If you can't find a regular dentist or if you have a toothache, the Academy of Dentistry will help you find one and will direct you to a dentist who's on call for after-hour emergencies.

Monday to Friday 8:30 a.m. to 5 p.m.
234 St. George St. (967-5649). Emergency Service, after hours and weekends: 924-8041

Alexandra Park Community Health Centre
Dental appointments are only $8 each and there's a complete range of services. But there's also a formidable waiting list and priority is given to residents of the Spadina, Bathurst, Queen and Dundas area. Book well in advance.
Monday to Friday 9 a.m. to 5 p.m.
62-64 Augusta Ave. (364-2998)

Etobicoke Community Health Department
They offer free basic dental care to marginal income families in Etobicoke. Call for times and locations.
Civic Centre (626-4136)
Monday to Friday 8:30 a.m. to 4:30 p.m.

Dixon Hall Neighbourhood Social and Family Service Centre
Their low-cost dental programs for people on low and moderate incomes in the Shuter-Lakefront, River-Sherbourne area, excluding Moss Park. Call for information.
Monday to Friday 8:30 a.m. to 9 p.m.
58 Sumach St. (863-0498)

Springhurst Community Health Centre
It's a Parkdale clinic but they'll accept patients from other areas. Their rates are 100% of the O.D.A. schedule but that's less than many

Make Your Own Toothpaste

Colgate-Palmolive and Proctor & Gamble would have us believe that tooth care depends on expensive commercial toothpastes that come in non-biodegradable, throwaway tubes. But there's an alternative. With a few simple ingredients and a little know-how, you can make your own cheap, original concoction.
- You begin by making tooth powder. Mix 3 tbsp. of baking soda (to clean and sweeten your mouth) with 1 tbsp. salt (to clean your teeth and stimulate your gums). Next, add 4 to 5 tsp. of glycerine (you can add more or less, depending on the consistency you like) and 25 to 30 drops of flavoring (anise, fennell, peppermint and wintergreen are great). You might want to brighten it up with a few drops of food coloring. Mix thoroughly and add just enough water to make a paste. Store your toothpaste in any plastic squeeze bottle dispenser (mustard or ketchup types are fine). Your homemade original will not be as slick and smooth as commercial toothpaste. But there is one consolation: You can make up to a year's supply for a family of four for less than $2.

dentists charge. There's a one to two week waiting list.
160 Springhurst Ave. (531-5712)

Hospital Dentistry

The following hospitals offer a complete range of dental services at reasonable rates. Call for information.

Etobicoke General Hospital
101 Humber College Blvd., Rexdale (744-3400)

Mount Sinai Hospital
600 University Ave. (596-4200)

St. Michael's Hospital
30 Bond St. (360-4000)

Sunnybrook Medical Centre
2075 Bayview Ave. (486-3000)

Toronto East General Hospital
825 Coxwell Ave. (461-8272)

Toronto General Hospital
101 College St. (595-3111)

Toronto Western Hospital
399 Bathurst St. (368-2581)

The Academy of Medicine
There's a 24-hour telephone service to help you find a doctor any hour of the day or night and they'll give you information about any medical service in Metro Toronto.
288 Bloor St. W. (922-1134)

Family Practice Units

One way to solve your family's medical problems is to register at a Family Practice Unit at one of the following hospitals. You need an appointment and you must have OHIP or interim insurance. Here's a list:

Mount Sinai Hospital
600 University Ave. (596-4331). Baycrest Division at 30 Baycrest Ave. (789-2911)

St. Joseph's Hospital
30 The Queensway (534-4251)

St. Michael's Hospital
30 Bond St. (360-4136)

Sunnybrook Medical Centre
2075 Bayview Ave. (483-4470)

Toronto General Hospital
657 University Ave. (595-3600, ext. 9) (for appointments)

Toronto Western Hospital
751 Dundas St. W. (369-5644)

Wellesley Hospital
146 Wellesley St. E. (966-5740)

Women's College Hospital
76 Grenville St. (966-7070)

Community Health Centres and Clinics
The following hospitals operate community health centres and clinics that offer a complete range of medical services for you and your family. For information contact:

St. Michael's Hospital
Broadview Clinic, 791 Queen St. E. (360-6590)

Toronto General Hospital
St. George Health Centre, 174 St. George St. (962-1270)

Wellesley Hospital
St. James Town Health Centre, 200 Wellesley St. E., Ste. 104 (966-5749)

Community Health Centres
These centres are staffed by family physicians and often include public health nurses and social workers as well as dentists. You need OHIP and, unless it's an emergency, an appointment. There's a doctor on call 24 hours a day in case of emergency. Although they're there to help

people in the areas specified, they often take residents from other areas.

Boyden Memorial Health Centre
Medical service.
562 Eglinton Ave. E. (482-9841)

Don District Community Health Centre
Medical and dental care. Serves area south of Carlton, Jarvis and Don River.
295 Shuter St., Ste. 102 (364-1361)

Flemingdon Health Centre
The centre serves both Flemingdon and Thorncliffe Park areas.
10 Gateway Blvd., Lower Level, Don Mills (429-4991)

Hassle Free Clinic
Its services are free and it offers general medical care, counselling and various outreach programs. Specializing in pregnancy, VD and abortion counselling.
60-62 Gerrard St. E. (363-6103)

L.A.M.P. Community Health Centre
Serves residents of the Lakeshore area.
185 Fifth St. (252-6475)

Lawrence Heights Medical Centre
3 Replin Rd., (787-1661)

Niagara Neighborhood Health Centre
The centre offers medical care to residents of the Bathurst-Shaw and Front-Queen areas.
289 Niagara St. (363-2021)

Regent Park Community Health Centre
The centre offers a complete range of medical services plus low-cost dental care to residents of Parliament-Don River and Gerrard-Shuter areas.
19 Belshaw Pl. (364-2261)

South Riverdale Community Health Centre
126 Pape Ave. (461-2494)

Springhurst Community Health Centre
Medical and dental services are available.
160 Springhurst Ave., Ste. 203 (531-5711)

Village Health Centre
108 Scollard St. (925-3843)

York Community Services
The centre serves residents of the borough of York (within a 5 mile radius).
1651 Keele St. (653-5400)

Alexandra Park Community Health Services
Medical and low-cost dental services are available. Priority is given to people in the area bounded by Spadina, Bathurst, Queen and Dundas Streets but they'll treat others.
62-64 Augusta Ave. (364-4107)

Hospital for Sick Children Medical Clinic
Part of this excellent medical clinic's a Walk-in clinic — you don't need an appointment and your child will be seen.
Daily 9 a.m. to 11 p.m.
555 University Ave. (597-1500)

University Settlement Community Health Centre
23 Grange Rd. (598-3444)

University of Toronto Dental Clinic

You don't get speedy service at the U of T Dental Clinic, but you *do* get smaller dental bills. Of course, there's a catch: you'll be put in the unskilled hands of an aspiring dentist. I know what you're thinking, but it's not all that bad. They've tested their skills on many a store dummy — which can't complain — before they touch you. And a testimony to their expertise is a long waiting list — they're booked months ahead. There's a full range of dental services. Students deftly clean, drill and fill your teeth, extract them at $3 or $4 a piece, and supply you with dentures for $150. At the orthodontics clinic the initial consultation is free. There is a fee of $20 (to cover the molds and X-ray.) For the fitting of braces — if they're suitable — the fee is $90 for the first year, $50 for the next, and $50 after that.

Apart from the incredibly low fee structure, the clinic has its advantages — it's bright, large, scrupulously clean, and features the very latest in dental techniques. And in case of emergency (a toothache), they'll take you at 9:30 a.m. or 1:30 p.m. The fee is $5. All work is carefully supervised and checked and that takes time, so plan to spend half a day — perhaps more — at the clinic. Registration fee is $10 and there's a long waiting list.

No new patients in July and August; closed at Christmas.

Monday to Friday, 10 a.m. to 2 p.m.
Dental clinic, 100 Elm St. (978-2784)
Monday to Friday, 10 a.m. to noon, 2 p.m. to 5 p.m.
Orthodontic Clinic (same address) (978-2792)

Pets

Ontario Humane Society
Because it can't advertise, most people aren't aware that the Ontario Humane Society operates two thriving and well-equipped veterinary hospitals one in Scarborough and one in Mississauga. They offer regular health checks, treatment, vaccination, surgery and sterilization for your pet at prices you can afford — as little as $25 for spaying a dog or cat and $18 for neutering a cat, $25 for dogs, including an overnight stay at the hospital. The services are not only for low-income groups or people from the immediate area.

Pets must be examined before sterilization and need vaccinations or a certificate to prove their shots are up to date.

OHS's main concern is animal welfare and you'll find the staff understanding and helpful. Consultation by appointment only.

Monday, Thursday and Friday 2 p.m. to 4 p.m., Tuesday and Wednesday 2 p.m. to 4 p.m. and 6 p.m. to 8 p.m., Saturday 10 a.m. to noon.
Scarborough clinic, 751 Kennedy Rd. at Eglinton (757-3606)
Monday 2 p.m. to 4 p.m., Tuesday and Thursday 2 p.m. to 4 p.m. and 6 p.m. to 8 p.m., Friday 10 a.m. to noon and 2 p.m. to 4 p.m.
Mississauga clinic, 3490 Mairs Rd. (279-5960)

Toronto Humane Society
T.H.S. brand new sterilization program is directed at cutting down on the growing number of unwanted kittens and puppies they're forced to take. And at their prices you can't afford *not* to have your pet altered. Spaying costs vary according to the age and size of the dog. They're busy but there are two vets to do the job. Your pet must be examined, and needs vaccinations at least three weeks before surgery, or a certificate to prove that shots are up to date. All sterilizations are by appointment, and to get one you must fill out an application. (It can be picked up at TSH.) And incidentally, all dogs must be licensed. Open seven days a week, 24 hours a day. At 11 Wellesley St. W. (922-1191).

Cars: Some Facts to Know

Paying the Right Price: Haggling

It's well worth it to wheel and deal and drive a harder bargain for a new car. Roughly, here's how it works: Take 20% to 25% off the sticker price of a standard domestic car, up to 21% off a compact (intermediate), and 10% to 15% off a small sub-compact. New car prices are lowest during the coldest winter months. The best time of day? Late at night when everyone's tired and wants to go home.

Saving Gas and Money

The easiest way to cut down on gas and expenses is to buy a light-weight, frill-free, gas-stingy car. Weight is the single most important factor in fuel economy. Big, powerful engines are gas-guzzlers and you can save a lot by buying a car with a smaller engine.

Cars: New vs. Used

You can save as much as 50% by passing up a new car and opting for a good, two-to-four-year-old used car. There's no doubt about it, used is better, price-wise, depreciation-wise and almost everyway-wise *IF* you get a good one.

The *Toronto Star's* Star Probe gets more complaints about new cars vs used ones. Most are warranty complaints. The Consumer Protection Bureau's files are filled with similar new-car warranty problems. If you really want to find out the full extent of the problem, buy a copy of Phil Edmonston's *Lemon-Aid* a book everyone should read before buying any kind of car, can or truck, new or used.

Of consuming interest:

- Air conditioning reduces your gas mileage by as much as 10%; power steering by 1% to 3%.
- Driving at 55 m.p.h. instead of 70 m.p.h. will save you 20% in fuel.
- Your mileage improves from 1% to 3% with radial tires — they stay cooler and "squirm" less. And remember air is free: Keep your tires inflated. Under-inflated tires wear faster and waste up to 10% in fuel.
- The more octane a gas contains, the more expensive it is. Tests show the performances are about the same. Save by buying the cheapest regular gas available.
- You'll save by changing your oil and filter every 1,000 miles.
- If you're willing to swear that you're a nondrinking driver, The Abstainers' Insurance Company can knock up to 20% off your standard rates.
- Traffic surveys show that many car outings are three miles and less. Try riding a bike or walking. Consider carpools and public transit.

Where to get things fixed

by
Patrick Conlon

Introduction

There are three things you should know about this directory of fixers before you consult it.

First, you'll probably be tempted to measure it more by what it lacks than by what it contains. No doubt you'll think of products we didn't include, but that's what second, expanded editions of books like this are for. What's more, we hope you'll judge this for exactly what it is: a good start at accommodating the current trend away from easy disposal and toward preservation. We hope this directory will lighten Toronto's trash bins.

Second, the cost of some repairs (even though they're averages) may seem a bit high. That's natural but we suppose you'll want to measure the cost of repair against replacement. The people we recommend aren't necessarily the cheapest in the city but most of them are considered the best — and, in many cases, the *only* sources for repair in each product category.

Finally, some of the entries may surprise you because they're not Toronto's old faithfuls. Most of them are recommended according to happy personal experience. They have all demonstrated honesty and fairness, both elusive virtues, and they're very good at what they do because they like what they do. Treat them with respect and without pressure — most of them are individualists who know they're in demand and won't sacrifice quality to a timetable. In all cases, they'll tell you immediately whether they can deal with your problem, or cheerfully refer you to someone who can if they can't. If you have a complaint, all of them want you to tell them first (instead of your neighbor) because they prize good will and respect the power of word-of-mouth. Few of them advertise their services. Over the years, they've discovered they don't have to.

Assembling this list has been interesting, challenging, maddening, stimulating, frustrating, wearying but (at last) rewarding. A special nod to co-author Wilma Fraser, and I'd like to thank editor Claire Gerus, whose patience and efficiency are exceeded only by her sense of humor. *Toronto Life's* Sandy Ross, who commissioned the article last year that spawned this project; and Annabel Slaight, who has an unerring instinct for filling the specialized reading needs of this healthy city. Thanks also, to the velvet-voiced Valerie Frith and Bob Martin for turning the chore of checking into an art. In addition, I'm grateful to a large network of unpaid "informers" who generously shared well-guarded names and sources, knowing when they did that they wouldn't be secrets anymore. But, finally, the weight of my gratitude goes to the ladies and gentlemen who agreed to be listed here. Most of them are as busy as they want to be and shy away from publicity. They also recognize that they're needed more than ever and perhaps their agreement to participate is the most commendable service they've provided. It also unites them and they know that a directory like this is the city's first real kick in the pants to planned obsolescence.

Patrick Conlon

A

Acoustic Problems

Fox-Richardson Ltd.
If you've got the standard highrise problem of living with the "boom-boom" of your neighbor's stereo, call Frank Fox. He and his selection of sound-absorbing materials might be able to help. Their standard ceiling tile, "Gold Bond", costs from 23¢ a square foot up; and there are others from $1 a square foot for 1" thick panels, up. If Frank can't solve your acoustical problem, he'll cheerfully refer you to someone who can. Oscar Peterson is one of his customers — Frank provided his recording studio with the correct acoustical personality.

5369 Maingate Dr., Mississauga (624-0776)

Acrylic

Lucidity
Phyllis and Irwin Manov believe that, if it's properly maintained, acrylic will outlast almost any other material. Their first-aid tip for scratches: an application of Brasso, followed by any top quality "Simonizing" wax. They can buff out deeper gouges and also re-bond joints that have given out, using an acrylic resin. A magazine rack that's come apart, for instance, would cost about $5 to fix.

154 Cumberland St. (961-5998)

Adding Machines

Robert Johnston Office Equipment Ltd.
Robert Johnston supervises a staff of six mechanics but has other specialists on call. He charges an average $35 per machine, including minor repairs, thorough cleaning, oiling and adjusting as well as a 90 day guarantee. It adds up to a good deal for customers who prefer old reliable machines to new, untried ones. The staff also repairs all makes and models of typewriters.

273 Queen St. W. (598-2345)

Air Conditioners

Harry Edwards Appliances Ltd.
Air conditioners have a nasty habit of quitting at the peak of a heat wave, but Bob Edwards (son of the founder) can usually fix your unit within a week. There's a $15 charge for pick up and delivery, with a $40 charge for cleaning and service. If more work is needed, they'll call with an estimate before proceeding, and then pay a house call within the warranty period if it fails again. (Warranty: 90 days parts, 30 days labor.) The company has been in business for 40 long, hot summers.

575 Mount Pleasant Rd. (481-3381)

Amusement Machines

Toronto Coin Exchange
If your old pinball machine eats your dime and then sits there in sullen silence, chances are Tony Crowe or

Frank Stegner can revive it for you. Although a complete overhaul could cost $1,100, the problem might only be a coil, relay or contact and for these you'll be charged about $25. They'll even make a house call if you can't dismantle the machine. Mr. Crowe is happy to dispense free telephone advice to frustrated players.

464 Gilbert (789-1806)

Antennas – TV & Radio

Town & Country Television Ltd.
Dave Van Ihinger installed east-end Toronto's first TV antenna on Kingston Road in 1949. Since then he's been regarded as one of the city's top specialists in repairing and designing reception systems. He charges $25 for a repair service call, which usually includes necessary labor but not materials. He also has a complete service shop for TVs.

882 Kingston Rd. (691-2000)

Aquariums

Nature's World
If the glass breaks in a 10-gallon tank Peter Tinnelly will charge you $3.50 to $4 to replace and reseal it. The broken diaphragm on a simple pump can be replaced and installed for $1.98 to $4, depending on the type. Mr. Tinnelly will also test water (salt or fresh) at no charge and offers free care and feeding advice for the tank's inhabitants.

2988 Bloor W. (233-9500)

Nature's World

Archery Equipment

Archery Craft Co. Ltd.
Harry Markham says many old, laminated bows are impossible to repair but, if so, customers will be informed on the spot. Ordinary wood arrows can have their knocks, points and feathers replaced for a fixed price of 15¢ per item. Bows are restrung with guidance from Canada's only major manufacturer of archery equipment.

543 Timothy, Newmarket (881-1414)

Art Objects

Odon Wagner Restorations
Vienna-trained Odon Wagner and his staff of six specialists will repair almost anything of value in china, glass, ivory or jade, as well as paintings. For art restoration, his shop uses a unique lamp which allows microscopic restoration of paintings. Cost depends on the extent of damage, but the basic charge is $15 an hour.

194 Davenport Rd. (962-0438)

Art Restoration

June Bramall
Not for those who just want a quick cleanup, Mrs. Bramall is a Conservator, whose members maintain the high standards of art restoration. Mrs. Bramall can bring almost any

painting into the foreground again, methodically working on tiny portions of the canvas at a time, gently repairing rips and reviving color and texture. Most local museums are clients but she gives every painting, regardless of value, the same care. Unless you have a "hang-the-cost" emotional attachment to the work, ask for a professional appraisal before you invest in Mrs. Bramall's assistance.

205 Trafalgar Rd., Oakville (844-9865)

Audio Equipment

Radio People
Two full-time technicians will restore just about any piece of equipment to full fidelity, at a $16 hourly service charge for receivers. To replace a transistor, rates are $30-$36, including parts. In addition, they have access to a large supply of parts, including some of the older tubes that are now hard to find. Routine repairs will take about a week.

84 Elizabeth St. (366-4572)

Ring Audio
Ring's shop has a reputation for speed and honesty and, what's more they encourage customers not to throw out old equipment before it's had a chance at rescue. If a customer wants to "exchange" an old set for a new one, they'll service the old one before re-selling it. There's a charge of $17 an hour for repairs, which usually take less than an hour. Worth noting: they're currently trying to enlist interest in an Audio Society which would combine lectures and workshops to heighten consumer awareness.

40 Irwin Ave. (967-6500)

Auto Radios

Kromer Radio Ltd.
Many shops charge a flat hourly rate but this one believes that's unfair because AM radios are easier to work on than the more complicated AM/FM stereo types. Service manager Albert Prinz' technicians will diagnose your problem while you wait. You may simply need a new antenna: the locking type is $10.50

and the ordinary, $8.50. Prices include installation. All work is guaranteed for three months. Old car buffs should note that the shop stocks most tubes, in case you want to preserve the radio in your '55 Chevy.

420 Bathurst St. (920-6700)

Automobiles

Ontario Motor League Car Inspection Centre
Regrettably for the exclusive use of OML members only, the service itself is almost an argument for signing up. (There's sometimes a waiting list to join.) For a fee of $30, the Centre checks about 500 different items on your car. The information is then analyzed and you're presented with a written report. Although the Centre doesn't sell parts, make repairs or recommend a garage, you can return with your car within 30 days if work has been done and then have it re-checked for $4. The Club has no vested interest in the treacherous world of repair garages in this city and, thus, you're assured of objectivity.

142 Vanderhoof Ave. (964-3067)

Automobiles – Old

Antique & Classic Automobile Restoration
The oldest car John Bottan has restored is a 1911 Model T but his personal favorites are Duesenbergs and Packards. Although he jobs out complicated upholstery work, his mechanical and body work is considered the best in the city and show judges always praise his painting. There is no average price for his work because so much of it depends on parts availability and just how authentic the restoration has to be.

191 Parliament St. (364-5674)

Awnings

Bartlett's
Although you're advised to remove and deliver your damaged awnings yourself to save money, the company will do it for $8. Bartlett's has specialized since 1888 in such problems as ripped seams and damaged frames. They'll give an on-site estimate first but they won't waterproof because they can't guarantee it'll "take" on old canvas. Minimum charge for repair is $25. Take note: the company provides a free booklet on awning care.

616 St. Clarens Ave. (534-2318)

B

Baby Carriages

Macklem's Baby Carriage Store
The first passenger in a carriage sold by Macklem's is now over 35 years old and likely rearing a new generation of customers. The only store in Toronto to re-cover hoods, they also upholster carriages ($25 up) and strollers ($10 up). Large English prams are a specialty. Macklem's uses strong supportive vinyl rather than thin manufacturers' materials. Tire replacement will cost $2.75 for a

Restored cars

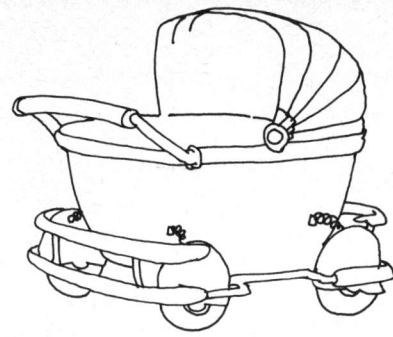

carriage. Customers must deliver and pick up their own carriage. Expect a two-week wait, but it's worth it.

2237 Dundas St. W. (531-7188)

Barometers

W.C. Pocklington
Bill Pocklington is the only known Canadian who can competently repair the old mercury-type barometers. Banjo barometers, for example, cleaned and with a tube replacement can run from $100-$400. Bill blows the glass tubes himself and then loads them with mercury, restoring an instrument that's useful as well as decorative. He can also fix the older aneroid types but he's not inexpensive and customers are advised to contact him before making the trip to Port Carling. Because barometer repairing is his hobby, he can't be pinned down to a time limit on repairs.

P.O. Box 424, Port Carling (705-765-3439)

Bathtubs & Sinks

The Bathtub Doctor
Ron Havimaki specializes in rescuing old cast-iron tubs and sinks, using a process invented in Switzerland 25 years ago. The fixture receives three coats of new enamel that will last for at least 15 years if not abused. The cost for a complete job is $240 for a tub and $65.95 for a sink. Isolated chips can also be repaired: three of them, for example, would cost $45. For more than three chips, the price is negotiable. Most standard colors can be perfectly matched and blended and the company does all its work right in your bathroom.

79 Langstaff Rd., Thornhill (889-1051)

National Glazing
Leonard Sanguine can re-glaze an average white tub for $159, charging $25 extra if it sits on feet, and taking about three hours for the job. One catch: you may be hard to live with because the tub will need five days without use to "cure." Mr. Sanguine can match almost any color and he also repairs chips, which cost $25 for one the size of a dime and $50 if it's as large as a quarter.

East Mall Shopping Plaza (621-1012)

Beds, Brass

The Brass Bed
Joshua Parker can replace missing parts with new brass, mend broken joints and modify old frames to accommodate standard mattress sizes. He charges from $100 to $150 to clean and restore a double or queen size bed, which usually includes any necessary minor repairs. He doesn't recommend a lacquer finish because it tends to chip and, what's more, he believes brass should be allowed to age naturally. Although his specialty is beds, he can fix almost anything in brass, brazing it with silver in a matching color.

12 Cumberland St. (922-5683)

Bicyclesport

Bicycles

Bicyclesport
Owners Mike Barry and Mike Brown, both former bicycle racers in Europe, not only repair bicycles but also build them to your own specifications.

A tune-up (overhauling brakes and gears, checking bearings and generally making your bike roadworthy) takes only one day but you must phone in and reserve a date for the repairs. Cost will run $12 to $15 for a five or ten-speed bike; and $10 for a three or single speed (including parts like bearings, cables, etc.). All work is guaranteed for one month at least, longer if you can demonstrate that your problem is their fault. They can find or make any parts required.

175 King St. E. (363-0525)

The Pedlar Cycle Shop
Taking only two or three days tops, Vance Wagdin will overhaul your brakes and gears and align your wheels and frame as well as checking your bearings. Depending on what the bike needs, a five or ten speed will cost $10 to $20 and a one or three speed will be $5 to $15. The shop claims it can find any part for any bike.

169 Avenue Rd. (921-2715)

Billiard & Pool Tables

Terry's Billiard Tables and Supplies
Fears to the contrary, minor rips or tears in the table-top cloth can be successfully mended, says Terry Haddock. But if damage is irreparable, he'll install a new wool/nylon blend for about $165 for a 4' by 8' table. He can also properly crate a table for moving, level it after installation and repair chips in the slate bed.

7310 Woodbine Ave. (495-0511)

Binoculars

Tieman Optical and Photographic Equipment Ltd.
Although he specializes in Carl Wetzlar binoculars, Mr. Tieman will clean and repair all types in a week to 10 days. He offers a free estimate on work and then guarantees it for six months. His shop is one of the few places that uses a collimator, a precise instrument that adjusts a binocular's line of sight.

1191 Brimley Rd. (438-5657)

Boats

Loftis Marine Services
Since 1938, John Loftis has mended the damage to thousands of hulls and although he's well equipped to repair fibreglass, he's one of the area's few remaining craftsmen who still works on the older wood types. Repairing a serious fracture in a 16-foot fibreglass runabout will usually cost about $250. Mr. Loftis also works with a naval architect to design boats.

17 Ruggles Ave., Thornhill (889-9116)

Loftis Marine Services

Books

Robert Muma
It started as a hobby for Mr. Muma over 25 years ago and now some of the city's most valuable old books are entrusted to him for restoration. But you can also expect the same care for a family literary heirloom. He'll bind it in leather that was tanned in Europe and promise you another 200 years existence as an object of pride. You are advised to keep valued books away from heat and out of damp basements: both conditions are as big a threat to the printed word as television.

118 Hazelton Ave. (921-1003)

BRASS, BRAZING: see
BEDS, BRASS

BRICK AND TILE: see
CEMENT AND CONCRETE

C

Cameras

M. Kominek Camera Repairs
European-trained Michael Kominek has been in the business for 39 years

Books to Learn By

We visited the *Can-Do Bookstore,* on Bloor Street just west of Bay, to find out just how often you'd profit from reaching for a book instead of calling a repairman. According to co-owner Sue Chaiton, "Most basic home repairs can be handled if you've a brain in your head and the right book." The hundreds of books in the store illustrate in how many areas you can be self-sufficient.

- Your best investment is probably the *Reader's Digest Complete Do-It-Yourself-Manual* ($24.95). You begin by learning how to choose tools, and you soon know how to solve power problems safely, fix and renovate plumbing, and do literally everything else needing repair in your home. The illustrations are so good that you feel you've a competent instructor close at hand. *How Things Work in Your Home* ($17.95) is another basic manual, but it's not as highly recommended.

- If you don't intend to become the "compleat home handyperson," but have a specific job in mind, the *Time-Life* series ($8.95 each) will serve you well. The *Paint and Wallpaper* volume tells you everything from mixing and straining to "Unconventional Methods for Unconventional Effects," and how to estimate the time involved in all kinds of jobs. If you get hooked on the feeling of independence and accomplishment, you can always buy the *Readers' Digest Manual* later.

- The Sunset series is excellent and inexpensive ($1.95 to $2.45) but most of their volumes are more concerned with design ideas and remodelling rather than how to fix things yourself. But their *Basic Home Repairs* is so inexpensive and instructive that even people without much patience for tinkering should own one.

- You'll also find specialty books like Stanley Schuler's *Floor and Ceiling Book* ($10.25) which tell you everything about building, repairing, soundproofing and finishing. For women, there's *The "You Don't Need A Man to Fix It" Book* ($9.25) by Jim Webb and Bart Houseman. It's amusing and includes a chapter on problem diagnosis which could be useful to anyone who has never investigated how things work, let alone why they go wrong. The excellent diagrams ensure that you won't be confused between tools which look vaguely alike.

- Experienced do-it-yourselfers will always tell you that the best way to save money is to spot trouble before it gets really serious. Hubbard Cobb's *Preventive Maintenance for Your House or Apartment* ($5.75) is designed to teach you how to diagnose in advance of trouble.

The staff at the Can-Do Bookstore is well-informed and helpful. If you don't see what you need, ask. Sue Chaiton says they could fill three stores with all the good manuals available for do-it-yourselfers, and she's happy to order the right one for you.

and can repair old cameras (including the bellows type) like Thorton-Pickard, Miraflex and Eastman. He'll also service simple Brownies but won't touch Instamatics and can't quote prices without seeing the camera first. His is the only place in Toronto that re-cements lenses and he's also, over the years, cannily stockpiled parts for discontinued camera lines. The *Toronto Star's* photography department is one of his customers.

405A Yonge St. (368-0850)

Caning & Wicker

Canadian National Institute for the Blind, Industrial Art Dept.
Although larger items will cost you more, supervisor Jean Martin says that most chairs can be re-caned for 38¢ a hole. He doesn't recommend patch repair work unless the item is new, because old caning tends to be too brittle. His people can also repair wicker that still has resiliency. Mr. Martin may be able to refer you to someone he's trained in your neighborhood and also give you a rough estimate.

1929 Bayview Ave. (486-2626)

Cane and Rush Seating
Marjorie and Tony Darling won't repair wicker but they charge a flat 45¢ a hole for caning, using techniques they learned from a friendly Ontario farmer. They plead for patience from customers, since this is a part-time activity for them.

18 Boswell Ave. (923-2465)

Carpets & Rugs

Armenian Rug Co.
Call Peter Khandjian and he'll either repair your rug in your home or take it back with him. He's a specialist in making cigarette burns disappear, charging a minimum $20 for his services. Peter also makes fringes by hand for high quality oriental carpets at $10 a foot.

476 Davisville Ave. (483-3300) — call first, please.

Cement & Concrete

Adit General Contracting
Dave Springett will repair anything from a small crack in your basement wall to a major crevasse in your patio or sidewalk. In addition, he designs and builds sidewalks and patios, for which there are no average prices since every job is different. The multi-talented Mr. Springett can fix your shingle roof, install aluminum windows and doors and even design and build an addition to your house. He also works with Robert Doto, a specialist in brick and tile repair.

151 Coleman Ave. (690-3197)

> **CHAIN SAWS:** see
> **LAWN MOWERS — POWER**

Chimneys

Toronto Chimney Service
Norman Lenz, Canada's only practising master chimney sweep, served a hard seven-year apprenticeship in Europe before becoming a full-fledged sweep and, with a little persuasion, he'll arrive in the centuries-old uniform seen in *Mary Poppins*. He and an assistant will arrive at your house and clean out the offending chimney for $35. Two or 3-storey houses will cost $45, and the whole process will take about an hour.

36 Rivalda Rd., Weston (742-9862)

Carpet Cleaning & Care

Renting: Deep water extraction, also known as steam cleaning, is the most common method of carpet care. A large machine can be rented for about $15 for four hours or $25 for a day, and small machines cost $15 for four hours or $20 a day. For the large machine, you can buy 24 oz. of shampoo for $3 to $4, which will do about 200 square feet of carpet. The small machine's shampoo is $3.50 to $4.25 per quart, and also does 200 square feet. Most people can do their living room, dining room and hall (an estimated 400 square feet) in a couple of hours, but when renting your machine for four hours, allow for travel time, too.

Hiring: Professional steam cleaning of a 400 square foot carpet would cost you $65 to $80 (shags usually cost a bit more); dry shampooing, about $55 to $65. Steam cleaning takes about two hours; dry shampooing about half the time. Dry shampooing does a better job, we're told, but can't (or shouldn't) be used on most shags and some brands of carpets. Check with your dealer.

How often to clean: Professionals suggest cleaning your carpets once a year, alternating between dry shampoo and deep water extraction systems, if your carpet can take the former. The frequency of cleaning your carpet will depend on your traffic volume.

General care: Coffee, tea and soft drink stains will rarely come out; your only recourse may to be rearrange your furniture. Pet stains should be cleaned immediately with one part non-alkalide dishwashing liquid to three parts lukewarm water. Let it sit, then clean again with one part white vinegar to three parts lukewarm water to remove the detergent and restore color. If the stain persists, call a professional.

China

A.W. Hockridge
Yonge Street has altered around them but, like some of the delicate figurines presented to them for repair, the Hockridges have stood frozen against time in the same location since 1900. They also repair jade and ivory as well as art glass and antique china dolls, using secret techniques that have been carefully transported from one generation to the next.

638 Yonge St. (922-1668)

Clocks – Old

Haze Clocks and Antiques
Years ago, John Haze made a splendid grandfather clock which now stands in his living room, serving as ticking testimony that he knows what he's doing. Mr. Haze concedes that some owners of old clocks simply want to bring them to life again and aren't too fussy about their time-keeping talent. Thus, at your option, he can do the minimum required to get a clock working or use his highly specialized tools to restore its case and movement completely: handy information for those whose budgets restrain them. His hourly rate is a bargain at $6.

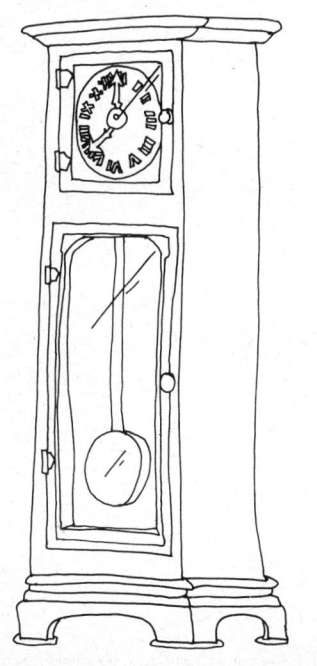

546 West Shore Blvd., Pickering (839-3434)

Murray McLeod
Once you surrender your old clock to Murray McLeod (he won't touch new ones), be advised that the bill for its repair won't be cheap. Complete restoration of a grandfather clock averages $225. He makes no compromises, preferring instead to restore all clocks to their original operating standards. Mr. McLeod offers a free estimate before beginning work, and doesn't swerve from it. He's also one of the few craftsmen in this area who can service old music boxes, replacing teeth and springs, but you'll have to consult our "Furniture, Antique" source if the cabinet is damaged.

62 Rockport Cres., Richmond Hill (884-5554)

Clothing

Cheeseworth's Cleaners and Weavers Ltd.
Since 1865, John Klaiber's shop has specialized in invisible weaving and mending, and he gets business mailed to him from all across the country. It'll cost an average of $20 to repair a cigarette burn, depending on the material: it's cheaper for tweed, for example. Service takes two to four days and includes free pick-up and

Cookware

Durable Release Coaters
Most people with Teflon-coated cookware are happy to donate it to the church rummage sale when its surface develops those inevitable scratches. But Durable's Dick Lund will rescue it for you by baking on a new finish, as long as you can remove all plastic attachments. For the low cost of $5, you can even restore your electric frying pan — unless you have one of those models with the control in a fixed handle.

4 Finley Rd., Bramalea (457-2000)

Cookware—Copper

Lyons Tinning
Gypsies once travelled through Europe tinning pots and pans to make them safe for cooking, but Philip Lyons is one of the very few people practicing the craft in Canada. He'll line old pots and pans with tin and also hammer out any small dents. Average size saucepans will cost $9; large soup pots; $15; and old brass syrup pails normally run $40.

5115 Maingate Dr., Mississauga (625-4611)

D

Dolls & Toys

A.W. Hockridge
Although Mr. Hockridge specializes in repairing china and antique glass, he also works on dolls, providing they're hand-made. He's not interested in the plastic, commercially manufactured dolls of the last 25 years. But Teddy Bears, puppets, antique and other valuable toys will receive expert care in the Hockridge shop. You'll be advised in advance if the repair costs exceed the toy's value.

638 Yonge St. (922-1668)

Ron's Ceramics and Doll Hospital
Anne Pitt learned what she knows from her father, who used to make dolls in their German village. Although she can repair the newer plastic types, she's in great demand for her work with antique dolls, and scours old books to make sure she is correctly duplicating their clothes. Anne also makes natural hair wigs for dolls requiring them. Her minimum charge is $6 to restring elastic. Patience is requested: her

work is time-consuming and restorations often take as long as a month. Lest your memory of the doll's original condition fail you during that time, Anne takes before-and-after photos for customers.

2975 Dundas St. W. (767-9306)
351 Waverley Rd. (694-9032) — Sundays

Doors

The Door Store
Sam Mirschak will hand-strip your ornate front door for $40 up, but you have to finish it yourself. His staff can also repair all doors. Normally, the job takes one to two weeks but if it means you're going to be without, say, a front door, it can usually be turned around within two days with an appointment. The store works principally with doors containing stained glass.

112 Queen St. E. (363-2539)

Draperies

Royal Cleaners
Salvatore Accardi cleans and alters about 500 pairs of drapes a year. He knows how to care for velvet and damask materials and he fully guarantees his work. Alteration prices are reasonable: shortening or lengthening is $3 per panel if lined, or $2.50, unlined. For pleated drapes, repairs are a flat $5 per panel. He charges $6 to fireproof drapes, although this is required more by offices and stores than homes.

1123 Broadview Ave. (425-0888)

Dying—Garments

Metropolitan Dye Works
Tucked away behind the Summerhill liquor store off Yonge Street south of St. Clair, Adam Inch's 40-year-old dye works is small but heralded. He can't guarantee his work because most of the new fibres are so fickle but he can usually tell you if it's going to "take." The cost of dyeing a woman's dress ranges from $12 to $25, depending on the length. Drapes are $5.75 for a four-by-eight-foot panel and double bedspreads are $15. Mr. Inch also dyes gloves, wedding gowns and coats.

1115 Yonge St. (922-9124)

E

Electric Motors

Electric Motors Service Co.
If the motor in your vacuum cleaner fails, Doug Colvin will usually advise replacement as the most economical course. But he can also repair others, like the motor on your furnace, for about $18 which includes replacement of the bushings and the switch. Mr. Colvin's 55-year-old store is one of the few electric motor repair depots left in the center of the city and he also specializes in fixing motors that propel pool and cottage pumps as well as roof fans and air conditioning fan motors.

687 Mt. Pleasant Rd. (485-0083)

Electrical Appliances —Small

Jackson Electric
If repairing your appliance is going to cost more than half the price of a replacement, Ed Ford will let you know. He strongly believes that older appliances are better than new ones and thus worth fixing. For a

What Happens When the Warranty Runs Dry

All new appliances are guaranteed these days but, luck and workmanship being what they are, some will inevitably fail just after the warranty expires. That's a situation that used to make buyers shrug their shoulders at Fate and pay the cost of repair, but attitudes, we discovered to our surprise, have changed.

- Perhaps it's newly-awakened consumer anger that's responsible, but we surveyed most major manufacturers of small appliances and learned that (with the possible exception of Sunbeam) all of them are hearteningly lenient when it comes to repairing products whose warranties have expired. If the problem is an obvious manufacturing defect, and the customer presents a product that clearly hasn't been abused, there won't be any charge for repair. There are limits to this elasticity, of course. Don't expect free service if you've tampered with the appliance yourself or if an unreasonable length of time has passed since the expiration of the warranty.
- "Unreasonable length of time" is a grey area whose definition is usually left to the person serving you, either at an authorized repair depot or at the factory itself. But, in most cases, if you present a product within six months after a one-year warranty has ended you can usually expect to leave without a bill. Most service personnel are harried, so you'll help your case considerably by flashing your friendliest smile and acting like a *most* reasonable person. Snarl or gripe, and the game's over.
- Obviously, it also helps if you can present an invoice with the appliance. But don't try to lie about the date you bought or received it: these days, most are code-dated on the bottom and the date of manufacture is easy to determine. Allowing an average six months' shelf life, the clerk can usually guess when the product was purchased. Without a receipt, some of them will ask you to sign an affidavit that certifies a date and rare is the customer who can look someone in the eye and then sign a lie.
- One final suggestion: save the carton and repack the appliance in it if service is necessary. That's tangible evidence that you care enough about the appliance (and, hence, haven't abused it) to protect it from damage in transit.

Perhaps the manufacturers' new relaxed attitudes actually reflects realistic self-analysis. They *know* they're not making 'em like they used to and unofficial warranty extensions are one way of apologizing for the high price of progress.

minimum charge of $4, he and his staff of five will repair toasters, kettles and irons, rarely exceeding $12 total cost. They'll imaginatively use a substitute part if the original is no longer available, and guarantee their work for a year.

344 Queen St. W. (364-9478)

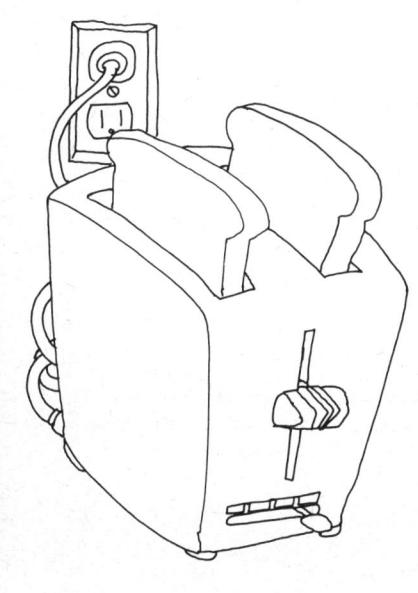

D.R. Stocks Electric Company
Don't look for a large sign identifying this shop; there isn't any. Instead, watch for a window that's packed with old toasters, vacuum cleaners, lamps and just about anything that plugs into the wall. Owners Mr. and Mrs. Kemp share Jackson Electric's policy: the cost of repairs should not exceed half the cost of the appliance when new. Although there may be a wait, customers return because the cheery Kemps' low prices more than compensate.

1046 Yonge St. (922-6041)

Exterior Cleaning & Restoration

Toronto Restorations
This company's sign is both familiar and stable around Toronto, in a business that has more than its share of fly-by-night artists. Estimator Bob David says his company prefers to use chemicals for most jobs unless sandblasting is deemed absolutely necessary. Estimates are free but you can expect to pay about 75¢ a square foot for a surface that is free of paint, more if stripping and repairs are required.

295 King St. E. (863-6077)

F

Fans (Hand Held)

Elsie Sawchuk
Elsie Sawchuk not only repairs but creates fans — she's produced 36 of them for one theatre production. You'll quickly be told if your fan is irreparable, because many of them simply haven't survived their years in musty trunks. But if the structure is basically sound and if the material covering it is still available, she can restore it for an hourly service charge of $5; time-consuming repairs will be taken on at a negotiable rate. Simple repairs such as adjusting silk are ready within a week. Ms. Sawchuk will even give you lessons on how to use your fan.

71 Gloucester St. (923-5161)

Fishing Tackle

Pollack Sporting Goods
Ed Greenbaum, an avid fisherman

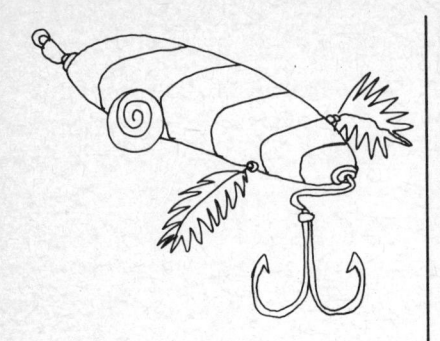

himself, supervises repair of all makes of reels and rods, and related equipment. Loyal anglers have been turning to this store for help since before 1930. He charges about $5 to repair a broken fibreglass rod, $3.50 to clean and lubricate a reel and $2 plus material to replace nets.

337 Queen St. E. (363-1095)

Flagpoles

John Ewing & Co. Ltd.
When this company opened for business in 1845, almost every Toronto home of substance flew the Union Jack. Today, few flags of any kind flutter on front lawns but on-site repairs to poles can be made or they can be replaced by the new aluminum or steel types. Re-roping of a 30-foot pole costs $65, painting a steel pole will run $2 per foot up to 340 feet.

2989 Kennedy Rd. (291-1675)

Floors — Wood

Darmaga Hardwood Flooring
Wally Darmaga sands, repairs, installs and refinishes wood floors, using techniques he learned from his grandfather who founded the family business. For 25¢ per foot for a normal finish, he'll sand your floor; for 70¢ a foot, you'll get a nifty staining job. He offers free polishing and maintenance advice and, where possible, will try to rescue an abused old floor by replacing damaged planks with others of similar age and grain. Hourly charge for repairs is $12. New plastic finishes have made maintenance easy but Mr. Darmaga says that industrial wax can reduce friction and prolong their life.

11 Johnson St., Thornhill (889-2544)

Frames — Picture

Goldframe
As long as its plaster base is neither too moist nor too brittle, Brian Dedora will restore the gilt to old frames, using 15th century Florentine techniques. He may also advise that the plaster be stripped to the wood and then refinished. His basic rate is $15 an hour, with gold or silver leaf running from $4 to $16 a foot. Dedora can also repair modern, more conventional frames and guarantees his work for ten years.

253 Gerrard St. E. (967-9176)

Furniture — Antique Repair & Refinishing

James Carlin
The Carlins have been mending or creating fine furniture for over 600 years and, in fact, one of them was official cabinet maker to Marie Antoinette. The Toronto company was established in 1930 and, despite his prestigious family credentials, James Carlin is usually flexible when it comes to repair work. Depending on its condition he'll restore, say, a Victorian side table for $100 plus, but if you only want a cigarette burn removed from its top,

it could cost you less than $25. His shop can also strip metal garden furniture and beds and even impose instant antiquity on a new wood piece.

233 Carlton St. (922-4012)

Bruce Saunders
Mr. Saunders specializes in carefully hand-stripping old pieces, repairing breaks, splits and cracks in the wood. For an average size buffet or sideboard, his charge would be about $65. His real specialty is restoring marquetry and repairing veneer, and he can arrange for pickup and delivery.

104 Edith Dr. (489-0977)

Furniture Stripping

Furniture Strip
If you bring them a pressed-back kitchen chair with several generations of paint on it, this company will probably lift the old coats off in minutes while you wait. But be advised: the chemical process involved often raises a slight furry nap on some woods that has to be sanded down before staining. Chair dipping will run $9, doors cost $17.50. If you want them hand-stripped, it'll cost two to three times as much. The service is especially useful for pieces that have lots of twists and turns to

Kay Benaco, of Furniture Strip

them, relieving you of hours of tedious rubbing.

9 Hanna Ave. (362-2066)

Furs

Avon Fur Co. Ltd.
Harry Cornblum will honestly tell you if your favorite muskrat is so far gone it isn't worth repairing — not because he wants to sell you a new one but because that's the way his family has operated for 53 years. Concern for the customer is paramount, and all major work is guaranteed for two seasons, with storage facilities on the premises. The average cost to clean a fur is $18.

686 Bathurst St. (534-7565)

G

Glass

Queen City Glass
There's many a cut lip twixt the brandy and the palate if the edges of your favorite snifters are chipped but they can usually be polished out. Crystal repairs and hand-bevelling can be done at $19 an hour. Clark Forster supervises Toronto's only hand-bevelling operation for larger pieces and his company resilvers mirrors for $4 per square foot, should you demand the absolute truth.

243 Victoria St. (364-6285)

Glasses (Eye)

Braddock Optical Co. Ltd.
One of the few remaining shops in the city to recognize the real value of good will, this branch of the Braddock chain will adjust any glasses without charge. In addition, they will solder metal frames while you wait, charging about $3 per break. Plastic frames can also be mended but since those repairs can't be guaranteed, the service is free.

280 Bloor St. W. (962-2020)

Guns – Antique

Lloyd Johnston
The oldest gun Lloyd Johnston ever

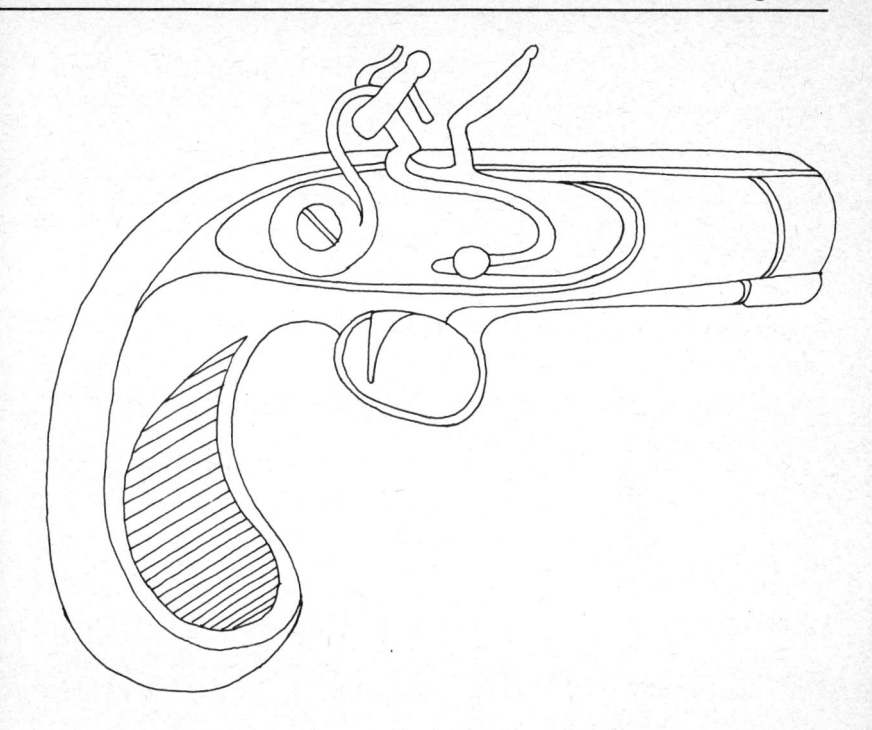

repaired was from Oliver Cromwell's day. He works only on guns at least 100 years old and is a stickler for authenticity — guns will only be modified to conform with their historic style. Warranties vary according to the work, but every job has one. If you own an antique gun, you can expect to be regularly consulted during a complex job. Changing the ignition system on a muzzle-loading British military musket (from cap lock to original flint lock) will cost about $100; engraving runs $15 per hour. Mr. Johnston does hand-buffing, but don't call him about re-blueing because only "modern" guns require it.

71 Fairglen Ave., Brampton (457-3435)

H

Handbags

Laurentian Leather Goods
Although he was once commissioned to make a camel saddle, owner Leslie Volgyesi really specializes in repairing less spectacular leather goods. He'll add extra pockets to wallets or longer straps to handbags, but can also design from scratch. In addition, he'll make needlepoint bags, which cost between $50 and $70.

Toronto Dominion Centre (368-4061)

Handwriting

Ebsen Graphic Arts Service Ltd.
With typewriters so common and inexpensive, most people's handwriting has deteriorated to an indecipherable scrawl. Gather five or six of your friends together and for $100 each, Alf Ebsen will teach you the basics of calligraphy, an ancient craft that restores handwritten work to its proper beauty. Write on!

60 Logandale Rd. (222-4556)

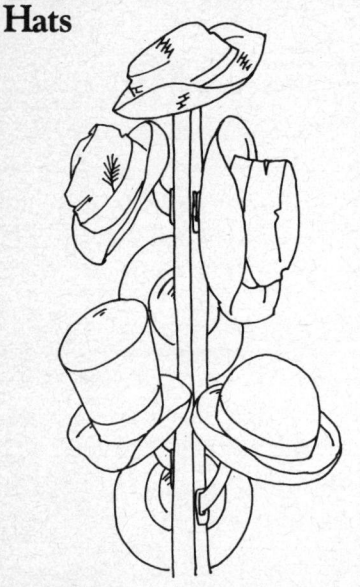

Hats

The Hatter
George Catleugh has been topping heads for over forty years. He'll clean and re-block your favorite fedora for $4, with a modest extra charge for any necessary repairs like a new band. He and his staff also design and make hats of any kind, men's or women's, at a basic charge of $15 an hour.

1794 Avenue Rd. (783-8233)

Hearing Aids

Union Hearing Aid Centre
Peter Keller runs the only hearing aid service in Toronto that will repair all makes while you wait. If it's going to be longer than a couple of hours, he'll loan you one until yours is ready. New microphones cost $18 to $29 but small adjustments are usually free. As well, Keller makes custom ear plugs for people like rock musicians exposed to high decibel levels, "to protect them from needing hearing aids later on." The plugs are $25 a pair.

137 Yonge St. (364-2264)

Humidifiers

Humidifier Sales & Service Ltd.
Here's a tip from Bud Durward on how you can retard lime buildup in your new portable humidifier: buy an extra belt or cloth, saturate it in a strong solution of vinegar and water and then install it in your unit. Then remove the original belt and saturate it, too. Rotate the two on a three to four week basis. If your unit needs work, it'll cost you a basic $14 an hour plus parts. Furnace humidifiers are tuned-up for a package price of $19.50 plus parts.

1693 Avenue Rd. (781-9191)

I

Insulation

Snowshoe Insulation
Instead of breaking down walls to insulate for lower fuel bills, Fred Silver's company will drill holes (from inside or outside the house) and then fill the gap with foam. An average two-storey detached brick

house, with about 2000 sq. ft., will cost about $1200. Many users report the process saves them an average 25% on their annual fuel bills.

22 Rivalda Rd., Weston
90 Courcelette Rd., Scarborough (699-0290)

Iron, Wrought

Jorret Metal Craft
Willy Jorgensen and his partner, Joe Ret, helped restore the elaborate fence, complete with cow-catcher gates, surrounding Osgoode Hall. They also design fences and repair railings and decorative iron work, including light fixtures. Trained in his native Denmark over 30 years ago, Willy charges a flat $12 an hour (plus materials) and gives a free estimate.

2105 Midland Ave., Unit 11 (292-1473)

J

Jewellery

Grant's Pawnbrokers and Jewellery
Owner Al Cohen directs repairs and restorations to most jewelry regardless of its age, using the city's best craftsmen. He also handles delicate enamel work but is quick to tell a customer if each piece is worth the cost of fixing it. In addition, he cleans jewelry and can restring pearls. His prices are fair and he never charges more than necessary — estimates are provided in advance. Diamond rings are retipped here at about $7 per claw, and charms are soldered to bracelets within two days for $2 each.

135 Church St. (869-0344)

K

Kites

Mamiko Suzuki, Ray Wismer

The Kite Store
Toronto's only store devoted exclusively to kites and how to fly them might not actually repair yours if you didn't buy it there, but they'll supply all the advice and materials you need to get it airborne again. You pay only for the material, which could be as cheap as a bottle of glue.

848A Yonge St. (964-0434)

L

Lamps

Artistic Lighting Studios
One of Toronto's posher homes is now lit by a camel's stomach, tastefully fashioned into a lamp by Jack Robbins. But he's also

equipped to transform almost any other object and makes basic repairs, like plug replacement, as well. Cost varies, depending on the task. An ordinary lamp can usually be rewired with a new plug and socket for under $10.

49 Avenue Rd. (924-6706)

> **LAMPSHADES:** see
> **STAINED AND LEADED**
> **GLASS**

Lawnmowers – Manual

Malacarne & Sons
The most common problem with the older types is rust due to neglect but the Malacarnes (see also "Sharpeners") will thoroughly clean moving parts, check the bearings, adjust and sharpen the blades for an average $7. Replacement of the wooden roller at the back will cost about $3 extra, with new drive gears running about $2.50 each and drive pins, $1.

201 Harbord (531-5603)

Lawnmowers – Power

Drake Sales & Service Ltd.
Mrs. Alice Drake has supervised the repair of about 4000 mowers a year since opening for business in 1949. Her shop has one of the city's largest stocks of parts. A gas-powered lawn mower will receive a minor tune-up for about $20, which includes thorough testing and sharpening of the blades. A major tune-up can run up to $50. Drake's will also service chain saws and snowblowers.

1855 Lawrence Ave. E. (759-9348)

Leather & Suede

Peter Pan Suede & Leather Cleaners Ltd.
Owner Paul Sears claims he gets work from across Canada. His shop repairs all types of leather garments, including elephant hide, and his staff can alter to fit. Cleaning, which includes replating and redyeing, runs to about $20 for a man's suede trench coat and $22 for a leather one. Prices include free pick up and delivery and they will provide summer storage of leather garments they clean that spring.

2531 Yonge St. (481-3341)

Lighters

Electric Shaver Centre
Owner Carl Fry specializes in Ronson, Colibri and Braun types, suggesting factory return or disposal for most others. His shop, in business since 1954, repairs about 3000 lighters a year and some can be fixed on the spot, except for the more complicated electronic kinds. Cleaning and reconditioning an old Ronson, including a new spark wheel, will cost about $4; a new valve

on a butane Colibri runs about $3.50.

11 Richmond St. E. (362-6487)

Locks

Eastway Lock & Door Co.
Susan Fleming will listen to your embarrassed confession that you've locked your keys in the car and then dispatch her husband Doug to let you in, charging a flat $35 at night and $17.50 during the day. Mr. Fleming can also repair and install home locks, panic bars and electric door openers with buzzers. If for any reason they can't accommodate your middle-of-the-night appeal, the Flemings promise to relay your call to someone who can.

94 Charlottetown Blvd. (284-7445)

Joe Vulakovic, Reilly Lock

Reilly Lock
Established in 1927, manager Edward Hartley reports that his store cuts an average 50,000 keys a week. If you lock yourself out of your home, they'll let you in for a minimum $25. Bring in the keyless lock from an old cabinet or box and they'll likely make a set for about $8. A sturdy old Yale door lock, for instance, can usually be restored and reconditioned for $26, much less than the price of a new one.

16 Isabella St. (921-5101)

Luggage

Evex Importers & Distributors Inc.
Repairs manager Gord Hopper cheerfully claims his service is one of the least expensive in town, noting that many leather goods stores send their work to him. But he's obviously busy and repairs take about a week, averaging $4 for a new handle and $5 for a new lock. He can restore old leather suitcases (like Gladstone bags, for instance), stitching their bindings and reconditioning and then redyeing the leather. Note: dyeing costs can exceed customers' expectations.

369 Spadina Ave. (864-1776)

M

Maps – Old

Langridge Ltd.
Jim Young supervises the map mounting department of this 82-year-old company. Most old maps, he says, are of paper bonded to linen, which has usually deteriorated. At a flat charge of $12.50 an hour, he'll mount it on a board after first repairing any rips or tears, and then treat the board so that the aged yellow tone of the map is preserved. Finished price depends on the amount of time involved — in some cases, as little as five hours.

83 River St. (366-1168)

Marble

United Marble
Since 1945, Paul Mably has repaired just about everything made of marble, including fireplaces, window sills and floors. He imports

most of his marble from Italy, Portugal and Spain and mends breaks or cracks with a special glue that's then finished to make it look like a vein. One break in the marble trim of a fireplace, for instance, can be fixed for $40 to $50.

46 Shaftesbury Ave. (rear) (922-6531)

Marine Instruments

Gabriel Aero-Marine Instruments Ltd.
If your old hand compass tells you you're facing north when that's Lake Ontario in front of you, you should probably throw it away because the cost of repair isn't justified. But Gabriel's will repair critical marine compasses, shipping them down to the 95-year-old company's head office in Halifax where they're fixed by sea-wise experts and then returned within ten days. They also repair other types of marine equipment like depth sounders, auto-pilots and radio-telephones. Their rates are $18 an hour on all work.

53 Colborne St. (363-8973)

Microwave Ovens

Roberts Electronics Services
Although they appear to be a recent phenomenon, microwave ovens have been around for awhile and Bob Szymanis reports his first service call was in 1961. Home users are sometimes alarmed by the possibility of radiation leakage around the door and for a flat fee of $12.50 Mr. Szymanis will visit your home and "read" your unit. He charges a basic $22.50, plus parts, for any necessary repairs.

516 Evans Ave. (252-4216)

Mirrors

Belgium Mirror and Glass Co.
Although they'll grind out minor chips on the edges, Shelly Dilman and his family really specialize in re-silvering mirrors. They won't pick up or deliver and you can expect an average two-week wait, but they're good, charging about $12 to resilver an 18" x 36" mirror.

1057 Eglinton Ave. W. (789-2155)

Mopeds

Toronto Motorbike Company
Gehl Martin's store sold over 600 motorized bicycles last year and her staff of five can repair just about any make. They can replace pedals and straighten forks and wheels. However, they'll encourage you to make all minor repairs yourself. If you need a new spark plug ($2.50), they'll show you how to install it instead of charging you for the service. If you have to leave your moped, they'll try to repair it within 24 hours.

1650 Yonge St. (482-3461)

Motorcycles

Firth Motorcycles
Harry Firth has been driving bikes for over 50 years and he recommends you take your Japanese or American-made back to your dealer for repair. But he's the city's only specialist in the classic British types, like Triumph and Norton, and he's been fixing them since 1930. He charges a basic $14 an hour for his work but can tune-up, say, a Triumph for $20 to $25.

1857 Danforth Ave. (698-9222)

Movie Equipment

Universal Camera Service
Alben Gabrovec learned his trade in Yugoslavia and can fix any eight, sixteen or 35 MM camera as well as projectors (including the sound amplifier) and related accessories. He charges a flat $8 an hour and guarantees his work for six months. Estimates are free.

1189 Bloor St. W. (534-7393)

Music Boxes

The High Fidelity Shop
Although he sells and services audio equipment, Bob Byrne also repairs those early music-makers without which no Victorian parlor was complete. He can replace and tune the teeth in the comb, adjust the governor and even sometimes identify the tune if the original label is missing. He will usually clean and overhaul a small music box (without drums or bells) for about $50 and does estate appraisals as well.

5197 Yonge St. (223-5325)

Musical Instruments

Geo. Heinl and Co. Ltd.
Now semi-retired from the firm he founded over 50 years ago, George Heinl is a skilled violin maker and the only Canadian allowed to repair Yehudi Menuhin's instruments. His company will also repair almost any other musical instrument but cost depends on the extent of damage.

201 Church St. (363-0093)

O

Outboard Motors

North York Marine
Hans Liebenau is one of the city's few outboard fixers who won't turn up his nose at a make he doesn't sell. With more than 20 years' experience, he works with four people to tune and repair, returning all replaced parts to the customer in a small plastic bag. Most makes (from 5½ to 18 h.p.) can be tuned for the season

for $20 to $30, depending on the parts required.

33 Glencameron Rd., Thornhill (881-5821)

P

Pens – Fountain

The Pencraft Shop
Dick Fraser and Joe Madden operate the only source in town for those ink sacs in old fountain pens that leak. A new one will cost you about $1.50, but it probably won't be as large as the original. Replacement nibs, should you want gold, are much more expensive — the range is between $5 and $50, depending on the make and the current price of gold.

137 Yonge St. (364-8977)

Photographs – Old

The Little Museum (Toronto) Ltd.
Shammai Ogden and his staff enjoy a challenge but they're swift to warn that many damaged photographs are impossible to repair. However, some of the work they've restored is over a century old. When possible, they remove stains, repair rips and tears and even retouch by hand, charging an average $20 an hour. One photograph with no stains but minor damage will cost between $15 and $20 to revive. Repairs are usually ready within three weeks.

882-A Eglinton Ave. W. (789-1219)

Pianos & Organs

Baldwin Piano & Organ Studios
President Barry Skinner charges an average $25 to tune a piano, more if the sound board has to be mended. Electric organs are repaired at a basic $15 per hour; if the instrument has to be totally rebuilt, all work is guaranteed for a year.

5192 Yonge St. (223-1801)

Emery Kada
Not for the battered rec room upright, Emery Kada specializes in tuning and repairing the pianos of serious musicians. He's rebuilt vintage Steinways and Heintzmans from scratch, including all wood refinishing; the cost of refinishing an upright grand piano can run from $350 to $700. (This includes special chemical treatments.) Mr. Kada is often called in by artists appearing at Massey Hall to tune their instruments before a performance.

4256 Marblethorn, Mississauga (625-8255)

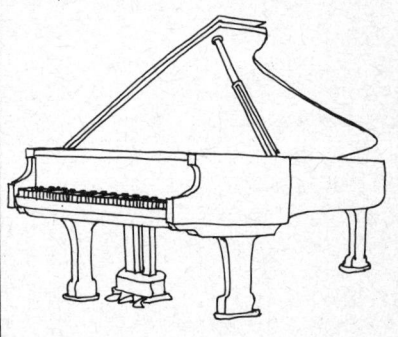

Pipes

Brigham Pipes Ltd.
Established in 1906, a Brigham still runs this major Canadian pipe manufacturer and they repair all types, as well as their own, including antique and meerschaum. Replacing an average stem will cost $4 to $5, but $10 if it's the amber type on a meerschaum. Simple cleaning and

Wally Watson, Brigham Pipes Ltd.

reconditioning, which includes scraping the carbon down to the proper thickness, averages $1.50 to $2.

Toronto Dominion Centre (368-5088)
11 Adelaide St. W. (368-5568)

Plants

Brian Murphy, The Plant Doctor
For an hourly rate of $15, Brian Murphy will tend to your indoor greenery — spraying, repotting, relocating and providing you with a care sheet. He can also nurse ailing plants back to life, and will design an indoor garden that takes into account the available light in your environment. Any materials he uses, like pots and soil, will cost you extra.

122 Carlton St., Apt. 4 (922-8558)

PROJECTORS: see
MOVIE EQUIPMENT

Q

Quilts & Comforters

Jahn's Bedding Specialties Ltd.
Using a machine that's unique in Ontario, owner Klaus Schulz cleans and disinfects the down from pillows, quilts and comforters. He then works the down in with new ticking and makes minor repairs to the cover. The cost for a 53" by 79" comforter is $75, but that, says Schulz, restores it completely and "makes it good for another 20 years."

579 Eglinton Ave. W. (483-9036)

R

Radios & Gramaphones —Old

Vintage Radio-Gramophone
Mike and Laurie Batch stock probably more original parts than anyone else in the city. They've been buying up vacuum tubes for over 20 years and they have schematics going back to 1921. Batch himself is an engineering technician. Estimates are free and Mike will overhaul an old radio that doesn't need major work for about $25. He can also refinish the wood cabinet for an extra fee.

1646 Bayview Ave. (481-6708)

Riding Apparel & Equipment

J.W. Barrington and Son Ltd.
Rooted in Ireland, this revered old

firm is managed here by Lisa Wesselo and is the first choice of most of the city's riders. They shorten bridles, stitch halters and stirrups, and repair saddles. Restuffing an average saddle, for example, will cost about $12 to $15. Affixing a leather chin harness to a hard riding hat will average $8.50. The store also repairs other leather goods, like handbags and briefcases.

51 Front St. E. (364-8461)

Roofs, Slate

O. Poirier Roofing Ltd.
Most modern roofers don't know how to deal with slate but George Poirier claims it will outlast asphalt by far if it's properly cared for. He replaces old steel nails with copper ones and also replaces the slate itself, using tiles he's picked up from demolition sites for correct blending. Minor jobs (3 or 4 missing slates) will cost $112; major ones, such as replacing flashing, with copper and new slates, will run about $800.

126 Victor Ave. (465-3678)

S

Sails

Triton Sails Ltd.
Joe Fernandes and his hearty crew specialize in repairs to all the running rigging on a boat: everything but the mast. For about $20 to $30, and assuming no major damage, they'll refurbish a suit of sails for a 30-foot boat.

229 Niagara St. (363-0472)

Sharpening:
Also See Lawn Mowers – Manual

Malacarne & Sons
Since 1904, the Malacarne family has been sharpening everything but precision instruments which need a fine edge, including knives, scissors, saws, axes, lawnmowers, chisels, wood carving tools and pinking shears. Average prices per piece: knives, 75¢ to $1.50; scissors, $1 to $3; saw blades, $2; axes, $2. They also sell a complete line of knives but will improve on the factory edge by honing it themselves free of charge.

201 Harbord St. (531-5603)

Shavers – Electric

Shaver Service Shop
For a basic $9.95 (including parts), Tom Gyokery will strip your razor right down, clean each part and turn the armature on a lathe to remove carbon build-up. He'll also sharpen the heads on older types and offers same-day service with a 90-day warranty. If you need a transformer installed for overseas use, an adaptor plug, he'll take care of that, too. Not long ago, a customer brought in a single-head Philishave made in 1931. Thanks to Mr. Gyokery, it now has a few more years of close shaves left.

509½ Church St. (922-7017)

Shoes

Bloor Subway Shoe Repair
Nick Morra will save you money if he

can, gently advising a cheaper alternative if it will serve just as well. Most rubber lifts can be replaced within five minutes ($2.50 up) but soles may take up to 20 minutes. His shop is also acknowledged as the only one in town that really knows how to properly install taps, according to a couple of budding hoofers of our acquaintance.

South entrance — Yonge/Bloor subway (925-5313)

Silver

Crown Silverplating
A lot of silver you turn over to your neighborhood jeweller for repair and replating ends up here. Harold and Carol Logan and their staff are equipped to handle most problems but because they're busy, you may have to wait up to six weeks for the return of your piece. Average cost of replating a cream-and-sugar serving set is $8; tea and coffee pots are $15 to $20, and trays over 20″ will set you back $40.

3881 Chesswood Dr., Downsview (366-6067)

Skates

Danforth Shoe Repair
Roy Follows succeeded his father who opened this shop in 1919. He does all of Bauer's warranty work in Toronto but he can also fix most other makes as well. A good pair of blades for professional-quality skates will cost you about $40 but you can pay less, depending on your blade choice. In addition, Mr. Follows replaces eyelets and rebuilds skates. Sharpening costs about $1 a pair.

1390 Danforth Ave. (466-0231)

Skis

Sport Swap
Barry Near leads a team of four ski repair experts, all of them familiar with the damage Ontario's rocks

inflict on downhill racers. It'll cost you about $12 per pair to have the gouges in the bases filled with new P-Tex and then polished with a wet belt sander to bring out the edges again. Barry will also fit you with a correct set of bindings. When the snow melts, the shop turns to repairing bicycles.

579 Mount Pleasant Rd. (481-0249)

Skylights

Skylight Services
Although they'll try to persuade you to replace it with a newer plastic type, because they honestly believe it's to your economic advantage, Fred Tompsett and Bob MacLeod can clean and repair the old glass kind, charging an average $100 which includes caulking. As rare specialists in skylight maintenance, they'll also install new ones you purchase elsewhere, charging a minimum of about $70 for two separate four by four foot units.

50 Bergen Rd., Scarborough (757-9933)

> **SNOWBLOWERS:** see
> **LAWN MOWERS — POWER**

Snowmobiles

Snow City
George Persichilli and his three mechanics specialize in snowmobiles but they'll repair just about anything with a small engine. A pre-season check of your snowmobile will cost $45, which includes a minor tune-up and adjustments to the steering, skis and carburetor. All work is guaranteed for 30 to 60 days, depending on its scope, and the warranty usually starts from the first day you use your vehicle.

1255 Kennedy Rd. (rear), Scarborough (752-1560)

Spot Removal

Century Cleaners
While most cleaners will throw your garment into a vat and cross their fingers, Jack Snitzer believes the stain should be removed before the garment's cleaned. Although his is the most expensive cleaning service in Canada, it's also acknowledged as the most successful in ridding garments of spots. Prices vary according to the cause of the stain, its properties and the time and materials needed to remove it. Sample price: small coffee stains on wool, $2.

3 Sherwood Ave. (485-1186)

Stained & Leaded Glass

Vanderboor & Sons
Bill Vanderboor works with any kind of leaded glass, stained or clear, and also makes it himself. He can usually give a rough estimate over the phone, assuming the problem is correctly described. Replacing two panes or pieces could cost from $15 to $25 but six to ten pieces could cost as little as $30 .... it all depends on the cost of his time and materials. Should he have to replace and relead an entire window, he will guarantee it for 20 years. He also repairs multi-paned glass lampshades and zinc windows.

821 O'Connor Dr. (751-8664)

Swimming Pools

Chrismanpool
Owner Ken Christman feels that

most pool problems could be avoided by simply keeping the chemistry of the water in balance. He provides free water testing and a free pool care manual but an on-site diagnosis will cost a flat $18. His company can restore vinyl liners as well as concrete and related equipment. When possible his staff will work underwater to repair a drain without emptying the pool.

1121 Bellamy Rd. N., Unit 7 (438-9631)

T

Taxidermy

Oliver Spanner & Co. Ltd.
Since 1880, this company has been mounting or repairing the one that didn't get away. With 38 years' experience, Cliff McCutcheon repairs and restores fish and game to its original life-like appearance, charging about $25 for a fish and from $15 to $75 for, say, a racoon. To stuff and mount a fresh raccoon will cost about $150. Cliff will also clean and restore hides and rugs, repairing splits and breaks in the skin. A polar bear rug will cost around $100.

7A Gilead Place (368-0861)

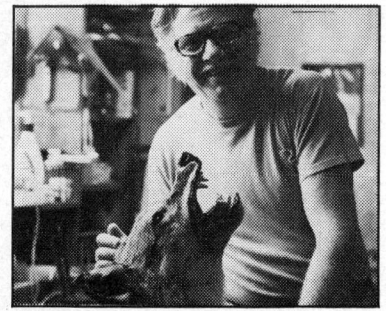

Oliver Spanner & Co. Ltd.

Television

Olympic TV
Ted Pendakis and his assistant charge a flat $8 for a black and white service call, $12.95 if color, but they advise customers to save that amount by bringing in their sets. Mr. Pendakis is known as an honest, reliable repair expert certified by the Ministry of Labour. His experience goes back to 1952.

8 Howard St. (924-5649)

Tennis Racquets

Harry Harrison
Rod Laver and many other stars of the tournament circuit get their racquets restrung here when they're in Toronto. It'll cost about $4 to replace an average grip and $2 to fit the present one to your hand. Restringing is $7 to $15 for nylon and $25 to $40 for gut. Doug Harrison runs the original store on Victoria Street and father Harry runs the new branch.

277 Victoria St. (364-4893)
1660 Avenue Rd. (781-4871)

Tents & Sleeping Bags

Soper's — American Tent Div.
If that's sky instead of tent canvas you're gazing up at, this company

will stitch a patch on and probably even match the color. Since 1875, says managing partner Harold Gallagher, his company has specialized in canvas. They'll replace the zipper on your tent for about $15, waterproof the material for $25-$30 and mend sleeping bags for an average $12 and up. You can also buy extra tent stakes at varying prices according to quality.

174 Wicksteed Ave. (425-6900)

Tools, Power

A&F Power Tools Co. Ltd.
Although this firm does most of Canadian Tire's power tool warranty work, Frank Soul and his associates will tackle any make. Repairs usually take a week to 10 days, averaging $7.50 to $9 to replace the armature in a do-it-yourselfer's drill and $6 each for a simple on-off switch. All of their work is guaranteed for 90 days.

638 Danforth Rd., Scarborough (261-7213)

Trains, Model

Model trains from George's

George's Trains
Model railroaders from all over Canada and the U.S. make tracks to George Olieux and his staff of ten. They're all enthusiastic model railroaders themselves, full of sympathy and helpful advice, and knowledgeable about all scales from Z, HO, N, 027 to more exotic ones. Most repairs average less than $10 and George's can also custom-paint locomotives, with prices varying according to the labor required.

510 Mount Pleasant Rd. (489-9783)

Typewriters

York Business Machines
Owner Kurt Langwisch collects old typewriters and his team of five mechanics will tackle one of any vintage making obsolete parts themselves if necessary. But they can also clean and overhaul the newer portables and desk types. Sample price for reconditioning an ordinary portable that doesn't require major repair: $18.

286 Eglinton Ave. W. (481-5673)

U

Upholstery

Mitchell Interiors
Ron Mitchell has been knocking the stuffing out of furniture for 48 years, repairing or restyling it if the customer desires. He also makes drapes, pillows/sheets either from material supplied by the customer or his own stock. Rates for recovering vary, but an average price for a two-piece corduroy set is $300-$350.

201 Weston Rd. 2nd Floor (762-1168)

V

Vans – Customizing

Philip Ebejer, Van Madness

Van Madness
Larry Batug, Phil Ebejer and Ken Sroka are creative van artists who will design a mobile signature for you, including the installation of beds, bars, insulation, closets, toilets and stereo equipment. They occasionally feature special installation packages at bargain prices but usually charge $15 for a simple roof vent, $25 each for basic round portholes and $20 for a tire carrier.

154 Vaughan Rd. (652-1212)

Vinyl

Doctor Vinyl
If there's a rip in your vinyl, leatherette or Naugahyde sofa, Norm Lee (or one of his five specialists) will visit your home, heat-weld the two pieces together, rebuild the surface and then regrain it to match the rest. After a few days of use, you probably won't be able to locate the repair site and it'll only have cost you around $25. Mr. Lee also fixes swimming pool liners and vinyl car roofs and interiors.

132 Fourth St. (259-2453)

W

Watches

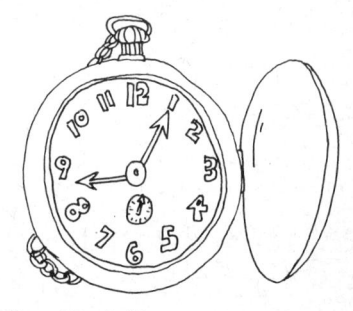

Albert Hockridge
Albert Hockridge has also been working on pocket watches since 1928 and is one of the few who will repair them. He can also fix watch cases and those complicated watches known as repeaters. He prefers to judge each problem on its own before quoting a price.

9 Irwin Ave. (924-3980)

Wheelchairs

Doncaster Medical
Vice-President David Harding says he runs the largest wheelchair repair service in Toronto, processing nearly 60 per month. Most overhauls cost $25 to $50, depending on the cost of parts, and they'll replace bearings and tires, refurbish upholstery and

adjust brakes. Minor adjustments are free. Mr. Harding will lend chairs without charge while patients wait for repairs and his prices include pick-up and delivery.

140 Doncaster Ave., Thornhill (889-9111)

Wigs & Toupees

Artistic Hair Creations
He won't reveal their secrets but Robert Rybka tops a lot of male and female TV and movie performers, avoiding synthetics and using only human hair for his craft. As well as repairing and altering them, he also designs wigs and toupees. He'll clean and style most hairpieces for $10 to $15 but the cost of repair depends on the damage.

176 Davenport Rd. (921-5571)

Window Shades

Toronto Window Shade Co.
In addition to manufacturing shades since 1930, Jim Duke's company cleans and repairs all venetian and roll-up types. He charges 75¢ to 80¢ a square foot to clean, re-tape and re-cord venetian blinds. A new roller in a 36" roll-up shade costs $3 if you do it yourself; $1.50 more if they install it. Pick-up and delivery is a flat $6.50.

1 Holmesdale Rd. (653-2411)

Windows – Screen & Storm

York Installations
Mr. and Mrs. Clarence Rose run a thriving family business that specializes in custom repair work. They'll install new windows, aluminum or wood, as long as no brick work is involved and also replace screening, glass and fix the wood frames on storms where possible. A service call is a minimum $15 but that usually includes the glass for one or two small panes.

127 Manville Rd., Unit 3 (267-9306)

Z

Zippers

Gold's Luggage Shop Ltd.
Zippers on everything but garments can be repaired by Sy Sobel and his eight assistants. They can usually return the item to you the same day and they'll tell you if it isn't worth repairing. But for luggage, sports bags, garment bags, club bags — in fact, anything you travel with — repairs average $5.50 per zipper. If it has to be replaced, it'll cost about $15 for a 14" one, and between $25 and $30 a 32-inch. Warning: if luggage requires dismantling to repair the zipper, the job could cost as much as $50.

212 Queen St. W. (598-3469)

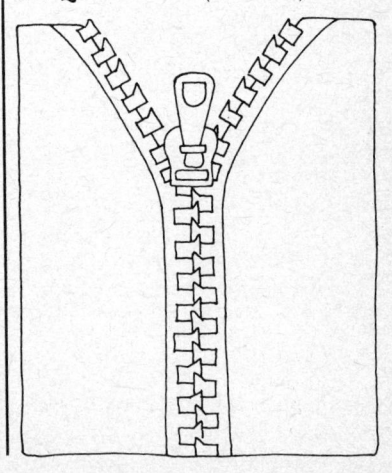

Do-It-Yourself Courses

If there's a high school, community college or YM-YWCA in your neighborhood, you probably have access to first-class instruction in basic home repairs. The courses generally last 20 weeks — long enough to brighten some winter evenings. Fall catalogues are ready in July, so sign up early for the most attractive courses.

- If you're serious about becoming a self-sufficient homeowner, the Toronto Board of Education offers a broad range of general and highly specialized courses. In *Home Maintenance and Improvement* you learn about basic carpentry, electricity and plumbing — how things work and how to make simple repairs. The next step is the *Home Handyman* course that prepares you for electrical rewiring, pipe layout for plumbing renovations, plastering and brickwork.
- Once you've mastered these basics, you might want to move on to specialized courses in *Household Appliance Repair* or *Television and Radio Service.* If you're both energy-conscious and budget-wise, *Heating and Oil Burner Service* might interest you. For those plagued by summer breakdowns in refrigeration and air conditioning at home or business, a winter's worth of study and practice can eliminate long, hot waits for the repairman in August.
- If tinkering with machinery just doesn't excite you, you might get a special surge of confidence from knowing how to refit a Victorian sofa from frame to cover in an *Upholstery* course, or from *Woodworking and Metal Craft,* in which you bring delapidated objects from home and learn to refit them step-by-step. For those who feel lost even in a hardware store, there's *Interior Design (Practical)* to familiarize you with materials and basic techniques — and avoid disappointment in your first efforts.
- Once you've mastered the home arena, you can proceed to the car. Twenty winter evenings of study is a small price to pay for basic competence with fickle automotive machinery, or at least being able to look your mechanic in the eye. Courses range from auto body repair, through engine tune-ups, and overhaul of electrical components.
- The YWCA offers special courses for women in home repair, carpentry and even motorcycle maintenance. Their philosophy is not that women require special training, but that they might feel more comfortable in the YWCA setting.
- A complete directory of all adult education courses in Ontario is available from the Ministry of Colleges and Universities. The facilities are excellent, accessible and designed to prove that ignorance is no excuse.

Tools for the Handyperson

Tenants generally require fewer tools than do homeowners, as the building caretaker does most repairs in rental units, but apartment dwellers should keep some basics on hand. Here is a guide to the "indispensables" for both owners and renters. Remember, Canada is going metric, so be sure to check whether you need imperial or metric tools and parts before you buy.

The Tool	Uses
Claw Hammer	Use it to drive and remove nails, frames and baseboards; drive a chisel; straighten metal and make that stiff bicycle seat go down. When driving a nail, tap it to start it, then get your thumb out of the way before you start really pounding. **$4 to $10**
Screwdrivers	Use them to screw screws in and out and to get your bicycle tire off (being careful not to puncture the tube). There are three head shapes: common (straight), Robertson (square) and Phillips (crossed) — keep a few sizes of each. Or get one screwdriver with interchangeable bits and extra bits stored inside the handle. A plastic handle is a must for safe electrical work. **individual drivers $1 to $3; all-in-one drivers $5 to $8**
Adjustable Crescent Wrench	Use it for opening and closing plumbing pipes and faucets, and on nuts and bolts on bicycles, electrical boxes, or anything else. For plumbing, use one that will open at least 1½ inches, and remember, a longer handle means more leverage. You'll probably find it useful to keep a couple of sizes around. **$3.50 to $9**
Measuring Tape	Use it to measure anything — length of wire, door size, diameter of drain pipes, or the height of your nephew. Try to get one with both imperial and metric units, with a lock to keep it extended, and a spring to pull it in. A 10 foot (3 metre) tape is probably a good length for you. **$3 to $8**

Tools (cont.)

Clamps — If you do much gluing, especially of wood, plastics, metals, etc., a few small clamps to hold pieces together while they dry is a must. If you don't do much gluing, try a big book instead.
$1 each

Level — Use it for hanging doors, fixing cabinets, repairing the sidewalk, repairing an eavestrough (make sure it slopes), replacing table legs, and leveling the stove. A small one should be adequate, but try to get one with horizontal, vertical, and 45° angle leveling bubbles.
$4.50 to $8

Gas Pliers — Use them for nuts and bolts, for plumbing and electrical work, on bicycles, to twist out a dent on a frying pan, to hold things still, to twist wires, and a million other odd jobs.
$2 to $5

Pointed Pliers — Use these mainly in electrical work and in tight spaces where the gas pliers won't fit. They also have a sire cutter included near the joint.
$2 to $5

Saw — It will cut window frames, baseboards, kindling for the fireplace, a board for your broken fence, or anything else. For most household chores, a crosscut saw (about 10 teeth to the inch) will do fine, although other types of saws are available for more specialized work.
$6 to $10

Step ladder — Use it to paint the ceiling, hang plants, fix the light, hang curtains, clean the eavestrough, put up Christmas lights, and change the screens. For indoor work, a 6 foot ladder will do for most exterior work on a one-storey house. If it's windy or you fall a lot, get an 8 foot ladder for outdoor work. Above one-storey, you can rent an adjustable ladder. Wooden ladders are generally cheaper, but metal ones are unaffected by moisture and tend to be more stable.
$14 to $20

(cont.)

Plunger If your toilet, tub or sink stops up, it's an absolute necessity.
$2 to $3

Chisels Use them to notch doors for a new hinge or lock, clear out old or smooth out new putty in a broken window, cut shims to adjust a door frame, and narrow a board to fit into the space it should. A package with a variety of sizes is handiest, but if you want only one, a ½ inch or ¾ inch chisel is likely the most valuable.
$1 to $3 each
$18 to $20 for a package

Glass Cutter If you have kids who occasionally hit balls through windows or break table tops, this is really a must.
$1 to $3

Hand Drill With a little elbow grease you can hang a plant or basket chair, add a hole for wires for a new plug, or provide a drain through the patio. Get a variety pack of bit (drill) sizes to go with it. If you do a lot of drilling, it might be worth buying an electric drill, but for most people the added expense isn't worth it.
pack of bits $1.50 to $8
Electric drill $12 to $25

Smooth Plane Use it to shave a bit off that sticking door or window, smooth out a dent in the woodwork and to make your homemade picture frames fit squarely at the corners. For very small jobs a block plane may be better and for big jobs you may want a jack plane, but a 6 to 8 inch smooth plane is a good bet for most household chores.

And don't forget:
masking tape, electrician's tape, a variety of nail types and sizes, extra fuses, rubber washers for faucets, extension cords (one with a caged light), a variety of saw types, a few light bulbs, a vise-grip for plumbing that resists being opened, a metal set square or universal square (or both), a variety of screws, nuts, bolts and washers, a couple of files, an extra light switch or two, a couple of male and female plugs, and a soldering gun (and solder) for fixing the toaster (unplug it first!).

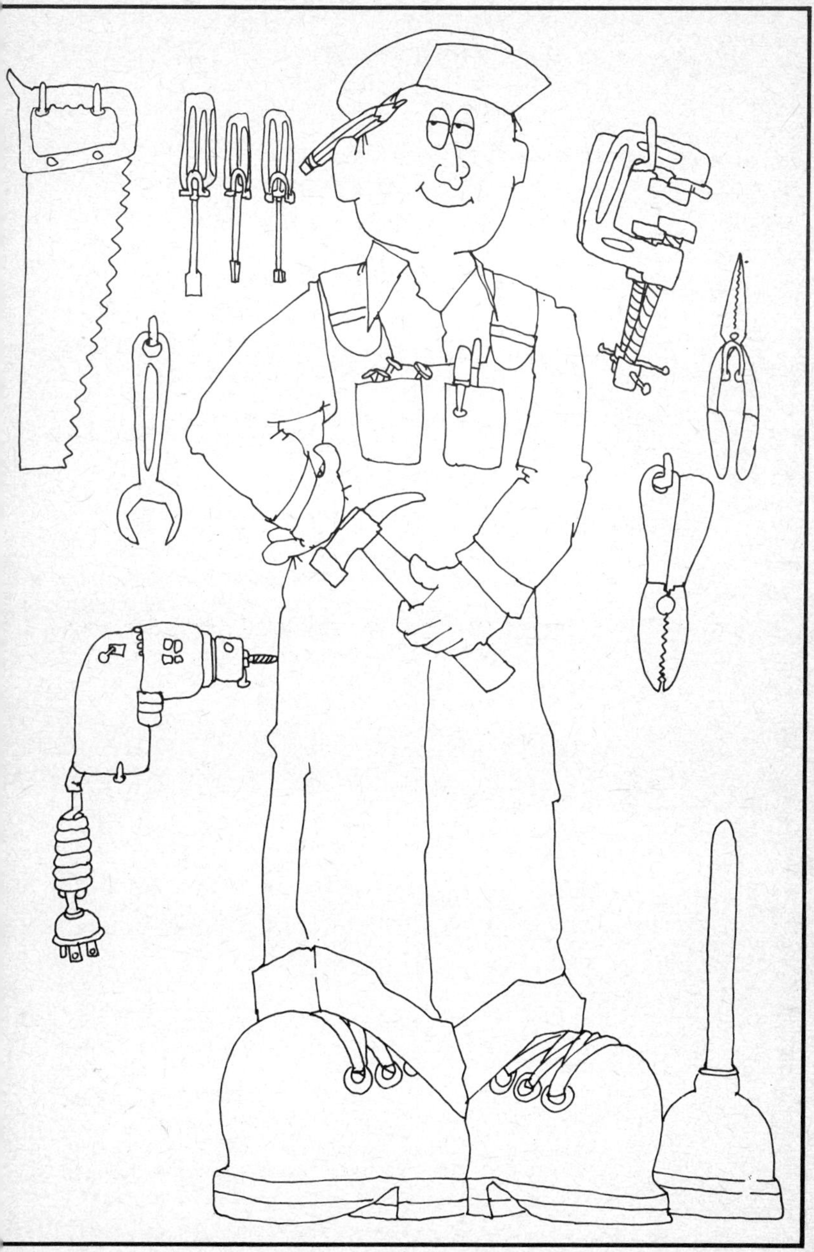

Index

A.O. White Supply Co. **53**
A.W. Hockridge **128**
Aardvark **44**
Abbey Auctions **7**
Acoustic Problems **117**
Acrylic, Repair **117**
Action Service Contact Centre **97, 99**
Adding Machines, Repair **117**
Advice from Some Experts **4**
Agincourt Community Service **101**
Air Conditioners, Repair **117**
Albert Britnell Bookshop **88**
Alexandra Park Health Centre **109**
Alternatives to Supermarket **30-31**
Amusement Machines, Repair **117**
Annual Sales **45**
Antennas, TV & Radio, Repair **118**
Anthony's Villa Restaurant **32**
Apartment Rental Tips **46**
Appliances **130**
Appliances, Repair, see Electrical
Aquariums, Repair **118**
Archery Equipment, Repair **118**
Around Again **88**
Art, Library **48**
Art Gallery of Ontario Rental Service **48**
Art Objects, Repair **118**
Art of Haggling **16**
Art Restoration **118**
Art Supplies, see Gwartzman's
Auctions **7**
Audio Equipment Repair **119**
Auto Radios, Repair **119**
Automobiles, Inspection and Repair **120**
Automobiles, Old **120**
Avon Furs, Repair **78**
Awnings, Repair **120**

B

Baby Carriages, Repair **120**
Bagel Restaurant **41**
Bakeries **22, 23**
Balaban's Produce Company **26**
Bali Indonesian Restaurant **40**
Banks, see Credit
Bankruptcy, see Debt Counselling
Barber, see Hairdressers
Bargain Hunter Press **13, 44**
Barometers, Repair **121**
Bathtubs and Sinks, Repair **121**
Bay-Bloor Radio **56**
Bazaars & Special Sales **11-12**
Beggar's Banquet Restaurant **42**
Benny's Denim and Leather Boutique **68**
Beds, Brass Repair **121**
Bicycles, Repair **122**
Big Sister Thrift Shop **70**
Billiard and Pool Tables, Repair **123**
Binoculars, Repair **123**

Black Whiskers Fashion **68**
Bloor and Gladstone Library Films **82**
Bloor Bathurst Information Centre **96**
B'nai Brith Bazaar **11**
Boats, Repair **123**
Boards of Education **83**
 see also Do-it-Yourself
Bodega Restaurant **38**
Boo Boo's **69**
Books & Records **88-92**
Books, Repair **123**
Books to Learn By **124**
Brass, Brazing, see Beds, Brass
Brick and Tile Repair, see Cement & Concrete
Britnell's Bookshop, see Albert Britnell
Bruce of Crescendo Hairstylists **71**
Bruce's Green Plants and Flowers **56**
Bumpkin's Restaurant **32**
Bumpkin's Take-out Restaurant **32**
Buy and Sell **13, 44**

C

Cafe May Restaurant **38**
Cameras, Repair **123**
Campus Legal Assistance Centre **108**
Canada Customs Auctions **9**
Canadian General Electric **47**
Can-Do Bookstore **124**
Caning and Wicker, Repair **125**
Canoes, see Liftlock
Capriccio Dining Room **40**
Car, Buying a **113**
Cars: Some Facts to Know **113**
Care-Ring **99 101**
Carpets **52**
Carpet Cleaning & Care **126**
Carpet Shop **52**
Carpets and Rugs, Repair **125**
Cashway Lumber Co. **59**
Cedarbrae Library, Art Rentals **48**
Cement & Concrete Repair **125**
Centennial College **84**
Central Hosiery **69**
Central Neighbourhood Food Club **30**
Centre, Cinema **81**
Chain-Saws Repair, see Lawnmowers, Power
Chair-Man Mills **58**
Cheap Credit: The Subtle Art of Chargemanship **104-105**
Cheese **23**
Children's Clothing, New & Used **77**
Children's Storefront **102**
Children's Own Storefront **92**
Chimney, Repair **125**
China **52**
China, Repair **127**
Chinese Restaurants **37-38**

Chocolate **26**
Church Street Community Centre **108**
Cinema Archives **81**
Cinema Lumiere **81**
Cinemas **81-82**
Classic Books **89**
Cleaning Your Own Carpets **126**
Clearance Outlets **68-70**
Clocks, Old, Repair **127**
CLOTHING **68-80**
Clothing, Repair **127**
Coles Bookstores **89**
Colleges **83**
Collegiate Sports **86**
Comforters, see Quilts
Community Information Centre of Metro Toronto **97**
Community Information Directory **99**
Community Information Fairview **97**
Community Legal Aid Services **108**
Community Service Grocery **30**
Compasses Repair, see Marine
Concrete, Repair, see Cement
Consumer Protection Bureau **46**
Continental Salvage **44**
Cookies, see Dad's
Cookware, Standard, Repair **128**
Cookware, Brass & Copper, Repair **128**
Country Style Restaurant **33**
Credit **98, 100, 103-106**
Credit Counselling Service of Metropolitan Toronto **98, 105**
Crippled Civilians, see Society for Goodwill
Customs Auctions, see Canada
Cutting Your Heating Bill **65-67**
Cycles, see Peddler Cycle Shop

D
Dad's Cookies **22**
Danbury Sales **45**
Dansk Warehouse Sale **45**
Darrigo's Food Markets **26**
David Warsh Textiles **53**
Dawes Rd. Library Theatre **82**
DeBoers Warehouse Sale **45**
Dental Clinic, see University of Toronto
Dixon Hall Neighbourhood Centre **109**
Do-it-Yourself Courses **151**
Do-it-Yourself Places **59-60**
Dolls, Repair **128**
Don Vale Food Club **31**
Don's Discs **89**
Donuts **22**
Doors, Repair **128**
Door Store **129**
Downsview Volunteers **101**
Downsview West Information Post **97**
Draperies, Repair **128**
Dry Goods **53**
Dufferin-Eglinton Information Centre **97**
Durable Release Coaters **128**
Dyeing, Garments **129**

E
East York Board of Education **83**
East York Library **84**
Eating Better for Less **20**
Eaton's Warehouse **45**
Egerton's Restaurant **33**
Eggs **26**
Electric Motors, Repair **129**
Electric Motors Service Co. **129**
Electrical Appliances Small, Repair **131**
Elinka's Restaurant **42**
Elte Carpets **52**
Emergency Shelter Information **55**
Energy, Saving **62-67**
Etobicoke Board of Education **83**
Etobicoke Central Information **97, 99**
Etobicoke Community Health Dept. **109**
Etobicoke Library **84**
European Meats and Sausages **28**
Exterior Cleaning and Restoration **131**
Extoggery Limited **73**

F
Fabric & Drapery Mill **94**
Fairview Electronics **56**
Fans, Hand-held, Repair **131**
Fantastic Flea Market **12**
Fashion Mine **74**
Federal Store Fixtures **54**
Federal Trustee, Bankruptcy **98, 105**
Fenton's Restaurant **43**
50¢ Bookstore **90**
Film Library Rentals **82, 83**
Fish Restaurants **38**
Fishing Tackle, Repair **131**
Flagpoles, Repair **132**
Flea Markets **12**
Floors, Wood, Repair **132**
Flying Down to Rio **74**
Food **18-31**
Fortune Housewares **54**
Frames, Picture, Repair **132**
  see also U-Frame-It
Frank Vetere's Pizza **40**
Free Firewood **67**
Free Haircuts **72**
Free Movies **82**
French Restaurants **38**
Fruits & Vegetables **26**
Full Moon Teahouse & Imports **28**
Furniture & Appliances **44-52**
Furniture & Antique Repair & Refinishing **132**
Furniture Revival Centre **59**
Furniture Stripping **133**
Furs Repair **78 134**
Furs, see Avon, Paul Magder

G
G & W Rent-All Ltd. **60**
Garage Sales **12**
George Brown College **84**
German Restaurants **38-39**
Glass, Repair **134**
Glasses, Eye, Repair **134**
Global Cheese **23**
Gold Shoppe **15**
Goodman, Rod **4**
Gordon, Lynn **4**

Gramaphones, Repair, see Radios
Greek Restaurants **39**
Greenspoon Wreckers **48**
Greenwood Food Club **31**
Griffiths Delicatessen **38**
Groaning Board Restaurant **33**
Groceries, see FOOD
Grocery Comparison Chart **24-25**
Guns, Antique, Repair **134**
Gwartzman's Canvas and Art Supplies **93**

H
Hadassah Bazaar **11**
Haggling, see Art of Haggling
Hairdressers **71**
½ Price Boutique **54**
Handbags, Repair **135**
Handwriting **136**
Handyman Rentals **60**
Harbourfront **82, 85**
Hats, Repair **136**
Health Foods **28, 29**
Hearing Aids, Repair **136**
Heat **55**
Henri The 2nd **46**
Hobby Supplies **93-95**
HOME **44-63**
Honest Ed's **18**
Horizon Stores **92**
Hospitals **110**
Household Rentals **58-59**
Housewares, see HOME
Housing Rental Agency **55**
Humber College **84**
Humidifiers, Repair **136**
Hungarian Restaurants **39**
Hunt's Bakery Thrift Shop **22**

I
I.O.D.E. Second Appearance Shop **77**
Indian Restaurants **39-40**
Indonesian Restaurants **40**
Information Centres & Services **96-111**
Insulation Repair **62-67 136**
Iron, Wrought, Repair **137**
Irving and Associates Auctioneers **8**
Italian Restaurants **40-41**
It's Your Move **50-51**

J
Jackson Electric **129-131**
Japanese Restaurants **41**
Jewelry, Repair **137**
Jewish Restaurants **41-42**
Joe Singer Shoes **78**
Junior League Opportunity Shop **75**

K
Karma Co-ops **31**
Kelly's Stereo Mart **57**
Kennedy Rent-All **60**
Kensington Market **19**
King Sol Outdoor Store **86**
Kingsway Cinema **81**
Kite Store **94**
Kites, Repair **137**

Knob Hill Farms **18**
Kwong Chow Chinese Restaurant **37**

L
Lakeshore Multi-Services Project **102**
Lamps, Repair **137**
Lampshades, Repair, see Stained and Leaded Glass
Landlord and Tenant Advisory Bureau **46, 55**
Lawline **108**
Lawn Mowers, Repair **138**
Lawrence Emporium **69**
Le Trou Normand Restaurant **43**
Leaded Glass, Repair, see Stained and
Leather and Suede, Repair **138**
Legal & Bankruptcy Counselling **105-107**
Legal, Consumers & Human Rights Services **107-108**
Leisure **81-95**
L'Elégante Ltd. **73**
Library House Films **82**
Liftlock Fibreglass Company **87**
Lighters, Repair **138**
Loans, Interest-free **100**
Locks, Repair **139**
Lord Stanley's Restaurant **34**
Lori's Shoes **79**
Luggage, Repair **139**
Lumber, see Cashway
Lyons Tinning **128**

M
Maher Shoes Warehouse Outlet **79**
Make Your Own Toothpaste **109**
Malcolm's Hairdressing **71**
Maps, Old, Repair **139**
Marble, Repair **139**
Marine Instruments, Repair **140**
Markets **19-21**
Marvel Beauty School **72**
McTamney's Pawnbrokers **14**
Meat & Poultry **28**
Metropolitan Dye Works **129**
Metropolitan Toronto Police Auctions **10**
Metro Toronto Conservation Authority **85**
Michi Japanese Restaurant **41**
Microwave Oven, Repair **140**
Ministry of Consumer and Commercial Relations **55**
Ministry of Housing **55**
Ministry of Transportation Auctions,
Miranda's Second Time Around **75**
Mirrors, Repair **140**
Moishe's Tel-Aviv Restaurant **42**
Mopeds, Repair **140**
Mortgages **61**
Motorcycles, Repair **141**
Motors, Repair, see Electric
Mount Pleasant Lunch **34**
Movie Equipment, Repair **141**
Movies, see Film Library
Moving **50-51**
Mr. Oliver's Restaurant **38**
Multi-Service Centres **101-102**
Municipal Government Information **96**

Municipal Reference Library **84**
Music Boxes, Repair **141**
Music Library **84**
Musical Instruments, Repair **141**

N

National Film Board Library **82**
National Gym Clothing & Sporting Goods **87**
National Sound **57**
Neighbourhood Information Post **96**
Neighbourhood Legal Services **108**
New Yorker Cinema **81**
North York Library **49 82 84**
Nth Hand **90**

O

Of Consuming Interest **96**
OISE Films **81**
ORT Bazaar **11**
Office of the Ombudsman **55**
Old Ed's Restaurant **35**
Old Favourites Bookshop **90**
Old Spaghetti Factory Restaurant **40**
Olympic Wholesale **19**
Ombudsman **55**
Ontario Condominium Association **55**
Ontario Humane Society **112**
Ontario Legal Aid Plan **107**
Ontario Legislature Dining Room **35**
Opportunity Shop, see Junior League
Organ Grinder Restaurant **41**
Organs, Repair, see Pianos
Original Stitsky's **94**
Other Art Supplies **93**
Other Books **90**
Outboard Motors, Repair **141**
Outdoor Stores **87**
Ovens, Microwave, Repair **140**

P

Paperback and Record Exchange **91**
Paint Centre **59**
Parkdale Community Legal Services **108**
Parkdale Golden Age Foundation **101**
Parkes Restaurant **35**

Pasquale Brothers **23**
Paul Magder Furs **78**
Pawnbrokers **13-14**
Peking Palace Chinese Restaurant **37**
Pennington's Wearhouse **70**
Pens, Fountain, Repair **142**
Peter Pan Restaurant **36**
Phillips Consumer Service **47**
Photographs, Old, Repair **142**
Pianos and Organs, Repair **142**
Pick Your Own, Fruits & Vegetables **27**
Pinball Machines, Repair, see Amusement
Pioneer Women's Annual Bazaar **11**
Pipes, Repair **142**
Plants **56**
Plumbing Mart **60**
Poor Alex Theatre **81**
Poor Faygees Crêpes Restaurant **36**
Positively Sunshine **56**
Projectors, see Movie Equipment **143**

Public Libraries **84**

Q

Quilts and Comforters, Repair **143**

R

Radios and Gramophones Repair **143**
Records-on-Wheels **91**
Recreation, Cheap & Free **83-86**
Recycled, Clothing **70-76**
Recycling for fun and profit **7-17**
Referee, Small Claims Court **98, 105**
Regent Park Community Services Unit **102**
Regent Park Food Club **31**
Rent Review Offices **55**
RESTAURANTS **32-43**
Revue Repertory Cinema **81**
Rexdale Community Information **97**
Riding Apparel & Equipment, Repair **143**
Robin Barker Hairloom **71**
Rons Ceramics and Doll Hospital **128-129**
Roofs, Slate Repair **144**
Round Records **91**
Roxy Cinema **81**
Royal Cinema **129**
Rugs, see Carpets
Rummage Sales **12**
Ryerson Polytechnical Institute **84**

S

Sai Woo Chinese Restaurant **38**
Sails, Repair **144**
Salvage **48**
Salvation Army **15**
Sam The Record Man Annual Sale **89**
Samina's Tiffin Room Restaurant **39**
Sanderson Library Films **82**
Sara Lee Thrift Shop **22**
Savage Shoe Factory **79**
Scarborough Community Services, see Information
Scarborough Library **82 84**
Screening Room Cinema **81**
Sears Warehouse **47**
Second Childhood **77**
Second Nature Boutique **75**
Second Time Around, see Miranda's
Seneca College **84**
Share **101**
Sharpening, Repairs **144**
Shavers Electric, Repair **144**
Sheriff's Auctions **10**
Shoe Bin **79**
Shoes **78-80**
Shoes, Repair **144**
Shoppe D'Or **76**
Silver, Repair **145**
Singer Shoes **78**
Sinks, Repair, see Bathtubs
Skates, Repair **145**
Skis, Repair **145**
Skylights, Installation & Repair **146**
Sleeping Bags, Repair, see Tents
Snowblowers, Repair, see Lawn Mowers
Snowmobiles, Repair **146**
Society for Animals in Distress **112**

Society for Goodwill Services **17, 44**
Soundproofing, see Acoustic
Special Information Directory **96**
Sport Swap **88, 145**
Sporting Goods **86-88**
Sports Repair Services **87**
Spot Removal **146**
Springhurst Health Centre **109**
St. Jamestown Food Club **31**
St. Lawrence Market **21**
St. Lawrence Sales **70**
St. Vincent de Paul **14**
Stained and Leaded Glass, Repair **146**
Stephanie's Belgian Chocolates **26**
Stereos **56-57**
Stitsky's **94**
Stoke-on-Trent China Company **52**
Stork, A. and Sons **28**
Student Legal Services **108**
Sunbeam Appliances **47**
Sunbeam Shoe Company **80**
Sunkist Fruit Market **26**
Sunnybrook Meat Packers **28**
Swimming Pools, Repair **146**

Tarogato Restaurant **39**
Taxidermy **147**
Television, Repair **147**
Tenant Hotline **55**
Tennis Racquets, Repair **147**
Tents & Sleeping Bags, Repair **147**
Teperman and Sons Wreckers **48**
Thistletown Community Service Unit **102**
Thrift Shops **14-17**
Thorncliffe Information Post **96**
Tile, Repair, see Cement and Concrete
Tips for Would-Be Borrowers **100**
Toby's Discount Children's Wear **77**
Toby's Goodeats Restaurant **36**
Tools for the Handyperson **152-155**
Tools, Power, Repair **148**
Toronto Barber College **72**
Toronto Hebrew Services **105**
Toronto Island Food Co-op **31**
Toronto Library **49 83 84**
Toronto Symphony Rummage Sale **13**
Toronto Transit Commission Auctions **10**
Toys **92, 93**
Toys, Repair, see Dolls
Toyerama **93**
Tramps Restaurant **36**
Trains, Model, Repair **148**
Tribe **76**
Trou Normand Restaurant **43**
Typewriters, Repair **148**

U
U-Frame-It **49, 52**
University of Toronto Dental Clinic **112**
Upholstery, Repair **148**
Usher's Surplus Foods **19**

V
Van Fike Advanced School of Hair Design **71**

Vans, Customizing **149**
Vegetarian Restaurants **42**
Vidal Sassoon Hairstyling **71**
Vinyl, Repair **149**
Volunteer Service Centres **99**

W. Jacques Auction Services **8**
W.H. Smith's Bookshops **91**
Waddington's Auctioneers **9**
Walkin Shoes **80**
Ward Nine Senior Link **101**
Warden Woods Community Services **102**
Warehouse Sales, see Dansk, DeBoers
Warehouse Shoe Mart **80**
Warranties **130**
Watches, Repair **149**
Weaving, Invisible, see Clothing, Repair
Wellington Sales **70**
West Hill Community Services **102**
West Metro Senior Citizens Services **101**
Weston's Bakery Thrift Shop **22**
What Happens When the Warranty Runs Dry **130**
Wheelchairs, Repair **149**
When Things Go Wrong **98**
Where the Cheapest Loans Are **106**
White, Supply, A.O. **53**
Whole Foods Trading **29**
Wholesale House **70**
Wicker, Repair, see Caning
Wicker World **57**
Wigs & Toupees, Repair **150**
Williams Pawnbrokers **14**
Willie's **77**
Window Shades, Repair **150**
Windows, Screens & Storms, Repair **150**
Wine Art **94**
Wing On Company **58**
Woman's Bakery Thrift Shop **23**
Wonder Bread Thrift Shop **23**
Woodgreen Community Centre **108**
Woodgreen Produce and Grain Store **31**
Wreckers, see Salvage

Y
YM-YWCA, YMHA & YWHA **84**
York Board of Education **83**
York Community Services **102**
York Library **84**
York Parks & Recreation Dept. **85**
York Services to Seniors **101**
York University Films **82**

Z
Zippers, Repair **150**